ILLUSTRATED
HISTORY
of
BRITAIN

Whatsoever · thy · hand · findeth · to · do · do · it · with · thy · Might ·

In the NINETEENTH
CENTURY, the Northumbrians
show the World what can be
done with Iron and Coal.

ILLUSTRATED
HISTORY
of
BRITAIN

Martyn Bennett

Trafalgar Square Publishing

NORTH POMFRET, VERMONT

First published in the United States of America in 1992 by
Trafalgar Square Publishing
North Pomfret
Vermont 05053

Produced by
Robert Ditchfield Ltd
Combe Court
Kerry's Gate
Hereford HR2 0AH
United Kingdom

Library of Congress Catalog Card Number: 91-65937
ISBN 0-943955-45-9

1 3 5 7 9 10 8 6 4 2

Typeset in Great Britain by Action Typesetting Ltd, Gloucester
Printed and bound in Hong Kong

FRONTISPIECE: *Iron and Coal* by William Bell Scott

For my Mother

The Battle of Trafalgar by J M W Turner

Contents

INTRODUCTION

BRITAIN IS AN ISLAND only in so far as it is separated by sea from the adjacent continent of Europe. There has never been a period when the nations of the British Isles have been culturally isolated from other national groups. The very formation of British ways of life, government, social structure, arts, architecture and, not least, history are all products of the relationships between those people who live in the Isles and those who do not.

This brief account can provide no more than an outline of the many facets of British history, some of which the reader will already know. There are the great and lesser kings and queens of the nation and there are the familiar events: King Alfred's struggles against the Vikings, the defeat of the Armada, the Civil War and the death of General Gordon at Khartoum. But it is also hoped that there is something new for everyone; the sheer violence of the early nineteenth century may come as a surprise to those who believe that British history has been a quiet story of progress towards the united group of nations that we see today.

The study of history is not a luxury: it is a necessity for all societies to examine their origins and past. Only through this can we understand the path by which a nation has travelled to the present-day or begin to comprehend the institutions and the attitudes of individuals within a society. The study of history is the attempt to come to terms with the experiences, events and emotions of the past and relate them to the world we know.

We must be wary of assuming that history is made only by the tiny minority of the people who wield power. It is not. No history can ignore the experiences of the broad range of people. The motives and decisions of the monarchs and rulers of Britain were generally responses to the needs of ruling the ordinary people of the country. In the early period of British history, it is only rarely that the people advanced to the centre of the stage, as when they spoke with Richard II in 1381, but they were always there — they had to be governed, taxed, enlisted, fought and even bought and sold. This book attempts to view history in that way, as a story of all the people, not just of the famous. Some of the characters and events thrown to the centre of the historical stage here may therefore be novel, but I hope they may become better known. They deserve this, for their lives are no less important to the British story than are those of the more familiar leading characters.

Martyn Bennett

1. AN UNWRITTEN TIME

FROM THE STONE AGES TO CELTIC CIVLISATIONS

'Britain is an island in the ocean and was once called Albion.'

The Venerable Bede.

TIME CHART

c.250,000 BC	Swanscombe on the Thames is inhabited.
c.8,000 BC	British mainland is separated from Europe.
c.6,000 BC	Influx of people from the European Continent.
c.4,750 BC	Neolithic Age (New Stone Age).
c.2,800 BC	Bronze Age begins. Beaker People move into Britain from the Rhine Valley.
c.2,700 BC	Stonehenge site is first built upon.
c.2,500 BC	Avebury Henge is begun and Stonehenge redeveloped.
c.1,000 BC	Iron Age begins in Europe.
c.600 BC	Hallstatt Celts start to migrate to Britain.
c.400 BC	La Tène Celts begin to occupy Yorkshire.
c.100 BC	Belgae Celts migrate to Britain.

THE PREHISTORY OF BRITAIN is shrouded from us, largely because there is no written evidence of the human habitation of the isles. Instead, our knowledge is dependent upon the study of archaeological remains. Many of these suggest that there were religions based upon astronomical observations. This evidence is still visible today in the form of stone circles such as the most famous, Stonehenge, and collections of monoliths like the 'observatory' of Ballochroy in Argyll, or single standing stones as in Rudston churchyard in Yorkshire.

Though not all of the remains of the past are so dramatic, some are as telling. In 1935 skull fragments were found at Swanscombe dating back to the interglacial Hoxnian period, which ended around a quarter of a million years ago. During this era entire cultures existed for thousands of years, alongside woolly mammoths and rhinoceri and at a time when Britain was still part of the continental land mass. These early inhabitants of Britain can be traced through archaeology, and their ritual of death more than their pattern of life has been handed on to us in the very soils that they tilled.

In general terms there was a shift in patterns of life, away from hunting as the main form of subsistence to farming. Crops were cultivated and some animals kept whilst others were still hunted. Tools changed too, from stone-based ones in the Stone Ages (Palaeolithic is the Early Stone Age, Neolithic the New Stone Age) to bronze, which was the first metal used by the inhabitants of Britain for work purposes. Stonehenge in Wiltshire is probably the most famous structure. This henge underwent several phases of construction. Initially begun some 2,700 years before the Christian calendar started, it continued to hold the religious imagination until the Iron Age which superseded the use of bronze.

Previous pages: Stonehenge, Wiltshire.

Opposite: A single standing stone, known as the 'Fish Stone', near Glenusk, Powys. The purpose of these Bronze Age monuments is not known; perhaps they have a religious significance, as is surmised with Stonehenge, but this is uncertain without written records.

A fine beaker pot buried, in the tradition of the Beaker Folk, in a grave at Barnack, Cambridgeshire.

THE CELTS

INTO LATER BRONZE-AGE BRITAIN came an influx of settlers from continental Europe. The new people were more technologically advanced than the successors to the Beaker people (so named because of the distinctive shape of their pottery) and instead of being entirely dependent upon bronze they used a stronger metal: iron.

The Celts originated in central Europe during the millenium preceding the Christian calendar. They developed out of the bronze-using people termed by archaeologists as 'Northern Alpine Urnfield' culture. Great finds were made near Hallstatt in Austria and these point the way to their progress. These were the earliest Celts but their society was already quite developed and superior to that of the bronze-using people. At Hallstatt they mined salt and this was the basis of the community's wealth. Their superiority was expressed in their artwork and skilled craftwork. Their burial techniques shared similarities with those of the Etruscans, but involved the elaborate use of four-wheeled carts placed within wooden chambers covered by earth mounds. The body was laid under the cart. In the grave were placed personal ornaments decorated with the most beautiful artwork bearing the basic designs which were to be passed on throughout the history of the Celtic races. Even the buckets placed with the bodies at Hallstatt showed the craft which was to be associated with Celtic society.

Further discoveries at La Tène on the edge of Lake Neuchâtel confirmed that Celtic society underwent dramatic changes. The finds at La Tène, made initially in 1864, revealed bridge-type structures in the area which had once been the course of the River Thiele. The quantity of finds around the bridges suggested that they were used for throwing votive offerings into the stream. These objects were of a more advanced design than those at Hallstatt and suggested that power and wealth had shifted westwards from the earlier settlements around the Austrian town. The burial sites later found in the Rhineland and in the Marne region of France, though reminiscent of the La Tène finds, also showed distinct differences from the earlier Celtic peoples. Burials now involved a two-wheeled chariot, not a four-wheeled cart. This chariot was for some centuries to be the most important feature of Celtic weaponry.

CELTS ARRIVE IN BRITAIN

THEIR WARLIKE NATURE gave them the drive and their military ability enabled the Celts to spread westwards as well as eastwards, and by the sixth century before the birth of Christ, they had crossed the seas to the British Isles. As early as 600 BC there were Celts in Scotland along the north-east coast. These were Celts who were of the culture found at Hallstatt. They were aristocratically hierarchical and a fierce people. Initially there appear to have been few women in the Scottish colonies, but no doubt the settlements became permanent and more representative of the whole of Celtic society and not just a large raiding party.

During the ensuing century further influxes of Hallstatt Celts arrived along the south and east coasts of what was to become England. Their better agricultural techniques, made possible by their use of the stronger iron tools, and also their superior military weapons enabled them to establish a supremacy amongst the native population who were still bronze users. The settlers moved inland from the coasts over the next two hundred years and became established across much of the country.

Around the year 400 BC a second wave of Celts began to settle in the British Isles. These were of the La Tène culture and brought with them their arts, crafts and the two-wheeled chariot. They settled in Yorkshire and in Sussex in particular (later in Ireland), and seem to have been chiefly engaged in agriculture. However, their warlike nature was exercised in the numerous cattle raids which provided wealth as well as excitement. The legends of Ireland which come down to us, contain many tales of such exploits, and it is impossible not to believe that this activity formed a major part of the way of life experienced by these people on the mainland. La Tène culture appeared in Ireland in the last century before Christ, having come from Britain, but there had been a movement there directly from the Continent a century or so earlier. This mirrored the pattern of migration to Ireland of the Hallstatt Celts, following their settlement in Britain.

The last influx of the Celtic races into the

Early Bronze Age gold regalia from Bush Barrow, Wiltshire.

British Isles took place about a hundred years before the Romans appeared on the south coast. These Celts were known as the Belgae and were renowned as a particularly fierce people. At the same time they practised a more efficient agriculture and introduced the plough into the isles. In addition they were fine craftsmen and produced distinctive art and, in particular, beautiful enamel work and pottery. They also utilised coinage. In effect, then, they were far more than just militarily superior: they were an economically advanced culture. They established larger settlements than had been usual and from these developed the towns which became Winchester, Colchester and St Albans.

THE CELTS AS WARRIORS

MUCH OF THE SUCCESS of the Celts was due to their military prowess. Their developed culture expressed itself in the weapons of war, as much as in the beautiful objects which they made. Indeed utility and beauty were often united in the same artefact. Two of the most striking finds which have illustrated many classrooms and formed the basis of the decoration of many model figures of the Celtic warriors, were beautiful works of art. Quite probably, despite later depictions based upon

The Celtic horned helmet found in the Thames.

Reconstruction of a Celtic chariot, a characteristically light structure designed for mobility rather than armoured protection.

them, they were never used as weapons. One of the items, the horned helmet found in the Thames near Waterloo Bridge in 1868, may have been made for a statue, or as a piece of 'parade' dress. It is of bronze and was once enamelled but as protective headgear it would have been of limited value; against a heavy sword stroke it would have split apart. Nevertheless, from such evidence we can assume that the basic pattern does represent the design of a real battle helmet.

The other item, the shield found at Battersea, again in the Thames, in 1857, was made early in the first century AD. This was constructed of bronze in thin sheets bound together and backed by wood or leather. It was decorated with a symmetrical design, based upon grotesque creatures joining the top and bottom roundels to the central boss, containing an owl-like representation. The shield was decorated with glass, probably imported from Italy or perhaps the eastern end of the Mediterranean, and the decoration is seemingly influenced by Roman design. It, too, is for parades, not for battle.

In Lincolnshire earlier examples of Celtic parade armour have been found in the River Witham. There, as well as an intricate shield, a sword and the gilt-bronze mount from the scabbard were discovered. This and other sword finds indicate that the sword was the most important weapon of the Celtic warrior. The Halstatt culture had developed the long sword and, later, daggers supplemented them. Large numbers of daggers, for a sophisticated market, had been produced, in Britain, in the Thames valley, though the industry declined after the third century BC, when a newer sword, developed by the La Tène culture Celts, made the dagger obselete. Spears were also used by the Celtic soldiers as were slings which served instead of bows and arrows. Archery was not a developed skill amongst the Celts.

The chariot was the favoured fighting vehicle of the Celts and it continued in use until the first century BC on the Continent, when it was superseded by the cavalry as the most potent military force. In Britain, however, the chariot was still in use when the Romans invaded. It was a light structure with spoked wheels, drawn by two stout ponies harnessed to a central shaft. The chariot was open at front and back, allowing warriors to

The ornate, ceremonial Celtic shield recovered from the Thames at Battersea.

Above: Burrough Hill Fort, Leicestershire — the south-east entrance.

Opposite: Maiden Castle, Dorset.

dismount or to fight from a precarious position between the horses, balanced on the shaft and using the harness for support. The two sides of the chariot were made of wicker and braced by a wooden frame attached to handles. They could then be fitted with bronze accoutrements and were often elaborately enhanced; one example was described by a Roman observer, as being covered completely in silver, which may well have been no exaggeration. The horses which replaced the charioteers in importance were likewise highly decorated with armour constructed in a similar style to the shields already described.

CELTIC FORTS

HILLS HAD PROVIDED natural defensive settlements for some five or six hundred years before the Celts began to settle in Britain. They were easy to fence off and offered visible and quickly recognisable loci for the scattered settlements of prehistoric tribes. Some of these were little more than embanked structures built on hills like the one on the site of Loughborough University campus and the now disappeared site on nearby Beacon hill in Leicestershire. They may have been part of the network of 'old straight tracks' outlined by Alfred Watkins in the 1920s. Others were massive structures with timber defences. These walls were, at first, simple walls made and braced with timber, but later the rear of the wall was braced by earth banks, stabilising and strengthening the structure. This type is epitomised by the fort at Hollingbury in Sussex. The building of these forts accelerated during the years in which the Celts were making the country their home. New developments appeared, such as the production of vitrified silica-based stone walls in the north-east of Scotland. These were made by building a loose stone wall and then setting fire to piles of wood surrounding it — thereby fusing the stone into a mass.

The Belgae introduced newer methods, either through friendly relationships or as a

Celtic horse-bit with enamel decoration.

A Celtic bucket found at Aylesford, Buckinghamshire.

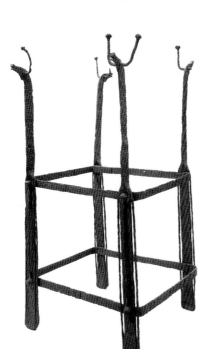

Celtic fire-dogs with ox-head motif.

reaction to their influx into the country. The single ditch forts were replaced by ones with many ditches. The best example, Maiden Castle in Dorset, has three ditches around its sides and a very complex series at its western gate to cover this vulnerable part. Examples in the east of the country have wide flat-bottomed ditches named after the fort at Fécamp in France; these were introduced by the Belgae. Inside the forts there was a great deal of evidence to suggest town planning. Streets were organised as at Danebury in Hampshire where there were five rows paralleling the ditch line. Some of the sites were zoned, placing different trades and enterprises in different areas of the township. Some had mints to provide coinage and others show signs of developed industrial activity.

In the extremities of Celtic Britain, small defensive structures known as brochs exist. They are to be found in the western and northern isles off Scotland. These were fortified private houses, with a tall tower, or blockhouse, surrounded by an enclosure which in time of danger would harbour the flocks of the owner. The best surviving example is Broch of Mousa which still stands some 40ft (12m) high. There are other examples at Dundornadilla in Sutherland and Glenelg near Inverness.

THE ARTS

THE ART of the Celtic world was altered subtly in the British Isles. The artists and craftsmen depended largely on the patronage of the nobility to further their arts and crafts. The earliest of these would have come across from the Continent with their masters and so the earliest examples of their work are generally continental in design; but once in Britain there were additions, such as the hatching which was favoured by Bronze-age chiefs. Some of this island's finest work was done in the Yorkshire area by the Parisi tribe who had transferred from the Marne area of France. Belgic influence fully modified the La Tène art by the end of the last century before the Christian calendar.

Iron was used in the creation of decorated articles as well as bronze and a great deal of the

The Desborough bronze mirror, early first century AD.

ornament was meant to be seen on the object whilst in use. Thus cauldrons, or pots to be suspended, would have their most decorative details on the lower edges where they would be noticed. The horse cap, designed to be worn by a chariot pony, would have been seen to its best advantage by the charioteer looking down on it from his position of the chariot.

Around Britain there were, flourishing in the years just before and after the Roman invasion, centres participating in what has been described as a rapidly developing art-culture which was progressing far faster than that on the Continent. Many of these centres were in Ireland, where, it seems, the best sword-scabbard work was done, although there is the suggestion that the Parisi may have been able to produce such work too. In north Britain there was a great artistic tradition and

the area which is now Dumfriesshire had a particularly vibrant artistic community.

Some of the finest work is seen on the backs of Celtic mirrors, which were not simply practical items of the fastidious Celts, but were status symbols. The design had Mediterranean origins but was turned to beautiful effect by the Celtic Britons. Examples are generally found in the south of Britain; one of the best was located at Desborough in Northampton-shire.

Many of the items of everyday life were designed for beauty as well as practicality. Fire-dogs, made of iron, to support logs in the hearth, could bear ox-head motifs as with the one found at Lords Bridge in Cambridgeshire. Pottery too bore artistic designs. Two types could be produced on wheels in Britain – the footed bowl and the pedestalled urn. Most of

these were coloured black or grey and the latter type could be used for the ashes of the dead. Other pottery was also produced, again to a very high standard. Enamelling was also practised but generally as a single-colour background before the Roman invasion. Glass, too, was added to decoration and this was a tradition found in the Hallstatt culture, where glass was often used to good effect in conjunction with enamel work. It seems that much of this production was carried out in the eastern areas of Britain. The areas occupied by the Belgae are particularly fruitful in archaeological finds which include enamel work.

The Roman invasions drove Celtic art underground. The need for the art had gone — the destruction of the Celtic hierarchy removed its purpose. It had been highly dependent upon the patronage of the Celtic nobility, who used art on weapons, their furniture and the majority of their possessions, from their smallest brooch to their chariots. The Roman invasion wrecked the nobility and the system of patronage. It was not until the influence of the Christian church was felt that Celtic art found itself a new patron. Although its designs and ethos were kept alive, and occasionally appeared during the four centuries of Roman occupation, native art was dormant.

CELTIC LANGUAGE

THE SETTLEMENT of the British Isles by the Celts brought not one, but two chief languages. That in the Scottish Highlands, which still lingers there and probably entered the country via settlers in Ireland (where it is also still spoken), is the Goidelic or Q-Celtic. The latter name is derived from the pronunciation of the letter q^v from the Indo-European languages, later the letter q, as a k (it was written as c). The other is P-Celtic or Brythonic. In this language the q sound became p. This means the word for head in Q-Celtic is cenn and in P-Celtic is penn. The latter became Brittonic, the language of the Brittones who inhabited the British Isles when the Romans landed here. Brittonic is the language which as the Celts were pushed west after the Romans left, became Welsh, Cornish and Breton across the Channel.

The Pretanic Islands

The earliest recorded name for the British Isles was that of the Pretanic Islands, where the people of Pritani or Priteni lived. It seems to be a Celtic name of the Brythonic form. In the Isles lived, by the time of the Roman conquest, thirty-three groups, who had often warred with each other and were still hostile towards each other when Caesar landed. Scotland had about sixteen of these groups and the area of England and Wales, seventeen. Some of these groups had probably originated from the same place on the Continent as the tribes recorded by the Greek geographer, Ptolemy of Alexandria, in the second Christian century, and have the same or similar names. In the Sutherland region of Scotland were to be found the Cornavii, whilst in the Welsh border lands were the Cornovii. The first part of the name is also part of Cornwall and, on the other side of the Channel, Cornouaille. Similarly the Dumnonii held the Forth and Clyde parts of Scotland and Devon and Somerset.

The principal tribal settlements of Celtic Britain were those of the Parisi, who lived in the area of east and south Yorkshire, whilst the Brigantes settled in the Lancashire and north-western part of England. Lincolnshire and the East Midlands were home to the Coritani. East Anglia had the Iceni in the north and the Trinovantes in the south. The South Midlands were settled by the Dobunni and the Catuvellauni. The South was occupied by the Dumnonii in the west, the Durotriges, the Atrebates and the Cantiaci in the Kent area. Wales and the later Marcher counties were lived in by the Deceangli, the Ordovices, the Cornovii and the Demetae.

The last influx of any size, was by the Belgae who settled in and influenced the area of London, Kent and the South and East Midlands.

It was not a homogeneous kingdom. In particular the South was marred by tribal rivalries as each struggled for territorial gains. This eased the way for the Romans to conquer the Island and for them to subvert the Celtic civilisation. Naturally, it was not expunged, and, just as the Celts had borrowed from the native Bronze-age cultures which had been found in the British Isles, so the Romans used, adopted, and often adapted to the culture they found in the Pretanic Isles.

2. A FAR-FLUNG PROVINCE

ROMAN BRITAIN 55 BC–AD 410

TIME CHART

55 BC	Caesar's first invasion.
54 BC	Caesar's second invasion.
AD 43	The Roman invasion begins.
51	Caradoc defeated.
60	Boudicca's Rebellion.
69–70	Wales conquered.
105	Occupation of Lowland Scotland ended.
122–8	Hadrian's Wall built.
143	The battle of Mons Graupius: Lowland Scotland reoccupied. Antonine Wall built.
154	Brigantian revolt.
163	Antonine Wall and Lowland Scotland abandoned.
196–208	Wars in Britain.
208–12	Britain divided into two provinces.
212	All free people in Britain accepted as Roman citizens.
259–74	Britain part of Gallic empire.
296	Picts attack the north of the province.
306–12	Britain divided into four provinces.
313	Christian religion tolerated. Three diocese established.
367	Barbarians' major attack on the province.
396	The last attempt to stabilise Britain's defences.
410	The legions leave Britain.

JULIUS CAESAR'S INVASIONS

BELGAIC INFLUENCES were strongest in the south-east of the country. It is from their immigration that the up-grading of British society is dated. Urban development was one facet of this; trade increased and links with the Romans through occupied Gaul grew. To the ambitious Caesar, the mineral wealth of the Pretanic Islands looked tempting, but it was probably more a matter of military necessity that a Roman army should land there and try to force allegiance from the tribal kingdoms. The Belgae had lent aid to their people who lived in north-east Gaul and valuable trade links with the Dumnonii and the Durotriges helped the Veneti in the Brittany area hold off the Romans for some time. Knowledge of the land over the sea was lacking and Caesar's first military venture was a reconnaissance mission following the failure of ambassadorial relations established through Commius, King of the Atrebates in Gaul.

In the last week of August in 55 BC Julius Caesar landed two legions on the south coast. He attempted first to land in the protected area

Above: Roman ships depicted on Trajan's column in Rome.

Opposite: Julius Caesar.

Hod Hill, Dorset. This hill fort succumbed to the invading Roman force in AD 43. The Romans then constructed their own fort in a corner of the British fort. This is visible at the top of the picture.

(now Dover), but the white cliffs were lined by the Belgae warriors, alerted to Caesar's intentions. The Roman fleet sailed along the coast to where the cliffs disappeared into low beaches. The landing site of this, the first Roman invasion, was probably between Walmer and Deal on the flat beaches. The Britons had kept pace with Caesar's fleet and were already on the shore awaiting the landing. The legionaries, ill-equipped as they were, without any small boats, had to get ashore under withering missile attack from the shore. Even so, the Britons were driven from the beach and Caesar established a camp. Some tribal leaders offered allegiance to Rome, but they were too quick: the war was not lost. Violent storms wrecked the Roman fleet and left Caesar stranded. The Belgae forces attacked a foraging party and then mounted an attack on the main camp of the Romans, convincing Caesar that he ought to return to Gaul.

The following year a larger campaign, with five legions and 2,000 cavalry was launched. This landed near Sandwich in the first week of July, 54 BC. The alliance of tribes was fairly fragile. When things went well, as on the occasion when the Britons defeated the

Romans whilst they tried to establish a camp, it was fine. However, when the Romans defeated an attempt to repeat the success, it failed. Caesar offered the Catuvellauni peace terms which ensured protection for his allies, the Trinovantes, but little in the way of harsh dictates. He, as much as Cassivellannus, leader of the Catuvellauni, was ready for peace. The Roman forces left Britain, with Caesar probably thinking in terms of another invasion the following year. Events far from the north-west of the empire left this plan unfulfilled.

Caesar had to deal with a revolt in Gaul over the ensuing two years. Towards the end of the revolt his old ally, Commius, deserted his former friend and left his Gallic kingdom for the Atrebates in Britain. With him went a major migration of Belgae, who formed the last main influx of these advanced Celts into Britain. Their influence began to spread north and eastwards through Britain and in their wake the tribal kingdoms developed and strengthened their unity. Whilst tribes developed internally, empire-building became evident as military domination followed cultural change. The Catuvellauni were not completely overthrown by their contact with

Rome and although they were supposed to pay tribute to Rome, they thrived on the neglect of the capital. Within a generation they were ready to ignore the dictum of leaving the Trinovantes alone. Cassivellannus himself would probably have benefited from the Roman invasion, as would have the other British kings. Increased trade with the empire had followed in Caesar's wake, and the valuable metals mined in Britain gave the leaders of society a new wealth. New luxury goods could be bought and a new sense of position seems to have affected the kings and queens in the Isles. The capital town of the Catuvellauni moved from Wheathamstead, perhaps because of its associations with the defeat there by Caesar, to Verulamium (later St Albans). From there their aggression began under the new king, Tasciovanus, and it continued.

By AD 10 the Trinovantes' lands had been subsumed by the conquering Catuvellauni and a new capital was built, next to the old Trinovantes' centre at Colchester. The new capital, Camulodunum, superseded the conquered people's capital, and from it King Cunobelinus (Cynfelin or, to later people, Cymbeline) not only ruled the expanded territory, but began to press his empire westwards. Soon the Catuvellauni had taken over most of Kent and were pushing into Atrebates lands. Incursions into the middle lands of England put pressure on the Dobunni as tentacles were pushed into the Cotswolds. In AD 40 Cunobelinus died. In his later years his aggression was tempered and one of his sons, Adminius, was friendly towards Rome. Two other sons were not: Togodumnus and Caratacus (or Caradoc in Celt language) defied Rome and drove Adminius from his base at Verulamium. He went to Rome to solicit help. The two brothers expanded further into the Cotswolds and began to put pressure on the Atrebates. Adminius's attempt to secure Roman intervention had ended in a fiasco when the invasion fleet established for the task failed to get further than Boulogne. Encouraged by this, Togodumnus and Caradoc pushed south through Atrebates lands and reached the coasts. King Verica of the Atrebates, once again, like Commius before the Gallic revolt, was an ally of Rome and fled to the empire. Like Adminius he was well received. Things had gone far enough.

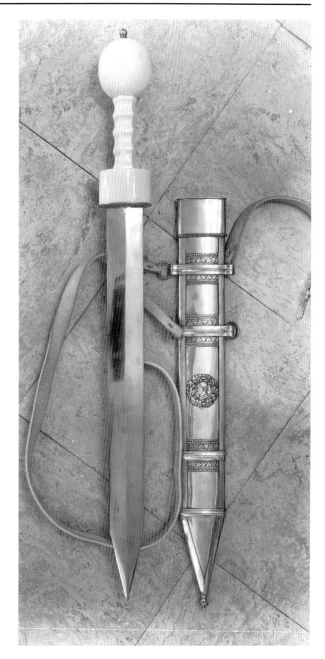

Facsimile of a Roman sword.

Had Rome been sleeping? Certainly for most of the ninety or so years after Caesar had left Kent, there had been little interest expressed in Pretanic affairs. The structure of Rome had changed after Caesar had left, with an Emperor becoming the chief executive figure. After Caesar's murder there had been a short period of instability which ruled out any involvement in Britain. Once Augustus Caesar had established an effective rule by 27 BC, he may have entertained taking up Caesar's plan; certainly he patched up relations with the

ROMAN INVASION

Roman eagle and standards from a sword found at South Shields, Tyne and Wear.

Atrebates, now ruled by Trinocommius, son of Commius, but with pressing affairs in central Europe, he made no further progress. Augustus was succeded by Tiberius who likewise took little interest in British affairs, despite the aggression of the Catuvellauni. It was to Gaius (the Emperor who has come down to us as the unstable Caligula) that Adminius appealed for help to so little effect.

Togodumnus and Caradoc felt confident enough in their power to demand of the empire that Verica be extradited to Britain following his flight to Rome. It was the final straw. The Emperor now, following Gaius's murder, was Claudius and to him the threat of a hostile power on the north-west border was not to be tolerated. An invasion was ordered.

Iᴺ AD 43 ᴛʜᴇ ʀᴏᴍᴀɴs launched the invasion that marked the establishment of Britain as a province of Rome. The initial landing was made at Richborough in Kent by Aulus Plautius with 60,000 men in four legions and 20,000 auxiliary troops. He drove inland towards the Thames, meeting little opposition. Most of the Britons had disbanded after the immediate threat of invasion seemed to have abated, due to delays on the other side of the Channel. Nevertheless, both Caradoc and Togodumnus attacked Plautius when the Romans reached the Medway, somewhere between Rochester and Aylesford. The army assembled by the brothers consisted of bands of poorly trained and weakly disciplined levies, supporting the aristocracy of Celtic society in their chariots. The Romans crossed the river on both flanks of the Britons, firstly to their left with the auxiliaries, and secondly to their right with the II (Augusta) Legion. This split the charioteers into two groups and weakened their opposition. On the second day the Britons attacked the legion's bridgehead and almost defeated the legionaries, but the increasing numbers available as the other legions crossed the river meant defeat for the Britons.

Togodumnus may well have been killed during the battle and the fighting was left to Caradoc. The Romans crossed the Thames and moved on Camulodunum. The Emperor Claudius joined them for the final victory and entry into the capital. Part of the Roman army went into the West under Vespasian and conquered the Durotriges and the Dumnonii. Over thirty skirmishes and battles were fought and many hill-forts, including those mentioned in the previous chapter, fell to the Romans: Ham Hill and Maiden Castle in Dorset were amongst them. At the latter the Romans launched a massive attack on the east gate and drove in the defences there. At Hod Hill in Dorset a large artillery bombardment was launched on the chief's house; this resulted in the surrender of the fort.

Within the next four years the Romans pressed north towards Lindum (Lincoln), into the Midlands and Ratae (Leicester), through to Shropshire. Although the main aim of the invasion, the defeat of the Catuvellauni and

Bronze head of the Emperor Claudius, found in the River Alde, Suffolk.

the restoration of Verica had been achieved and the friendly nations', the Iceni's and the Atrebates', security ensured, the flight of Caradoc into Wales meant that the north-western borders of the province were not secure.

Caradoc had been installed as a leader of several tribes in Wales, notably the Silures, and he was making attempts to win over the Iceni and the Brigantes who were north of the Humber. The new governor of the province, Publicus Ostorius Scapula, found soon after his arrival that the Silures were penetrating deep across the Severn. He drove them off quickly, but in AD 48 began the hunt for Caradoc. The governor started to destroy the tribal lands systematically, and by AD 50 was pushing deep into Wales. Realising that this policy of the Romans was damaging his support and ruining his resources, Caradoc turned on the legions, in the summer of AD 51, to try and defeat them in a major battle. Further, it was hoped that this would inspire more of the native peoples to turn on the invader. It has not been easy to find the site of this battle: no precise details have survived, but it is possible that it was on the Severn at Cefn Carnedd between Caersws and Llanidloes. As many as 10,000 Britons gathered at the hill but they were outnumbered by the Romans. The legions forced their way up the hill under the cover of the locked shield formation known as the Testudo (the tortoise), and drove the Britons off. Caradoc's wife and brother were captured and he fled to claim the hospitality of Cartimandua, Queen of the Brigantes. She was an ally of Rome and could not afford to risk helping Caradoc, so he was handed over. Caradoc was shipped as a curiosity to Rome where his evident nobility won him his life and relative freedom. It had been the last great gamble. The provincial status of Britain was assured.

A Roman legionary, as he might have appeared.

THE ROMAN MILITARY MACHINE

THERE WAS NO DOUBT that the Romans had imposed their will on the south of Britain by sheer brute force, aided by judicious alliances. Some of these latter were to collapse under the strains placed upon them by Rome, but this only meant that the Romans were able to impose their control over more of the country, with again, the use of brute force. Although the Romans were impressed by the Celtic cavalry they saw in action against them in Gaul, and by the charioteers which harried them at the battle on the Medway, there was no doubt that the legions were superior to the native opposition. Celtic cavalry units were absorbed into the Roman army, but chariots were rejected; the age of the aristocratic mobile attack force was over.

Legions were the mainstay, but not the only part of the Roman army. They were indeed self-contained armies in their own right. Each consisted of 6,000 men in ten cohorts. Nine of the cohorts had 480 men and one, the first, had 800. Each cohort was a tactical unit in its own right and within it were six centuries, each of 80 men, except the first one which had five double-sized centuries. In addition the legion had its own surgeons, engineers, armourers, carpenters, and a whole range of support services. Some had cavalry units attached, although these fought generally with the cavalry itself during battles. Each legionary was equipped with two chief weapons: the *pilum*, a javelin or throwing spear, 7 ft (2.1 m) long, and a *gladius*, a stabbing-sword. The *pilum* had two purposes: firstly to kill and secondly to disable enemies by sticking effectively into shields. If the *pilum* had been hurled at short range, the legionary could guarantee to have reached the struggling warrior before he had removed the impediment from his shield. If the first *pilum* missed then the Roman had a second. The legionary wore a bronze helmet lined with an iron skull cap on his head, and a segmented plate armour breast and back plate, the flexibility of which enabled him to move lithely when at work or in a fight. Under it was a leather jerkin and a tunic.

The soldier was not just a fighting man; he was a construction labourer too. The great forts and encampments which were built over the province were constructed largely by dint of the legionaries' labour. It was they who changed the face of Britain then and have left the lines of development for us to see. Many of Britain's great towns grew from the centres which Rome established here and which the legionary built. For more temporary arrangements each soldier carried two 7ft (2.1m) wooden stakes as his contribution to the camps constructed at the end of a day's march. Marching camps were surrounded by ditches, inside of which the dug earth was piled into a wall surmounted by the stakes carried

A reconstruction painting of the great fortress built by the Romans at Chester.

by the legionary. Thus was the legion self-contained.

The legion was not the only force. There were auxiliary troops which included cavalry, infantry and mixed units. These formations were between 500 and 1,000 strong and formed not of Roman citizens as were the legions, but of people from conquered or client nations. In the Province of Britain, the auxilia formed a crucial part of the occupying forces. The troops which manned the two walls built to keep out the tribes from Scotland were furnished by such forces. Some of the auxilia were brought in from abroad, but, as time passed, they were raised in Britain too.

The earliest forts built in Roman Britain were constructed of earthworks and timber walls and this continued throughout the first century AD. Their layout, however, followed a pattern which was repeated in later, stronger, structures. In the centre was the headquarters

Roman parade helmet with face-mask, found at Ribchester, Lancashire.

31

building, surrounded by barracks, granaries and stores. Each fort had four gates, the main one facing the enemy. From it ran the *Via Praetoria*, to the headquarters and then, as the *Via Decumana*, on towards the opposite gate. The two side gates were joined by the *Via Principia*. The area in front of the *Via Principia* was the *praetentura*; behind it was the *retentura*. Smaller roads were *Via Quintana* and they linked the buildings to one another. Around the inside of the wall was the *intervallum* road providing drilling space, greater communications and free access to the wall. Overall the shape of the fort was that of a playing card, rectangular, with rounded corners. Not all followed the exact pattern, but this was the general form.

As the Roman occupation became more settled, the forts became stronger in structure, built of local stone. The best example of the earlier type can be seen at Longthorpe near Peterborough. This was constructed before AD 48, probably for the Legion IX. It is not of the typical pattern and could not contain a full legion. It is called a vexillian fortress, built to be a headquarters for a legion. Another example of an early fortress is at Hod Hill, the old hill-top fort. It is irregular in shape, being adapted to fit in the corner of the old fort. Other examples can be found at Great Casterton, near Stamford, Waddon Hill near Bridport in Dorset, and Cirencester. The later forts used in many cases the same materials of wood, wattle and daub and earthworks. Good examples have been found at Inchtutil on the Tay and Fendoch at the end of the Sma' Glen. Three major fortresses must be mentioned here: Caerleon (Isca) in Monmouth, Chester (Deva) and York (Eboracum). These were the three chief military centres in the North and West, and an exploration of all three is strongly recommended. They were stone-built and, outside, settlements of the native populations developed to provide services for the large numbers of soldiers within. Other aspects of these towns will be looked at later on. At the same time as these fortresses were reconstructed in stone, other forts were similarly rebuilt. The period which saw this work also saw the building of Hadrian's Wall; a response to the need to protect the province.

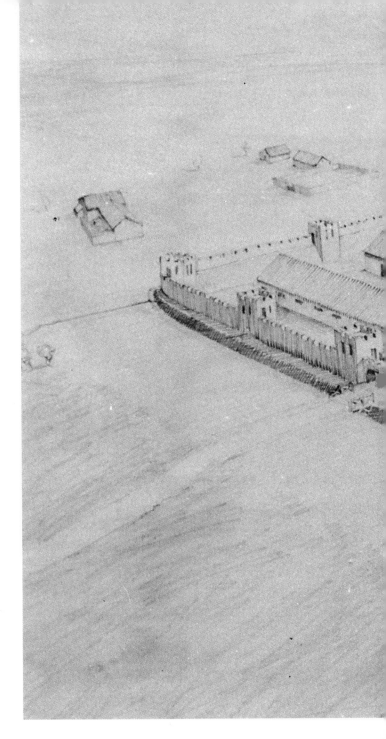

A sketch reconstruction of Segontium auxiliary fort, Caernarvon.

BOUDICCA

THE CAPTURE OF CARADOC did not end the trouble in Wales. Encouraged by the Druids' opposition to the Romans, the Silures continued to fight against the invaders throughout the following decade, and the Ordovices battled on until near extinction in the 70s AD. When the fighting was nearing its end, the Roman forces moved in, mining lead

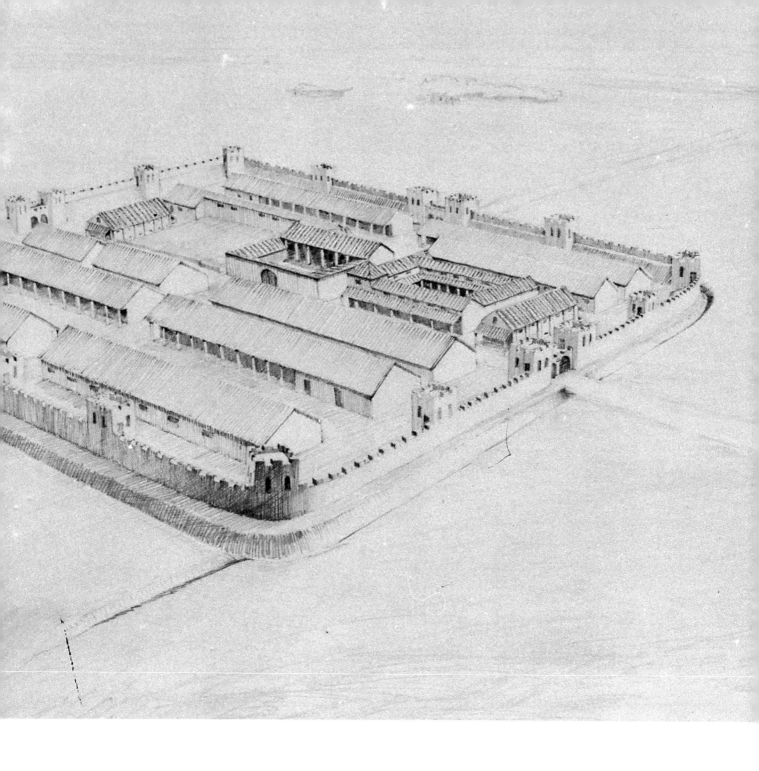

in the North-east and, later, gold in the south-west of Wales. The face of the province changed as a result of the military campaigns in the West. Most of the legions were withdrawn from the South and East to cope with the threat of incursion, and the area took on a more civil aspect. Colchester became the first chartered, or self-governing town, a little like boroughs in later centuries, which to Romans were called 'colonia'. Towns like this were usually filled at first with plots of land doled out to veteran legionaries. In this part of

the province a civil administration, the Roman hierarchical bureaucracy, developed in place of military rule. However, trouble had not entirely disappeared. In AD 60 there was a revolt by the Iceni from the Norfolk area.

The Iceni had been disarmed in the early 50s AD after a minor revolt, but this was not the only grievance in the East. The Trinovantes had fully expected that they would regain the site of their capital, which had been supplanted by Camulodunum following their conquest by the Catuvellauni,

after the latter had in their turn been beaten by the Romans. Instead the site was absorbed into the colonia. There seems also to have been a new rising generation of the Catuvellauni waiting themselves to exact revenge upon the conquerers. The crisis started when the King of the Iceni, Prasutagus, made the Emperor Nero co-heir to his throne with the Queen Boudicca. Nero had no wish for partners. Instead, he aimed to incorporate the Iceni lands into the province and when King Prasutagus died, he set out to achieve this. Roman soldiers went into Iceni territory and began to take over whatever Nero considered his property. The royal family resisted: Boudicca was flogged and her daughters, the eventual heirs, were raped. The Iceni people were furious. Sensing the spirit of the moment, Trinovantes and Catuvellauni joined what had become a major revolt. Boudicca led the angry tribes and in AD 61 Camulodunum colonia was attacked and the veterans and their families were massacred. Londinium (London) was sacked, Verulamium (St Albans) was destroyed and the Britons turned on the Roman forces under Governor Suetonius Paulinus, after first defeating Legion IX. Suetonius with 10,000 men defeated Boudicca's vast army (estimates put the figure at up to 230,000; it was probably much less) between Towcester and Atherstone, possibly at Mancetter. The Queen died; possibly she committed suicide. The governor sacked the Iceni territory, pausing only when he realised that he was actually destroying future Roman wealth.

THE ROMANS WITHDRAW FROM SCOTLAND

NERO, like his co-heir to Norfolk, committed suicide, and a civil war developed in Rome which hindered any activity in the British province. It was not until Vespasian became Emperor that the province could be put in order. It was long realised that the borders were insecure and

The finer houses of Roman Britain were colourful buildings with at least one floor mosaic. This roundel from Corinium (Cirencester, Gloucestershire) depicts Ceres, goddess of agriculture.

that conquest of Wales and the North had to be undertaken to secure the Roman hold. Under Vespasian, three governors achieved this. Troops were freed from middle Britain by extending the civil administration, and new town construction was begun. Isca (Caerleon) and Eboracum (York) were constructed as the main military bases for South Wales, and in the north of England, Deva (Chester) was constructed to watch the newly suppressed North Wales. The province began to grow northwards, across the Clyde and the Forth into the Scottish Highlands. A series of forts was established around the main garrison town of Inchtuthil on the Tay. The work of conquering the northern tribes and the imposition of military rule, was the responsibility of Governor Julius Agricola. He defeated the Caledoni under their leader Calgacus at Mons Graupius (possibly near Inverurie). But after the withdrawal of Agrippa in AD 84, long term plans for the conquest of the whole of Scotland were abandoned, despite geographical expeditions into and around the region. Furthermore, much of this northern territory was abandoned. By the end of the first century AD legions and auxilia were withdrawn and the northern border had to be pulled back past the Forth and Clyde, and eventually to the Tyne and Solway in the reign of Emperor Trajan.

In the first decade of the following century there was serious trouble for the Romans. The northern area was unsettled as the people of the North attacked Roman fortifications. The war was finally over by the time the Emperor Hadrian visited the province in AD 122.

NEW ROMAN TOWNS

WHILST NORTH BRITAIN may have been unstable, and unlikely to fall easily under Roman control, the South was being turned into a full Roman province. Under Agricola a period of urbanisation took place. New colonia appeared at Lindum (Lincoln) and Glevum (Gloucester); and Camulodunum and Verulamium were rebuilt. Urban develop-

The great Roman Bath House at Aqua Sulis, now known as the town of Bath, Avon.

ments were made at Isca Dumoniorum (Exeter), Calleva Atrebatum (Silchester) and Corinium Dobunnorum (Cirencester). The hill-fort which formed the loci of the Durotriges was abandoned in favour of the new site built on the edge of the recent Roman road into the West. The new town was Durnonovaria, later Dorchester, the amphitheatre in the town appearing in Thomas Hardy's *The Mayor of Casterbridge*. Also the setting for a novel was the spring at Aqua Sulis which, as the town of Bath, featured in Jane Austen's *Northanger Abbey* and *Pride and Prejudice*. In many of these the native Celtic aristocracy found homes and used their wealth to build the amenities which made life civilised. It was Rome's intention to spread civilisation amongst the conquered nations – after all, a civilised people would require Roman goods. Towns were constructed by the native peoples – not by order, but they were encouraged and expert advice and skills were provided by the Romans.

The coloniae too, though primarily for the veteran soldiers, were home to the native populations. As with the great fortresses, services grew up in and around the towns. Verulamium already had a large number of colonnaded shopping streets when Boudicca sacked the town. Shops appear to have been narrow-fronted, long buildings. The front was probably open to the street during trading and closed with shutters at night. A fine example can be seen at Catterick. Most buildings in the first century AD were wooden; later they were replaced with stone. Even the wooden buildings were of quite splendid decoration and structure; one at Cirencester shows evidence of fine frescos inside. Even when the larger shops had been replaced with stone buildings, there would still be smaller concerns constructed of timber. Indeed the picture of town life in Roman Britain seems to differ very little from the life of small towns much more recently. Not all of the medieval wooden-framed buildings have been removed from modern towns for example. Shops then, as now, would be bought up, taken over, expanded into the next premises and refurbished in the usual nature of trading.

Other features of the towns included the principal buildings, which were the civil equivalent of the military camp's head-

Above: Roman sewer system at Jewry Wall, Leicester.

Opposite: A sketch reconstruction of the forum at Corinium (Cirencester, Gloucestershire). There is evidence of a free-standing column in the forum dedicated to the worship of Jupiter.

quarters. These were the forum and the basilica. The latter formed the whole of the fourth side of an insulae (the block of land between the roads in a grid pattern street) of which the forum filled the centre. The remaining three sides of the insulae were fronted by porticoes or even shops. The basilica was the council hall from where the town was administered by the magistrates and the forum was an open-air meeting-place for public occasions or market stalls. London had these buildings before the end of the first century. Also, somewhere off-centre, were the bath-houses providing public health facilities with hot rooms for opening clogged pores, cleansing rooms for scraping the dirt off and out of the pores, with a tool called a strigil, and finally the plunge into the cold bath to close the open pores. Natural oils, lost during the process, could be replaced with substitutes available at the baths. Public lavatories were usually attached to the baths and they were

flushed by the waste bath-water. Fine examples can be seen at Chesters on Hadrian's Wall and parts of the bath-house sewer can be seen at the Jewry Wall site in Leicester. Perhaps a doubly rewarding example can be observed through the glass floor of the Roman Bath pub in York. The greatest example is, of course, the huge bath at the once-named Aqua Sulis — Bath. Water for the baths and for the sewerage system could be piped in from the nearest high source. The excess water, not required by the bath-houses or the domestic or other consumer, was channelled into the sewers to shift the detritus. This detritus is of use to the archaeologist. From the human waste we can analyse the diets of the Romano-British peoples and define what crops they grew and ate.

Just outside the walls of the bigger towns were amphitheatres, the entertainment centres of Roman Britain. Best-known from films like *Ben Hur*, as chariot-racing centres, they may not have been quite so glamorous in Britain; it does not seem as if the sport was widely pursued here. Instead many forms of blood sports were practised; executions for treason drew crowds and games of athletic ability also took place there. There are fine examples to be found at Dorchester, Caerleon and Chester. However, the last may be sacrificed to a 'Roman-world' theme centre.

By the second century, as the province became richer, the houses in the towns grew more impressive. The expensive town houses in the early Romano-British period were simple timber structures with five or six rooms. The walls, despite being of wattle and daub, were plastered over and decorated with murals. The windows were glazed and the roofs tiled. These grew, sometimes incorporating the original building but often completely from scratch, into Mediterranean-style houses of masonry. In these, proper concrete floors could be inserted and a hypocaust heating system installed to circulate hot air under the floors. Newer houses were, if possible, built with two wings around a central garden or courtyard. These were built to be beautiful homes, and a house at Leicester had a mural around all of the courtyard: a complete frieze of animals, birds and flowers.

The Multi-angular Tower, York. This was the south-west corner tower of the Roman fortress. The base is Roman and to the right is the line of the Roman city wall.

HADRIAN'S WALL

HADRIAN'S VISIT TO THE NORTH of the province at the end of the war, in AD 122, resulted in the construction of the wall named after him. It was a reversal of the policy of Agricola. Instead of concentrating on the conquest of the North, the Roman province was now geared to preventing the attacks of the northern tribes. The Ninth Legion, stationed in York had been defeated and disgraced. It seems to have been cashiered as a result of the war and this made the Romans

Bronze head of Hadrian found in the Thames by London Bridge.

more circumspect in the North than they had been before. The trouble had sprung from the tribes in south-west Scotland. These were probably the red-haired people who had caused trouble for Agricola earlier and were going to wreck any future attempts to incorporate Scotland into the province. They were described as being distinct from the rest of the Celts in Britain, with their red hair, and they carried round shields and great swords; they also drove chariots. Whilst not yet called Picts by their enemies, (this came about in later centuries) it was under this name that they were to make further incursions into the troubled province. By the end of the Roman occupation, the North was inhabited by three tribes, the best known today being the Picts. Pict was likely to have been a nickname, based on their habit of decorating their bodies with paint. A tall people, they spoke P Celtic, unlike the Scots who spoke Q Celtic and who called the Picts Criuthni. (This is the Q Celtic way of saying Pretani – Britons). There were two tribes of Picts, one to the north of the Highlands and one to the south and east. The Scots came from the north of Ireland and had migrated to the Western Isles and onto the mainland by the end of the Roman occupation of Britain. Pretani, or Britons proper, inhabited the southern Lowlands of Scotland and were to be unnaturally divided from tribal relations by Hadrian's Wall.

The wall was to be a spectacular construction. The scope of the structure was great, stretching from Pons Aelius (Newcastle-upon-Tyne) in the east (although it was later extended to Wallsend) across the country to

the banks of the Solway and Bowness on Solway near Carlisle. It was eighty Roman miles long. Every mile was marked by a milecastle, a small, almost square fort giving access to the north. In between each milecastle were two turrets. The wall was, for the most part 8ft (2.4m) wide, mounted on a base some 10ft (3m) wide. It is likely that this had been the intended width, but the piecemeal construction by three separate legions and the speed required in construction, resulted in many modifications and changes to the original design. The extreme western end, between the River Irthling and Bowness, was constructed to the same pattern but made of turf and fortified with wood. The section between North Tyne and Newcastle was the full width of 10ft (3m) and the last piece between Newcastle and Wallsend was again 8ft (2.4m). Sixteen forts for the housing of the garrisons stationed at the wall were built and linked by a road called the Stanegate. The area containing the forts was demarcated by a ditch, built as a boundary, not as a defence work. In front of the wall was a ditch, except where the crags or heights upon which the wall was built rendered the digging of one

impossible or unnecessary. There are many places from which the wall can be explored, but perhaps the area of Chesters cavalry fort near Chollerford on the North Tyne, and Housesteads infantry fort, 8½ miles (13½ kilometres) to the west are best, and the wall in the vicinity holds views of beautiful rugged grandeur. The forts contain excellent examples of Roman military architecture with bath-houses, granaries, barracks and headquarters.

THE ANTONINE WALL

HADRIAN'S WALL marked the boundary for the period of his reign. The succession of Antoninus Pius brought renewed vigour. In any case, it has been argued, Hadrian's Wall did little to cure the problems in the borders, and the real trouble, the Caledonians, were a long way north. The new push resulted in a wall of turf on cobble foundations, fronted by a ditch and supported by nineteen forts. Further north than the Antonine Wall on the Clyde-Forth line, a few of the old forts built

Hadrian's Wall: Housesteads infantry fort. In the centre of the picture is the headquarters building with the commandant's house below it. In the top right corner are barracks. Outside the fort at the bottom of the picture are some of the dependent civilian buildings.

under Agricola had been reoccupied. This frontier could not be held for long. Serious revolts in the area of the Brigantes, south of Hadrian's Wall, caused the Antonine Wall to be abandoned in AD 154. Five years later a return to Scotland was made but for only three years or so did the Antonine Wall form the northern border of the British province. The forces in the country were too stretched and Hadrian's Wall again became the frontier.

CRISIS

AT THE END OF THE SECOND CENTURY the Roman province of Britain was placed in its most serious crisis by a combination of events outside and from within. Upon the assassination of the Emperor Commodus there was a mammoth power struggle in which the governor of Britain, Clodius Albinus, took part. When he was left with only one rival, Septimius Severus, Albinus crossed into Gaul to fight for the throne. He was defeated. In his absence, tribes in Wales rose against Roman rule and the Brigantes again rebelled. The wall was attacked and empty forts were demolished. The villages which had grown up around the military towns were also destroyed. These were the settlements of the indigenous people, quick to realise that a good living was to be made from permanent settlements of soldiers. In effect they were suburbs. There were significant settlements at Eboracum and Isca (York and Caerleon), but there were lesser ones dotted throughout Wales and England. The villages were often linear − that is, following the line of the roads out of the forts. They were not walled or fortified in any way, and in the second century, they were wooden. In the rising which followed Albinus's attempt to assume the purple (wear the purple robes of the Emperor), they were razed.

The new Emperor, Severus, restored order in Britain and by AD 208 felt able to visit the province: by this time, most of the wrecked fortresses had been rebuilt. Severus died in the province and his son, Caracalla, was proclaimed Emperor in his place, at Eboracum in the head-quarters building, the foundations of which can be seen in the undercroft of York Minster. Caracalla, after a defeat, then came to

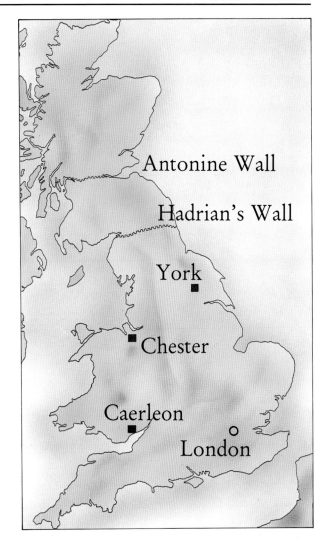

The two Roman walls, the main fortresses and the provincial capital.

an accommodation with the Caledonians and engineered peace with the Brigantes. The northern province entered on a hundred years of peace.

ROMAN VILLAS

PEACE IN THE PROVINCES resulted in prosperity. In the Roman province great estates were built up by those who profited from the occupation. In Wales, some of these have been measured at up to 6,000 hectares, and many were a thousand hectares in extent. In the centre of these estates stood villas, the economic unit like a large farm. Villas contained a wide range of buildings, from luxurious dwellings to stables, barns and mills. Some were occupied for centuries by the same families, some were confiscated from the

Reconstruction of a Roman kitchen at Corinium Museum, Cirencester. Food was cooked on the raised stone hearth on the right.

losers in the various civil wars and some were bought up by Continental entrepreneurs from the third century AD. In some cases the villas were home to two or more families at one time, each participating in the economic activity.

Some of the villas were, not surprisingly, built on the site of earlier farms. Earliest examples, like the one found at Bazely Copse at Micheldever in Hampshire from crop markings, were simple three-room affairs built on an earlier farming site. At Sparsholt, also in Hampshire, there is evidence of a developing farm growing from a simple one-building affair to a large villa and finally into a stockyard and detached hall. In Hertfordshire at Gadebridge Park, the timber house and baths expanded into a complex villa system and then shrank, by the fifth century, to a simple two-room cottage with stockyards.

The residential area of the villa could be lavish. They were generally timber-framed and often faced with rendering, and the insides were plastered and often decorated with mural work. The roofs were thatched, tiled or slated depending upon the availability of local materials. Glazing was known, but many windows were left unglazed because of the expense: all windows would be shuttered. Most villas had mosaic floors in one or more rooms, whilst the other floors were covered with red tiles. There is little information about furniture in the villas, but there were sideboards, occasional tables and dining suites as in modern houses. Diners probably sat at tables in Britain rather than reclining on

Roman model of a ploughman and cattle found at Piercebridge, Co. Durham.

couches in classical style. There are excellent villa sites to visit in Britain: Bignor in West Sussex with its fine museum of villa life is one good example. In Gloucestershire the villa at Chedworth has its main buildings under cover, and Littlecote Park near Hungerford is being excavated. North Leigh in Oxfordshire has a fine mosaic floor in the excavated Triclinium (dining room).

The villa was the centre of a farming community and the province was an agricultural economy. The occupation of the country by the Roman army spurred on agricultural production by providing a large on-site consumer. The Celtic farmers would have had to produce more to pay the military taxes aimed at feeding the army. This seems to have pushed production further than the amount required for just subsistence and a bit extra to cover taxes. Iron-age and earlier cultures were able to produce excess food, and this must have continued and increased. Not all of the construction work done in Britain was undertaken by the legions.

With regard to agricultural methods, the use of the plough was extended. The light plough of the Iron Age first spread in its use and was then superseded in some places by the heavier plough which could turn the cut soil, unlike the earlier one. Many of the improvements made in the Roman period were developments of previous techniques and instruments, much of which went hand-in-hand. The use of iron-blade spades would facilitate better ditching, therefore better drainage and better crop-growing. Simpler, one-handed shears meant

A model of the Claudian temple at Colchester, Essex.

that fleeces could be trimmed more easily and effectively. It was Roman technology applied to the existing knowledge which improved the agricultural wealth of the country.

New crops too were added to British farms. Spelt, a hardy wheat capable of coping with the wet climate, had already supplemented the spring emmer, wheat and barley, enabling winter crops to be grown too and under the Romans its use increased. Oats and flax were also grown in greater quantities and root crops like turnips and carrots provided fodder and food for humans. The fields of the province were often in the same areas as the Iron-age ones, and often still surrounded by ditches. However, squarer and oblong fields were beginning to appear. On the livestock side, cows, sheep and horses were bred to better standards and goats were still raised for their hair. Pig stocks also increased in size. Geese and hens were raised for eggs and flesh too.

RELIGION

THE ROMANS LEFT MUCH of the native religion alone. They hated Druids for several reasons, including their use of human sacrifices in their ceremonies, their involvement in political affairs (remember, they encouraged the Silures under Caradoc) and for their part in education. Although the sacrifices may well have offended Roman dignity and humanity, they were not as dangerous as the Druidical role in politics and education.

The imperial cult, the deification of the dead emperors, was introduced into Britain. One of the first so honoured, was Claudius for whom a temple was built at Colchester. It was destroyed in the Boudiccan revolt, though the building was later re-erected. Similar temples, and their administrative offices were built in Lindum (Lincoln) and Londinium (London).

These were accompanied by the building of temples to the classical gods, Pluto, Jupiter, Neptune, Minerva, Mercury and others, as well as to the abstract gods such as fate, victory etc. In some places these gods and goddesses were intermingled with the local deities. At Aqua Sulis (Bath), Minerva, the goddess of wisdom and learning, was blended with Sul, the deity of the springs. Mars too, was absorbed by the local tribes, linked with Medocius at Colchester and Rigonemetos at Lindum. Worship was undertaken at various shrines or temples – the one at Aqua Sulis being a particularly beautiful example of combined classical and Celtic art.

Mithraism, the worship of Mithras, was imported into Britain from the Middle East via Rome. It demanded high standards of conduct from its adherents who believed that the bull of darkness and chaos had been slaughtered by Mithras. There were centres of worshippers at Londinium, Caernarvon and Housesteads, of which Londinium was the most important. The cult of Mithras appealed to soldiers and the merchant classes chiefly. Mithraic temples were small and rectangular, often with an apse at the western end.

Mithraism came into Britain at the same time as Christianity. The latter, until the Edict of Toleration in 313, was punishable by death, because of the refusal of Christians to swear loyalty to the Emperor. Certainly there would have been Christian sects in Britain by the second century, but as they would have been underground, little evidence has been found. There were several martyrs during this period, Julius and Aaron amongst them; but the most famous is Alban, killed at Verulamium (now St Albans) in the late second or early third century. By the time the edict was passed, there was a strong Christian presence. In 314 there were established three bishoprics: Eboracum, Lindum and Londinium, and possibly a fourth, Cirencester. One early 'church' has been found at Silchester in Hampshire; at Richborough, there is a timber-frame church and at the villa at Lullingstone in Kent there is a Christian chapel. Villas prove a rich site for evidence of Christianity – better than the urban environment. Christianity inspired a reaction and upsurge in other religions and new temples sprang up in various places.

Capital from the free-standing column at Corinium, illustrated on page 38. This face depicts Silenus, an attendant of Bacchus, god of wine and fertility.

THE END OF ROMAN BRITAIN

IN CARACALLA'S REIGN, Britain was divided into two provinces to prevent there being a pretender to the purple again from the country. Britannia Superior embraced the south of the province as far up as Deva (Chester). Britannia Inferior included the area to the north and the border lands. The capital was at Eboracum (York). The same sort of division, for similar reasons, was made in Syria. Whilst Britain was chiefly quiet, the south and east coast was being plundered by German tribes, sailing up the navigable rivers, raiding the ports from which coastal trade was plied. New forts were built on these chief rivers – there are examples to be found at Reculver in Kent and at Brancaster on the Wash.

In the following century, the Empire fell into chaos. The inhabitants of Britain (or of Rome, for citizens they had become) in 212, were not directly involved. Nevertheless,

there was less building work carried on during the third century. Britain and Gaul became a semi-independent empire as an experiment between 259 and 274; but it was short-lived and had little effect upon ordinary life. When Diocletian assumed the purple, he bound together most of the Empire. Britain remained aloof under Carausius until he was murdered. Britain was reconquered by Rome and the renegade legions and auxilia were defeated. When these were drawn south to fight the Empire's armies, the Caledonians, or Picts as they were now called, invaded the North. The province was re-ordered by Constantius Chlorus, the western Augustus (the Empire was now governed in two parts, one from Rome, the other from Byzantium – later Constantinople). He died at York in 306 and was succeeded by Constantine who became sole Emperor in 312. The province of Britain was again divided, into four. The southern part was now Maxima Caesarienis with Londinium as the capital and Britannia Prima with a capital at Cirencester. The northern became Flavia Caesarienis centred on Eboracum and Britannia Secunda with Lindum as the capital. After Constantine's death in 337 Britain became anarchic. The raids on the east coast continued to grow in number and seriousness and the Picts attacked the North. The Duke of Britain, the person in charge of the North, was defeated and driven from the wall in 367 when many tribes united to attack the province. It was two years before Count Theodosius was sent to restore order. Most of the damage had been done by this time and many of the barbarian tribes had departed with the booty.

The peace restored in Britain lasted twenty years until the Duke of Britain, Magnus Maximus, tried to take over the western empire. He left the province in 383 with most of the troops available. In his absence the Irish began to raid the west coast and to settle there. By 396 new attempts were made to re-establish order in the province, but Rome was under pressure from the central European barbarians and Britain was a far-off place, considered useful only as a source of reinforcements. In 410 the last legions were withdrawn and the towns were told to defend themselves: armies had left before and the province probably expected their return at some future date: but the far-flung province had been abandoned.

Above: Tombstone of Sextus Valerius Genialis, a Roman trooper, buried at Cirencester, Gloucestershire.

Opposite: Tombstone of Marcus Favonius Facilis, a centurion, buried at Colchester, Essex.

3. THE AGE
OF
BEDE
410–1000

THE LEGIONS DID NOT RETURN and the towns had to fend for themselves. To do so the 'High King' Vortigern, based in central Wales, who came to prominence after the Romans had left, began to allow Saxons – a general term embracing the three chief immigrant groups, the Angles, Jutes and the Saxons – to settle in Kent and on the east coast. Each had different geographical origins. The Angles, whose name was to encompass most if not all of the invaders when it became altered to English, came from the bottom of the Cimbric peninsula (today, this is south Denmark). The Jutes may have been their immediate neighbours to the north from the area of Denmark named after them, Jutland, or they may have come from the Rhineland. The Saxons hailed from northern Germany, around the lower part of the River Elbe. Vortigern's motive was plain. He needed their support against the greater enemy – the Picts and Scots.

Vortigern's reign ended when the Christian Church intervened to put a stop to the 'heretical' beliefs he held. Vortigern subscribed to Pelagianism, a Christianity which did not accept the concept of 'original sin': Adam's fall had not damned all mankind thereafter. To the followers of the British monk Pelagius, grace, or entry into heaven, was assured by the individual's good works. To the church in Rome this was heresy and Vortigern and the members of the British aristocracy who held these views were driven from power after Germanus was sent to quell

Saxon expansion into Britain in the two centuries following the departure of the Romans.

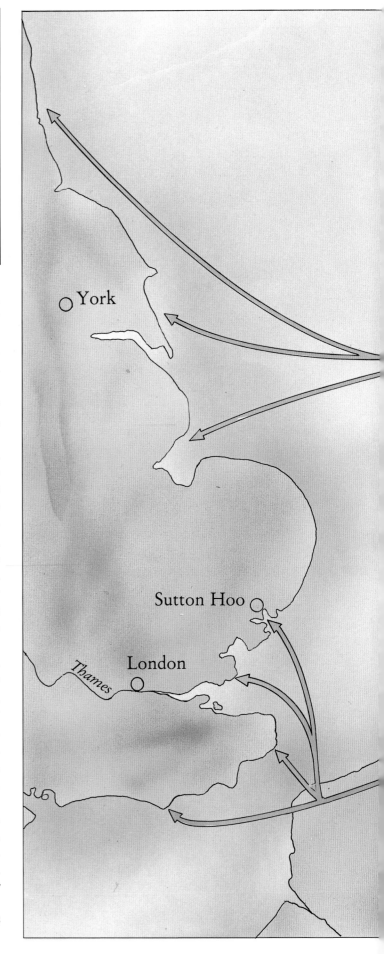

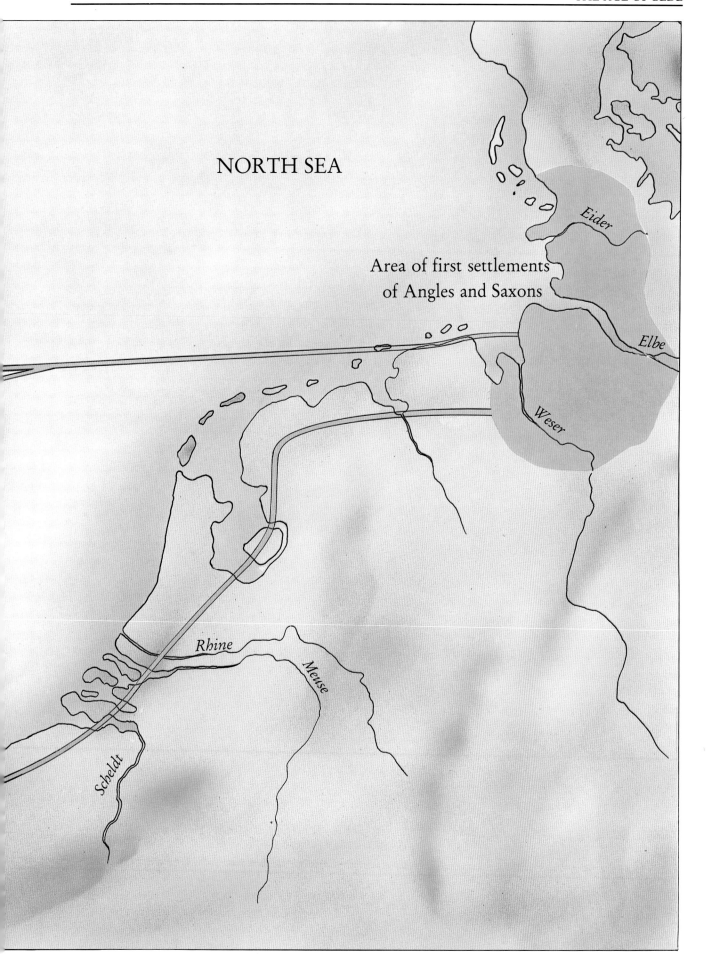

NORTH SEA

Area of first settlements
of Angles and Saxons

Eider

Elbe

Weser

Rhine

Meuse

Scheldt

TIME CHART

449	The date ascribed to the first landing of the new settlers.
446–454	The last appeal to Rome.
514 or 516	The battle of Badon halts the Saxon advance for half a century.
563	Columba sets up the mission at Iona.
570	By this year Northumbria's capital is at Bamburgh Castle.
577	The Battle of Dyrham; the West Saxons cut through the Severn Valley, separating Cornwall and Wales.
586–93	Northumbria fights and defeats the British coalition in the west of England.
597	Augustine begins his mission in Kent.
605	Bernicia and Deira united.
630s–658	Northumbria attempts to control Mercia and fails.
664	The Synod of Whitby.
670	Mercian expansion includes London.
757	Offa, the King of all England, comes to the throne.
793	The first Viking raids occur.
829	Mercia is taken over by Wessex kings.
843	Kenneth MacAlpine becomes King of Scotland.
866	York falls to the Vikings.
878	King Alfred holds back the Vikings after the battle of Ashdown. Most of Wales united under the first High King, Rhodri Mawr.
910	The beginning of the reconquest of England.
927	High King of Wales Hywel Dda accepts the overlordship of the English King Aethelstan.
945	Cumbria let to Malcolm I of Scotland by Edmund of England.
959–75	The reign of Edgar over England. It is followed by renewed Norse conquest.
1016	The establishment of a Norse empire based in England.
1040	King Duncan murdered by Macbeth.

Opposite: A belt-set from the early years of the fifth century. The design is Germanic and it may have been worn by one of the early Saxon mercenaries. Discovered in a grave at Mucking, Essex.

the heresy in 429. Germanus also led a successful attack on the Picts – his forces yelled 'alleluia' and off the Picts ran. Vortigern was not helped by the risings of the Saxon mercenaries. He had initially allowed three boat-loads, led by Hengist and Horsa, who were Jutes, to settle on Thanet – but once they were in, they and the Saxons wanted to expand inland. Vortigern was superseded by the orthodox Christian, Ambrosius, who gathered the Romano-British Christians about him but could not contain the Saxon incursions. The last appeal to Rome, probably made in 446, fell on unreceptive ears, and attempts by Ambrosius to re-enter the imperial fold came to nought.

There was no headlong rush into barbaric decline. For the majority of the one-time province, the departing of the legions was followed by a period of prosperity. Unlike Gaul, the slaves and peasants of Britain did not rebel wholesale. They may have rejected their overlords in some instances: Lullingstone's villa may have been overthrown by the local peasantry; the Picts did destroy forts on the decreasingly effective Hadrian's Wall; forts on the east coast were also wrecked. However, much of the decline experienced by Britain came not through violence but as a result of the fall-off in trade. Some outlying villas lost their markets as the Roman roads fell into disrepair. Markets, deprived of the produce, shrank and their buildings became empty. As wealth declined so did the ability and will to maintain the communal services of the towns. A few like Verulamium retained working aqueducts and waterworks. Indeed, new buildings were still built of masonry: Chichester kept going as a market centre until the middle of the fifth century, but then operations contracted. In the South-east the towns were absorbed by the Saxons and parts of towns were given over to ex-soldiers, as with Roman colonia. As the Saxons moved west, the Jutes through Kent, the Angles inwards from the east coast and the Saxons from Essex, Sussex and Hampshire, the British aristocracy moved ahead of them. Villas were abandoned and in many cases so were the slaves and peasantry. Many of the lower classes of society were no worse off under the new conquerers after all; they had little to lose and some Celtic tribes stayed on in the Fens for four centuries. On the other hand, the towns

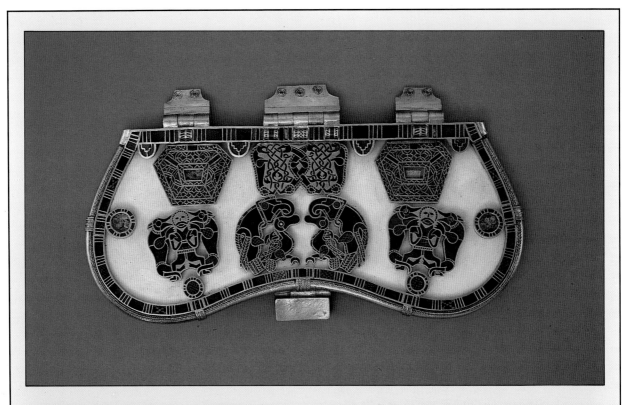

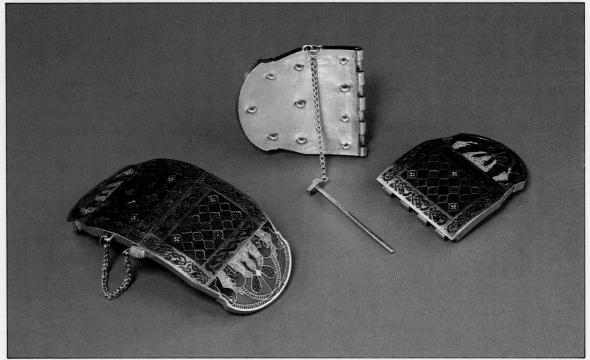

Sutton Hoo

A magnificent Anglo-Saxon 'ship burial' was discovered on the East Anglian coast at Sutton Hoo in 1939. Its wealth of treasures and weaponry suggested it was a royal tomb, probably that of Raedwald, King of the East Angles, who died in the 620s. Above is a purse lid from the tomb, below it are shoulder clasps of gold and garnet.

nearest to the Saxons became depopulated by the middle of the fifth century. Inhabitants moved to smaller sites which they found easier to defend. The towns were left with populations too small to undertake proper defence. Some towns were abandoned and others were reoccupied by the Saxons.

KING ARTHUR

AMBROSIUS WAS SUCCEEDED in his fight against the Saxons by the most mysterious of figures from British history: Arthur. He emerged from the declining Romano-British culture that persisted in the towns which attempted to maintain elements of the provincial administration. His activity against the encroaching Saxons followed the lead established by Ambrosius who had forced back their advances. Arthur, or Artorius, could have been born in the period when a fashion for romanised names was inspired by Ambrosius' successes, probably in the 470s. He came to prominence, not as king but as a war-lord, when Ambrosius died or retired. He established a following, a good cavalry unit perhaps – based on the late Roman *clibanarius*. It is not too great a leap from this to the romanticised Knights of the Round Table. Several years after Arthur died these soldiers received names. For instance, Kei and Bedewyr appear in the *Black Book of Carmarthen*. Arthur was a man of the West, perhaps Cornwall, although Wales has claims upon him too. Camelot has generally been identified as being at Cadbury in Somerset which was an occupied hill-fort at that time.

Arthur is associated with twelve successful battles. The last, Mount Badon, halted the incursions of the Saxons for some years. These battles seem to have ranged all over the South and the Midlands, from Chester to Caerleon in the West to Lindsey in Lincolnshire. Badon seems to have been fought in 516 or 518, but the place where it was fought is not easy to locate. Any of the places named Badbury between Dorset and Lincoln could be the site, yet so might one of the hills around Bath – Caer Vadon as it is known in the Welsh.

If the accounts written within the next few hundred years are pieced together, a little more comes to light. Despite the heavily Christianised stories which appeared (Arthur was portrayed carrying a cross on his shoulders at Mount Badon, for three days and three nights) Arthur was not universally successful in his dealings with the Church. One story has Arthur attempting to seize a man from the sanctuary of Cadoc's Abbey of Llancarfen. In the twelfth century in *The Life of St Padarn*, Arthur is referred to as Tyrannus – a tyrant without legitimate power. It may be possible that Arthur requisitioned Church property to support his military forces and that this is what the Church resented and recorded. Twenty-one years after the success at Badon, Arthur died at the battle of Camlaun, where Medraut also fell. This last battle became the fight against his treacherous son, Modred.

It was in the 1450s that Sir Thomas Mallory created *La Morte d'Arthur* chiefly from French romances which had built upon the earlier tales. Mallory's work did not create the full image of Arthur as *Regis quondam regisque futuri* (the once and future King) – this was done much later in the nineteenth century by Tennyson's *Idylls of the King* and given colour by the work of the Pre-Raphaelite artists. It is through this glorious mist that we must peer at the real story of Britain's defender against the Saxons, a man not in need of embellishment. Instead, it was perhaps the societies which created King Arthur which sought embellishment. When his body was discovered in 1190 it was used, if not entirely engineered, as a prop to the monarchy of the time. If Arthur was found to be buried as any mortal was, he could not rise with his knights again. Despite the fact that Arthur was from the Celtic fringes and fought against the races who brought the name England to the country, he has been appropriated by England as the saviour *Regisque futuris*, the future king. England thus sought the enhancement which the great Arthur brought.

SCOTLAND

IN THE NORTH, which had never fully succumbed to the Romans, the Picts were joined by the Scots who moved in from Ireland, and by the time Arthur defeated the Saxons at Badon, a Scottish kingdom had been

A Saxon king sitting in council and dispensing justice, from an Anglo-Saxon translation of the Old Testament, c.1000.

established by Fergus Mor consisting of Kintyre, Loarne and Oban. The Scots were Christian and received support from Ireland, which enabled them to hold off the Picts. They developed their hold over the next one hundred years and in 563 received the mission of St Columba, who united them under the house of Gabrain and its head, Aidan. The latter led the nation in its fight against the incursions of the Angles who had occupied the north of England. After his defeat at Degastan, the Scots influence declined in the west of the country. The Angles penetrated only the south Lowlands for any length of time; the real power in Scotland developed as the Picts and the Scots united. When the Scots went into decline as a political force after Aidan's defeat, the Picts were able to dominate the region. However, the Scots with their Christian traditions and their learning were not entirely subordinated. In 843 the Scots king, Kenneth MacAlpine, succeeded to the Pictish throne. When his successors were buried on Iona they were entitled the Kings of the Scots. Thus the kingdom became known as Scotia — later Scotland.

THE SETTLEMENT OF WALES

IN THE LANDS yet to become England the effects of the battle of Mount Badon lasted for only around fifty years and the Britons, the Celtic peoples, were driven ever westwards. The writer Gildas suggested in the first half of

coast and into the Severn Valley. The aim was to divide the Welsh Britons from those in Cornwall. In 577 the army of Cuthwine and Caewlin made its way into the region which linked Wales and the South-west, the area around Bath, Gloucester and Cirencester. The Saxon army defeated three local 'kings', Conmail, Condidan and Farinmail at the battle of Dyrham, seven miles north of Bath. The kings died and the towns fell to the Saxons. The Britons were now divided.

THE KINGDOMS OF ENGLAND

THE INVADERS had by this time developed a sense of their own 'separateness'; they no longer considered themselves linked to mainland European tribes, except by culture. By the end of the sixth century the separate kingdoms, referred to as the heptarchy, had been established. There were actually more than the seven kingdoms implied by the title as some were, at one time or another divided. Northumbria was the largest, stretching from the Scottish Lowlands down to south Yorkshire. This kingdom is commemorated on maps by the county of Northumberland. For some of the time this great kingdom was divided into two, Bernicia – the north-east of which is incorporated in the modern county to the north – and Deira to the south. The inhabitants of this kingdom were probably derived chiefly from the Angles, indeed they were named English by the great historian Bede a couple of centuries later. The kingdom of Lindsey encompassed Lincolnshire and part of East Anglia. It is recalled by the northern division of the modern county of Lincolnshire. The present Midlands cover what was once the kingdom of Mercia. Other kingdoms have passed more directly into British county or regional names. The kingdom of the East Saxons is roughly Essex, the South Saxon kingdom included Kent and also Sussex to which it left its name. West Saxons left behind the name Wessex, resurrected by Thomas Hardy in the late nineteenth century. The Saxons living in the middle of those in the east, south and west were the Middle Saxons, who left behind Middlesex.

In the middle of the seventh century, the most powerful of the kingdoms was

the sixth century that Badon brought peace and prosperity and he berated the kings of the Britons for casting off the Roman ways which, he felt, expressed not only the knowledge of Rome but also of Christianity. By this time the Britons were strongest in the area which was to become Wales. Gildas mentions only a few, but the most powerful of all seems to have been Maelgwn Gwynedd who ruled the Gwynedd area from Deganwy on the north Welsh coast.

As the Saxon invaders organised themselves into kingdoms centred upon the main aristocratic families which emigrated to Britain, they pushed on westwards, forcing the Britons back into Wales and Cornwall. The Hampshire dynasty, founded by Cerdic early in the sixth century, thrust along the south

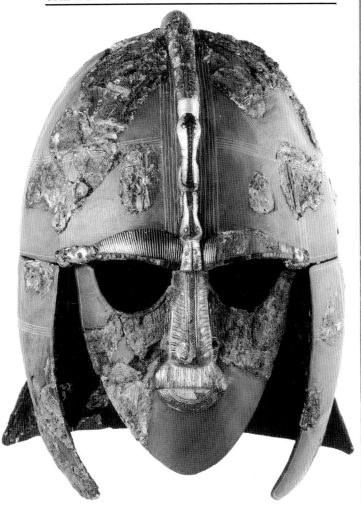

King Raedwald's helmet from Sutton Hoo.

Bamburgh Castle, Northumberland.

Northumbria. The kingdom grew out of the two kingdoms of Bernicia and Deira. Deira was secured in the middle of the sixth century under the king Aelle, descendant of Soemil who had separated the kingdom from Bernicia. At the same time as Aelle became king, the northern kingdom was entered by Ida, who went to war with the native Britons. Ida established Bamburgh as his capital. It is a place well worth visiting and the view of the castle, built at a later date, is one of the most dramatic scenes in northern England.

Ida went on the offensive against the British king Outigern. Then his son, Theodoric, was attacked by coalitions of Celtic tribes led by Urien of Rheged (an area incorporating part of Cumberland) and Rhydderch of Strathclyde. The alliance was successful until the point when it besieged Theodoric on Lindisfarne. During the siege Urien was murdered by a jealous rival and the alliance collapsed. Under the son of a nephew of Theodoric, Aethelfrith, the Britons were defeated at Catraeth (perhaps

Catterick — but this is open to question) around the year 600 and driven west. After one more war against the west Britons of the kingdom of Elmet (now still traced in place names in west Yorkshire such as Sherburn in Elmet), Aethelfrith, who was not a Christian, defeated the Scots Christian king Aidan, as mentioned earlier, and in 605 united Deira and Bernicia as Northumbria. He went on to defeat Britons near Chester, when, it was asserted, he murdered 1,200 monks at Bangor-is-y-coed for praying to the Christian God on behalf of his enemies. Aethelfrith was in turn defeated by the East Angles and killed. His sons were driven into exile and Northumbria was ruled by Aella's son, Edwin, who destroyed Elmet. In the face of Northumbrian aggression, the Britons of Rheged and Strathclyde declined in importance and the Scots and Picts never again attacked northern England.

The kingdom of East Anglia was formed as the kingdom of Bernicia was being forged and

Deira was secured under Aella. A new wave of immigrants settled in the south of the area and under King Wehha went on to subjugate the whole of East Anglia, claiming it for the royal family of Wuffingas, descendants of the son of Wehha, Wuffa. Raedwald, buried at Sutton Hoo, was of the Wuffingas family. Before Wehha secured the control of East Anglia, settlers had moved inland along the Trent and other rivers into the Midlands. A royal family named after an ancestor, Icel, and known therefore as the Icelingas dominated the region south of the Humber and east of the area named Wales.

Many of the settlements of the Southumbrians or Mercians — the dwellers of the Marcher areas on the edge of Wales, were gathered around the Trent. We can see their settlement names from suffixes such as -worth, -field, -ham and -ton which mingle with the earlier Roman ones like Caster, often recast as Chester; Birming*ham*, Wolver*hampton*, and Wiggin*ton* are West Midland examples. The latter is a word derived from the name of an erstwhile owner Wicka or Wigga; it therefore means Wigga's ton or tun, a settlement later corrupted to town. Other less prominent suffixes also date from this incursion along the Trent Valley. Ibstock in Leicestershire is named after a one-time settler named Ibbe or Ibba, who would have had some form of farm or stock there. Nearby Hugglescote would once have been Hucca's cot, a cottage or homestead. Next to Hucca's cot was another tun now called Donington le Heath following yet another invasion of the region after 1066.

The other kingdoms were generally older. Kent and the south Saxon territory was a direct result of the early incursions of the Saxons. Wessex was forged as Saxons pushed along the south coast from Hampshire and was consolidated by the military actions of Cynric and Caewlin when they finally divided the Celts.

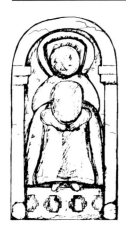

Madonna panel, possibly from the seventh century, at Deerhurst Priory Church, Gloucestershire.

CHRISTIANITY

THE HISTORY OF ENGLAND in the seventh century is dominated by the Christian conversion of the inhabitants and latterly with bringing England firmly under Rome's guidance. Within years of the departure of the Romans, St Ninian had founded one of the earliest monasteries at Whitehorn in Dumfriesshire. Germanus brought other monastic orders into the country. This Celtic Christianity naturally suffered a decline at the hands of the non-Christian Saxons. The Angles and Saxons brought with them their natural gods and goddesses. Many of these have passed into our everyday usage – Tiw, Woden, Thunor, Frig, for example, as Tuesday, Wednesday, Thursday and Friday. Tiw was originally a god of war supplanted by the far more vicious Woden who delighted in broken promises and bloodshed; he was also credited as the ancestor of the East Saxons. Thurnor took care of the farmers maintaining a watchful eye over fertility and the elements. Frig was married to Woden. There were others: Eostre gave her name to the Saxon month of April and later to the Christian feast of Easter; she was also a goddess of light. Superior to the gods and goddesses were the fates, past, present and future. They meddled with the deities' plans and wove a complex web of destruction around the gods, goddesses and humans. Religious buildings were constructed in England. Some, named Hearg (temple), have left evidence of their existence in place names such as Harrow; others, called weoh (sanctuary) can be traced to places like Weedon in Buckinghamshire.

Christianity was brought in by several missionaries, often called saints by following Christians. In 597 St Augustine arrived in Kent after Pope Gregory had sent him to convert the Angles, the natural beauty of whom he likened to Angels. But there were, in the border areas especially, native Christians and possibly several religious communities lingering from the days of the Celts. These made small-scale conversions and their laxity was criticised by Augustine – they were not fervent enough. Augustine converted the King of Kent, Aethelberht. The King of the Northumbrians in 617, Edwin, successor to Aella, succumbed to Paulinus who had ventured north from the mission to Kent. The Kent mission also claimed Raedwald of the East Saxons, although his kingdom was a little more tardy in taking on the new god. The

Panel carving on the Franks casket, made in Northumbria in the early eighth century. It depicts a pagan scene alongside the Adoration of the Magi.

successful mission founded Canterbury as the centre of English Christianity. York was established as a northern outpost, with Paulinus named bishop in 626. Aethelberht's successor, Eabald, nearly drove out the Christian mission but his conversion at the last moment halted the pagan reaction. Similarly, Raedwald's successor, Eorpwald, accepted Christianity, but on his death East Anglia returned to pagan belief until the 630s.

King Edwin was killed in battle against the Gwynedd King, Cadwallon, and Penda, the pagan King of Mercia, in 634. Penda went on to crush the Anglian Saxons and killed King Sigebert in 636. However, Cadwallon died in battle against King Oswald of Northumbria a year earlier and the reconstruction of Christian Northumbria began. Aggressive Christian attacks on Penda failed when Oswald died in battle against him in 643. Yet Penda was fighting a losing battle: his own son, Peada, was converted to Christianity in 654 and eventually Penda died in battle against Oswald's Christian brother, Oswiu. Mercia fell under his control and despite Peada's murder, the conversion of Mercia went ahead and continued under Wolfhere, another son and eventual successor to Penda. By 664 Northumbria, the strongest Christian nation, came under full Roman Church control eschewing the Celtic Church and its older notions of the dating of Easter. From within this great kingdom came one of the great Englishmen − Bede the chronicler

BEDE

IT IS PROBABLE that Bede was born at Wearmouth in 673. His parents sent him, at the age of seven, to be educated by Abbot Benedict at the local monastery. Later he was transferred to Jarrow, where in 686 he and Abbot Ceolfrid were the only surviving monks able to carry out divine service after an outbreak of the plague. At the exceptionally early age of nineteen Bede was made a deacon by the Bishop of Hexham – later Saint John of Beverley. Eleven years later he became a priest. For the next thirty years Bede compiled materials for his history of England, whilst working on commentaries on the scriptures. He provided us with a detailed record of monastic life in the early centuries of English history. The abbots, of whatever origin, were expected to undertake the most arduous of the duties. They, of course, had to officiate at the religious services conducted seven times during the church day, but they also had to labour in the fields which provided the monasteries with their food. In addition they worked on the scriptures, reading them and in some cases copying them out.

Bede completed the book, which is known to us as *A History of the English Church and People*, in 731, some four years before his death. He dealt with the centuries so far covered in this and the previous chapter, with the development of the English Church and the creation of the nation itself. It is a great and dramatic text, part of which details the history of the kings of Northumbria and portrays their attempts to dominate the whole of the North.

Naturally, to a man concerned with the work of his God, this period of conquest is imbued with the aura of a crusade: the extension of Northumbrian power into Mercia was the extension of Christianity also. Bede's bias is obviously angled towards the Christian peoples and against the pagans. Bede also attacks the Celtic Christians for their adherence to the older forms of the Christian calendar. The book contains many descriptions of petty miracles, some of an almost childlike nature. One concerns the remains of King Oswald which were to be transferred from Oswald's tree (now Oswestry) by the will of his niece at Bardney Abbey in Lindsey, then part of Mercia. 'The monks were

reluctant to admit it; for although they acknowledged Oswald's holiness, they were influenced by old prejudices against him even after his death, because he originally came from another province and had ruled them as an alien king.' However providence revealed the dead king's holiness: 'for throughout the night a pillar of light shone skywards from the waggon . . .' (Bede *op cit* Chapter 2, Book 3.). Bede was engaged in a struggle to assert the Christian religion at a time when other religions were still being practised. In some ways miracles were an extension of the process of conversion. Bede and the Christian Church had to prove somehow that their God was greater and more powerful than others – and miracles were a convenient way of doing this. Another part of the process adopted in Britain as elsewhere was the absorption of pagan festivals into the Christian calendar. The celebration of the birth of Christ – Christmas – was taken from other festivals including Saturnalia. Easter took its name from the Celtic goddess, Eostra.

Thanks to Bede's work we are made familiar with one of the women who demonstrated their ability to wield power in early England. Women such as Hilda or Hild were not unusual in the early history of England but some have been filtered out by the male Christian authors of the middle ages. Abbesses wielded great power in the areas under their control; they were fundamental to the development of the early Christian Church, and many became minor saints. Penda, the last pagan King of Mercia, fathered several holy children, amongst them two women, Cyneburg and Cyneswith.

Hilda herself was born around 614, a relation of King Edwin of Northumbria. For thirty-three years she led a secular life, yet had been converted to Christianity by Bishop Paulinus. When she gave up the secular life she went into orders, first in East Anglia and then at the mouth of the River Wear and went on to become Abbess at Hartlepool. The abbey there had been founded by a woman, Herutue, reputedly the first woman to become a nun in Northumbria. She became learned, and was taught by Bishop Alcuin, the man who

Opposite: The opening of the First Book of Bede's Ecclesiastical History, Folio 3 v. The Leningrad Bede (courtesy M. E. Saltykov – the Shchedrin State Public Library, Leningrad).

BRITA
NIA

Oceani insula cui quondam albion
nomen fuit inter septentrionem
et occidentem locata est germaniae
galliae hispaniae maximis euro
pae partibus multo interuallo ad
uersa. quae per milia passuum
dccc in boream longa latitudinis
habet milia cc exceptis dum taxat
prolixioribus diuersorum promon
toriorum tractibus. quibus efficitur
ut circuitus eius quadragies octies
lxxv milia compleat. Habet a meri
die galliam belgicam. cuius proximi
litus transmeantibus aperitur ciuitas
quae dicitur rutubi portus, a gen
te anglorum nunc corrupte reptacaestir
uocata. Inter pestuario manu
a gessoriaco morinorum gentis
litore primo. traiectu milium l
siue ut quidam scripsere stadiorum
cccel. A tergo autem unde oceano
infinito patet orcadas insulas ha
bet

Optima frugibus atque arboribus insula
et alendis apta pecoribus ac iumentis
uineas etiam quibusdam in locis ger
minans. Sed et auium ferax terra
marique generis diuersi. fluuiis quoque
multum piscosis ac fontibus pre clara
copiosis. et quidem precipue isicio
abundat et anguilla. Capiuntur
autem saepissime et uituli marini
et delfines. nec non et balenae. exceptis
uariorum generibus concyliorum.
In quibus sunt et musculae quibus. inclusam
saepe margaritam omnis quidem
coloris optimam inueniunt. id est
rubicundi et purpurei et hiacinthini
et prasini. sed maxime candidi sunt.
Sed et cocleae satis superque habundan
tes quibus tinctura coccinei coloris
conficitur. cuius rubor pulcherrimus
nullo umquam solis ardore: nulla
ualet pluuiarum iniuria pallescere.
sed quo uetustior eo solet esse uenustior
Habet fontes calidarum. habet et
fontes calidos. et de his fluuios bal
nearum calidarum. omni aetati
et sexui in distincta loca iuxta
suum cuique modum accommodos.
Aqua enim ut sanctus basilius dicit
feruidam qualitatem recipit. cum per
certa quaedam metalla transcurrit.
currit. et sit non solum calida sed
et ardens. quae etiam uenis metal
lorum aeris ferri plumbi

founded the ministerum at York – a kind of ecclesiastical university. Hilda was of the old, or Celtic Christian tradition, believing that the gentle St John was preferable to the strict Paul and she was opposed to the result of the Synod of Whitby's debate when the Roman doctrine prevailed. Hilda was in favour of resistance to this, only to be overruled by the majority of the Celtic Christians. Her wisdom was recognised as being so great that, according to Bede, kings and princes sought and applied her advice. Five of the religious men who were educated at her abbey at Streanaeshalch (Whitby) went on to become bishops, one of them a saint – John of Beverley. Of course the church would not permit a woman, even one of Hilda's greatness, to go on to such honour. The abbess lived sixty-six years, dying in 680.

Hilda discovered one of the greatest early English Christian poets – Caedmon. He was reputedly a swineherd who, according to Bede, at first eschewed all opportunities to sing. However, whilst avoiding a performance on his harp at a social gathering, Caedmon witnessed a vision in a barn. An unknown figure bade him sing of the creation, and Caedmon found that he could sing beautifully: what is more he could compose poetry on religious themes. He was presented to Abbess Hilda who took him into the monastery and had him educated. Caedmon was for the rest of his life capable of creating the most stirring verse.

Opposite: The title-page of Bede's Life of St. Cuthbert. King Aethelstan presents a book to the saint.

Below: This Saxon chapel dates from the eleventh century, built by Earl Odda at Deerhurst, Gloucestershire, in honour of his brother, Aelfric. It is likely that it was a rebuilding of an earlier structure within a complex of buildings, of which the Priory Church on page 67 is the most significant.

SAXON ARCHITECTURE

THERE ARE SEVERAL EXAMPLES of the buildings created in early England which can be visited today. Although most have vanished from above ground, they can still tell us of the environment of Saxon England. Under the great cathedral of Canterbury lies one of the earliest of the post-Roman Christian churches – St Peter and St Paul. It was built at the turn of the seventh century and was the chief of the Kentish churches – the oldest stone Saxon churches in Britain. These usually had a nave for the laity and an altar with a smaller section – an apsidal chapel – for the clergy. St Cedd's at Bradwell-on-Sea in Essex is a good example of this. Later developments seen at Canterbury, for example, were porticus, small cells at the sides of the nave.

The later type of church dating from the mid-seventh century came from Northumbria after the Synod of Whitby had united the English churches and after their rejection of the Celtic Christian observations. Fine examples of these churches can be traced in the ruins at Jarrow. They had squared ends, not the curved apse of the Kentish churches. There were often large numbers of porticus on each side of the nave, which possibly contained small altars or served as administration rooms. There is an excellent church, still in use, at Escomb, near Bishop Auckland in County Durham. It is of early Saxon date, and has a nave, a squared chancel and one porticus. The whole structure is just 50ft (15m) long. Some of the stone for its construction was lifted from the nearby abandoned Roman town at Binchester, and this can be recognised from the Roman carvings, now often inverted.

On an entirely different scale is the church at Brixworth in Northamptonshire. This church had a large nave flanked with porticus and at the east end an octagonal presbytery was placed at a much later date. Some of these Saxon churches were the resting places of the local kings or saints. At Repton in Derbyshire, St Wystan, a Mercian king, was buried in a chamber under the church. It was altered to have an ingress and egress to allow pilgrims visiting the tomb to file in and out in a continuous stream. A simpler crypt was the resting place of King Ince at Glastonbury Abbey.

A later innovation of the Saxon church builders was the use of a tower. There are interesting examples of these still to be seen. At Hough-on-the-Hill in Lincolnshire there is an excellent tower incorporating a stair turret which is almost circular in plan. Towers in that county have two distinct stages and are fairly plain on the outside. This style is shared by the Northumbrian towers which generally rise at an almost constant width, but have decorated sound holes and belfry windows surmounting them. There are a series of towers in East Anglia which are circular in plan: Haddiscoe Thorpe is a good example. The splendid tower of the church at Earls Barton in Northamptonshire is unlike the others, highly decorated, rising in four original stages, now surmounted by a later brick-work top stage. The outside of the tower has beautiful pilaster strip-work on it, a Continental innovation, often used to help keep rubble walls in straight lines. At Earls Barton they undoubtedly serve a chiefly decorative purpose.

Whilst the churches were built of stone, the architectural environment of Bede's England was dominated by wooden structures. At West Stow in Suffolk a Saxon village has been excavated and then reconstructed. There were several types of building. Small huts which were dwellings and perhaps workshops have been built with suspended wooden floors, a possible means of avoiding dampness. The walls of the larger 'hall', like those of Greensted church in Essex, are built of large solid timbers, whilst the huts may only have had planks for the front and back and the roofs may well have reached right to the ground. The hall was the central feature of the Saxon villages. Although the reconstruction of the one at West Stow is finished plainly, it is possible that they were decorated – the more elaborate, the more important or the wealthier the owner. This demonstrates the dangers of reconstructions. Once a feature from the past has been reproduced in three-dimensional form and seen in that way by many people, its appearance becomes accepted. With timber buildings it is very difficult to recreate the unseen work above ground and interpretations change. It is easier to change a two-dimensional image of the past than a three-dimensional one. Halls belonging to the aristocracy have been found at Sulgrave in

Saxon Buildings

Above: The Priory Church at Deerhurst, Gloucestershire, is one of the finest surviving Saxon churches in England. The core of the church probably dates from the seventh century, with flanking porticus added in the eighth and subsequent centuries. The tower is probably also Saxon in origin.

Right: The Anglian Tower in York. The stages of the city's defensive embankments can be seen to the right of the remains of the tower – Roman, Saxon, Norman and medieval.

Four images from the Anglian Cross at Rothbury, Northumberland. *Above:* a calf muzzling a branch.

Part of a figure of Christ.

Northamptonshire and at Porchester in Hampshire. There is at Yeavering in Northumberland the remains of a 'palace'. It may well be the place Bede referred to as ad Gefrin, which was the palace and council place of the Northumbrian kings. A large assembly grandstand has been found there and it could be the spot where Paulinus preached to the nobility in 627.

CULTURE

THE NATIVE CULTURE which had all but disappeared in the Roman province resurfaced when the occupying forces left. Designs similar to those which had existed before the occupation reoccur in British art. Some of the splendid Christian crosses which can be found around the country, exhibit details common to almost a millenium of Celtic art. One of the most beautiful creations from the 'dark ages' of Britain is the series of Gospels. Amongst these are the Lindisfarne Gospels, the Gospels of Chad and the Book of Kells. The script in which they are written is an Irish one called 'half Uncial' and it blends Celtic and Saxon art in a form known as Hiberno-Saxon. Certainly they originate in the British Isles, but there is argument over whether they come chiefly from Ireland or if,

indeed, they come from Northumbria, which had strong links with Ireland. Nevertheless, it is perhaps enough to acknowledge that they are works of great beauty, revealing the high standard of artistic achievement in a part of the world immersed in the so-called 'dark ages'. The use of colour defies prosaic description. This Hiberno-Saxon art went into decline by the beginning of the ninth century to be revived one hundred years later under influence from the Continent. By then it had changed to what is now known as the Winchester style. Art as well as power had also passed to the south of the mainland. One of the best examples of the later work is the charter for the foundation of the minster at Winchester itself. The colouring is more delicate and the use of the leaf pattern is most gentle and beautiful.

Images of nature are contained on the stone crosses, the northern ones revealing an affinity with the Lindisfarne Gospels. In the North-west several crosses contain the two first letters of the word Christos when written in Greek. The symbol is thereby called Chi Rho and the crosses are found in places such as Whithorn. These were early carvings, but the later work can be seen in friezework to be found at the church at Breedon-on-the-Hill in Leicestershire. They are what remains of the abbey there.

Learning in Britain came from two origins.

A crowd of eighteen figures.

Christ healing a blind man.

Many people received their education in Ireland and this annoyed some of the Christian scholars in the South-east. However notable schools were set up at Canterbury by Augustine and later by Alcuin at York. Theodore was perhaps the most influential man in the former city and he attracted a large number of disciplines to his school. The education available at these places was broadly liberal, grouped by the ninth century into the Trivium – grammar, rhetoric and dialectic – and the Quadrivium – music, arithmetic, geometry and astronomy. Law, Roman Law which later became known as Civil Law, was also taught at Canterbury, Jarrow and Monkwearmouth as well as at York. Metre was also taught at Glastonbury. The ancient writers such as Virgil were read, but to the Christian mind the pagan writers were a source of great misgiving. However, a wide range of books was made available in the better libraries, and certainly Bede would have had access to a good selection. By the tenth century a lot of the commentaries on the scriptures were being written in the vernacular languages.

This was also true of the *Anglo-Saxon Chronicle* which started in 890–2 and, in various forms, ran on until 1154. It began as a dynastic table of the wars between Wessex and the Danes but it became a kind of propaganda dispatched by the Wessex kings to the monasteries. Other kings and nations receive only passing reference. East Anglia is very rarely mentioned and it had no great chroniclers of its own. Apart from its inclusion in the eighth-century *History of the Kings*, Northumberland was well beyond the reach of the Wessex writers – but then it had Bede.

CHRISTIANITY IN SCOTLAND

FOLLOWING THE CORONATION of the Scot, Kenneth MacAlpine, as King of the Picts in 843, the four Scottish peoples began the long process of unification. Indeed, the old differences are still evident in the distinctive Highland and Lowland characters. One of the main factors in unification, in addition to the numerous cultural links between the Picts and Scots, was Christianity. One of the first missions had been led by the Briton, Ninian, in around 400, but he managed to create only small enclaves amongst the Picts and the great Patrick of Ireland described the place as full of pagans.

After Columba's mission in 563, successive abbots established enclaves of Christianity throughout the mainland, and even down through Northumbria. Columban Christianity was the old-fashioned Gallic type which

calculated Easter differently from Rome and favoured the teaching of the humane St John, not the authoritarian Paul followed by Rome. Whilst Hilda wanted the Columbans to resist Rome, they, in a spirit of meekness which much became them, conceded. The Pict king, Nechtan, adopted Roman Christianity in 710 and eventually Iona, too, accepted the authoritarian church. Some did not and after the mid-ninth century there were still arcane practices continuing into the next millenium and a few clergy were still marrying.

The family of Kenneth MacAlpine ruled until 997. The rough terrain of Scotland made it difficult for the kings to establish a strong administration. There was little in the way of an organised hierarchy and even the succession was complex. The Pictish kings permitted descent via the matriarchal line and the choice was not automatic. Gaelic tradition allowed for the choice of the strongest leader from the 'derbfine', the collection of people who had a king for a grandfather. As a result the succession swung between branches of the family based at Moray and Atholl. The last of MacAlpine's line was succeeded by Kenneth III who was killed by the man who succeeded him, Malcolm II.

Not content with this, the childless Malcolm murdered Kenneth III's son. Even so the latter's sister, Gruoch, had a son and married a second, ambitious husband – Macbeth. Malcolm II's successor, the young Duncan, had ambition unmatched by talent and met with military defeat in 1039. Capitalising on the King's unpopularity, Macbeth murdered Duncan and assumed the throne himself. His subsequent reign was not wholly successful, although in 1050 he felt secure enough at home to visit Rome. Siward of Northumbria, a brother-in-law of the murdered king, captured Cumbria which had been given to the Scots King Malcolm I in 945, and he aided Duncan's son, who killed Macbeth in 1057. The crown passed first to Gruoch's son, Lulach, but he was killed at Strathbogie after only four months on the throne. Duncan's son reigned as Malcolm III – the 'bighead'. Whilst at first it was an unsettled time, with Donald Bane claiming a right to succession, Malcolm III had actually established a family which was to reign for two centuries.

THE HIGH KINGS OF WALES

In WALES the collections of small tribal kingdoms survived into the ninth century. After the ending of the Roman rule, these kingdoms and their petty kings often declined into violence. Warbands surrounded the kings who, as with the earlier Celts, were also attended by bards who sang them into an Heroic Age. It was not a steady time. The kings were not entirely secure from the ambitions of the nobles about them.

Out of these shifting fortunes grew four large nations. In the South-east was the kingdom of Glywysing-Morgannwg which, after the fall of the three kings in the Severn Valley, bordered on the Saxon Wessex across the Wye. There was little border trouble and the place became insular and only drawn into the centre of Welsh politics in the ninth century. The South-west was the kingdom of Dyfed, which had once been the land of the Demetae. It had been settled by Irish peoples who had been absorbed into the cultural picture.

The central area of the country now known as Wales was occupied by the kingdom of Gwynedd, ruled at one time by the great Maelgwn Gwynedd. He held court at the centre of Celtic culture; moreover he exerted influence on a territory which stretched beyond the boundaries of Wales. His descendants, Cadwallon and then Cadwaladr, fought with the Mercians and the Northumbrians in wars intended to curtail Saxon power. Bede saw Cadwallon as a savage tyrant. Cadwaladr is recognised as the last British King. Once he was defeated, the kingdom of Gwynedd shrank back and fragmented.

The final kingdom was Powys in the North-east, a place again embattled by the aggressive Saxons. Three of its kings were involved in the battle at Chester in 616, and the nation was certainly drawn into helping Penda fight his losing battle against the new order of Christianity. However, in the late eighth century Offa, King of Mercia, built a ditch running from the coast of north Wales to the River Wye. The people to the west were now excluded from the land which had been the country of their ancestors. What was worse, they, the people who had settled the British Isles for over 1,500 years, were called Welsh –

foreigners, aliens in their own land.

In the ninth century Powys, Gwynedd and Dyfed all lost their ruling dynasties. In their places came the High Kings of all Wales. Rhodi Mawr was the first of this new breed, forming a kingdom centred on Gwynedd by 878 and creating a dynasty to rule all of Wales except Morgannwg. He fought the new invaders, the Vikings, as well as the Anglo-Saxons, receiving the soubriquet 'the Great'. After his death, his successor, Hywel Dda the Good, codified Welsh Law and the dynasty moved to Dyfed. Hywel Dda presided over a kingdom growing in culture and status. He held a parliament at Whitland and attempted to create a united Wales, by taking over Morgannwg and securing the friendship of Wessex. He, too, strove to halt the incursions of the Vikings, but parts of the south coast fell under their sway − Swansea is a Scandinavian name. After Hywel Dda's death, chaos reigned; between 949 and 1066, thirty-five Welsh rulers died violently − when one of the kings of Glamorgan died of old age in 1043 it was a newsworthy event. The last High King,

Above: Offa's Dyke is still evident at many points along the boundary between England and Wales. This section is at Hawthorn Hill, Knighton, Powys.

Below: Silver penny, thought to have been minted for Hywel Dda. The inscription reads *Rex Houel.*

71

Silver penny of King Offa.

Interior of Viking ship found at Gokstad, Norway. Note the shallow draught for speed over short distances.

Gruffydd ap Llywelyn, forged a new Wales in a series of violent struggles against Saxons, Vikings and other Welsh kings. In the end he was defeated by an invasion mounted by Earl Harold Godwinson, and murdered by his own side. His successors had to swear fealty to the English King, Edward the Confessor. The potential for a great Wales had gone into abeyance.

ENGLAND

IN ENGLAND the centre of power shifted away from Northumbria. The attempt to secure Mercia under Northumbrian overlordship failed when the surviving son of Penda, Wulfhere, took the throne of Mercia and threw out the Northumbrians. Mercia expanded to absorb the kingdoms of Lindsey, Essex and East Anglia. By 670 London, now a great sea port and the mercantile capital of England, had also been drawn into Mercian domination. In the West, Wessex similarly accepted the supremacy of Mercia. The Northumbrians again attempted to defeat the great southern rival, and indeed Wulfhere was killed. He was succeeded by Aethelbald who completed Mercia's domination of Saxon England. Offa, his cousin, became the strongest Mercian king and was termed *rex totius Anglorum patrae* – the King of All

England, a reign lasting from 757–96. Mercian rule lasted only until Offa's successor, Cenwulf, died in 821. Under Egbert, King of Wessex, Mercia was conquered and the lands formerly under Mercian control passed under the hand of Wessex. From then on all England was ruled from Winchester.

THE VIKINGS INVADE

Bᴇꜰᴏʀᴇ ᴛʜɪꜱ, however, the harbingers of doom had already appeared on the northern coasts. In 793, the *Anglo-Saxon Chronicle* reported that 'dire portents appeared over Northumbria and sorely frightened the people. They consisted of immense whirlwinds and flashes of lightning, and fiery dragons were seen flying in the air. A great famine immediately followed those signs . . .' The point of this heavenly warning was soon felt. That same year the monastery of Lindisfarne was attacked, its treasures were plundered, the monks slaughtered and the

Above: Lindisfarne.

Opposite: Wooden prow, thought to be that of a Viking ship.

church destroyed. It was one of the early manifestations of the coastal terrorism practised by the Danes and Norsemen with their longships – the Vikings had reached Britain. It was a great target.

Despite the decline experienced by Northumbria, there was relative peace; and peace meant prosperity. The churches had amassed considerable wealth, usually expressed in the accoutrements of the altar. Many – Lindisfarne, Iona, Jarrow and Monkswearmouth amongst them – stood on islands or on rivers; they were easily accessible to the shallow-draft longships in which the Vikings crossed the North Sea. These first raids were conducted by small predatory bands who administered a short sharp shock and returned home to Denmark. However, fifty years later much larger forces landed in

Northumberland and began to conquer and even settle great tracts of Northumbria and Mercia.

The Vikings came from both Denmark and Norway, although in the early days of the trouble the coast of Britain was raided chiefly by people who hailed from the former. Lindisfarne and Jarrow may have been attacked by Norsemen heading for Ireland via the coast of Scotland, for by the tenth century Norwegian Vikings were plundering the west coast of England, Wales and Scotland from their bases in Ireland. The Viking races were outside the civilised spheres of Europe. To describe the raid leaders as a collection of aristocratic thugs is not too far from the truth. Leaders had failed to bind them together for any length of time, although after 872 Harold Fairhair achieved supremacy in Norway. A

similar attempt had miscarried earlier in Denmark when Horik had become a victim of internecine strife in 854. Taking ship to the rich lands of Britain was an excellent step in many ways: the excess population could be settled overseas and young-bloods could be easily removed. Whilst the longships were technologically superior to the ships employed by the Anglo-Saxons, naval battles were won by the Wessex fleets, which kept the raiders from the south coasts. Nevertheless, London was attacked and in 860 Viking parties reached and sacked Winchester.

It was in the North that the great political changes occurred. In 865, as Kent bought the Vikings off at Thanet, a great army landed in East Anglia. The kingdom immediately came to terms and the army turned north. On 1 November 861, York fell and became known thereafter as Jorvik. Attempts by King Aella of Northumbria to recapture the town were unsuccessful. The Danes returned to East Anglia after failing to conquer Mercia and murdered the Christian King Edmund, who later became a saint for his martyrdom. In the following decade they turned on Mercia and

Wessex. They were opposed by King Aethelred and his brother Alfred, who defeated them in 871 at Ashdown. Two months later, the Anglo-Saxons were defeated at Basing and the King was killed. Alfred succeeded him. Luckily, the Danes returned northwards, but Alfred was forced to sue for peace and within a year a Viking puppet king (Ceowulf II) was placed in Mercia.

KING ALFRED

ALFRED proved a great king. His army was soon forced into guerilla warfare after defeat in 878. Whilst hiding in the marshlands of the Isle of Athelney, coordinating resistance and the movements of the western army at his command, he is supposed to have burned the cakes prepared by the hostess whose lodgings he was using. More importantly, if less charmingly, he successfully brought the armies from the West together at Egbert's Stone in the forest of Selwood. Seven weeks after Easter 878, he defeated the Viking army

Jorvik Viking Centre, York: reconstruction of a ship from Norway unloading skins and barrels of herring at the quayside, River Foss.

The Alfred Jewel, found near Athelney, Somerset: it is inscribed 'Alfred had me made'.

at Edington. This was a defeat so dramatic that the Vikings agreed to leave Wessex and the leader, Guthrum, became a Christian. After a year the Danes left the South.

Alfred went on to capture London and to hold the Danes north of a line along the Thames and Lea to Bedford and then along the Ouse to Watling Street. The area north was known as Danelaw. It can be discerned by the suffix of '-by' in placenames. The heaviest density of these names occurs in Yorkshire, Nottinghamshire, Lincolnshire and Leicestershire. Examples are Hax*by*, Hu*by*, and Sel*by* in Yorkshire, or Kettle*by* in Leicestershire. The suffix '-gate' in street names also reveals Danish links. In York there is Copper*gate*, the site of the most exciting archaeological Viking 'dig' in Britain. This is now the Jorvik Centre, a heritage museum of reconstructed Viking dockside and workshops.

In the 890s Alfred was again forced to fend off coastal attacks. He built up the fleet and has often been called the 'father of the Navy'. He did not create – he only developed what was already there – but he did turn it into an effective and successful force. Alfred and his successors, with a newly resurgent Mercia, set the western limits to which Danelaw reached by securing the positions of West Mercia and Wessex.

In the early years of the next century, the Wessex and Mercian Saxons went onto the offensive and under Edward the Elder and Aethelstan, the 'most brilliant of the English kings,' Northumbria was recaptured. Aethelstan created a civil service and organised a new coinage for the kingdom. He became an elder statesman in Europe, consulted even by the Holy Roman Emperor as well as by the Vikings and their close relations, the Normans. Yet all of this was short-lived. When the great King died in 939, the kingdom again fell prey to raiders. Edgar's reign (959–75), saw order briefly re-established, but the conquest of England followed within twenty-five years of Edgar's death. The Danes who had long settled in the North and East were easily persuaded to become a part of another empire – but this one was to be governed from within England.

4. CONQUERED PEOPLES

NORMAN BRITAIN 1000–1200

IN THE ELEVENTH CENTURY the British Isles underwent a series of major changes and upheavals. At the beginning of the century it was emerging from yet another battle between Scandinavian kings and the Wessex dynasties. At the close, there was the murder of the second monarch from a house imposed by conquest.

During the 980s the number of Scandinavian raids on England increased. At that time the country was at peace and united under the domination of a Wessex king who was also the acknowledged 'overking' of Scotland and Wales. As a result of the raids, large numbers of people were killed or thrown into slavery and vast quantities of treasure were taken back across the North Sea. To the Norwegians, it was clear that England was not in the state of preparedness it had once been. Responsibility for this state of affairs was laid at the feet of the King, ever after known as Aethelred the Unready. Thus encouraged, they launched a massive attack in 991. After defeating the Earldorman Brithnoth by foul play at the second battle of Maldon, they pressed on and attacked much of the eastern part of England. On the advice of the Archbishop of Canterbury and a number of weaker souls in the aristocracy, Aethelred made the first of the irregular heavy payments of tribute – Danegeld. It was little more than protection money, the premiums of which increased without a guaranteed policy.

Arundel Castle, West Sussex. The original structure was one of the first castles built by William I after the Conquest.

TIME CHART

1017	Edmund Ironside dies and Cnut the Great becomes King of All England.
1034	Duncan I on the throne of Scotland.
1035	Cnut dies and is succeeded by Harold I.
1037	Harold I becomes King.
1040	Harold I dies. Duncan is murdered. Harthacnut is crowned in England, Macbeth in Scotland.
1042	Harthacnut dies and is succeeded by Edward the Confessor.
1051–2	Godwin Earl of Wessex exiled. The Confessor promises the throne of England to William of Normandy.
1053	Godwin returns and forces Edward to renounce the Norman claim.
1057	Macbeth murdered, succeeded by his son who is also murdered, and then by Malcolm III.
1066	Edward dies. William becomes King after the ten-month reign of Harold II ends at Hastings with his death.
1067	Norman incursions into Wales begin.
1070s	Wars between England and Scotland.
1086–7	Domesday survey carried out.
1087	William I succeeded by William II. (William Rufus).
1091–3	Wars again. Malcolm III murdered by the English. Rhys ap Tewdwr murdered by Normans at Brecon.
1094–7	Reign of Donald Ban in Scotland ends when he is murdered by son of Malcolm III, who then becomes Edgar I.
1100	William II succeeded by Henry I.
1124–53	King David's reign marks a Scottish renaissance.
1135	Death of Henry I: accession of Stephen.
1139–53	Civil war in England as Matilda contests Stephen's right to the throne. It is ended on the succession of Henry II (1154) who ensures Scotland's subordination after a period when they had exerted power over northern England.
1162	Thomas Becket appointed Archbishop of Canterbury.
1165	War against the Welsh.
1170	Thomas Becket murdered.
1173–4	Revolts against Henry II. Scottish join in, but King William (1165–1214) captured and forced to submit to overlordship of Henry.
1189	Death of Henry II. Richard I crowned whilst on short visit to England.
1190–2	Richard I on crusade.
1199	Death of Richard I. King John comes to the throne.

AETHELRED AND CNUT

THE LEADER of the great raid of 991, Olaf Tryggvasson, and his ally, Sweyn Fork-beard, returned determined to repeat the success. However, their attack on London in 993 was driven off and they were instead forced to raid the coasts and immediate inland towns. Yet again Aethelred bought them off, this time with £16,000. Whilst Olaf agreed to become a Christian as a result of the negotiations, Sweyn remained aloof from this and the subsequent promise to stay out of England. He and others like him returned in 997 and there followed almost twenty years of warfare and tribute, neither of which secured England from attack. At Aethelred's death many of the nobility were ready to secure their own peace by accepting Sweyn's son Cnut as King instead of the rightful heir, Edmund. However, the young Saxon became King and was of very different mettle from his father: his warrior nature gave him the title 'Ironside'.

Edmund determined to fight for his inheritance: he went into the field, drawing Cnut after him, away from the siege of London that the Dane had begun. With a fine sense of strategic skill, Ironside held Cnut back at two battles in the West, dodged past him, relieved London, beat the invaders back from Mercia and attacked the booty-laden Danes at Ashingdon in Essex. His earlier victories had turned the hearts, consciences or equivalents – probably hopes of power and wealth – of the disloyal nobility and by the time of the battle of Ashingdon (or Assundum as the *Anglo-Saxon Chronicle* calls it), he had amassed a large army gathered from all parts of his kingdom. There, despite fighting bravely, his army was defeated by Cnut. At subsequent negotiations, perhaps to gain a breathing space, Cnut and Edmund Ironside agreed to split the kingdom. Cnut gained the North and Edmund retained Wessex. However, within weeks, Edmund was dead and in 1017 Cnut became King of all England.

This succession did not go undisputed. Aethelred had two other sons, Alfred and Edward. Despite the fact that their mother then married Cnut, the two sons – the aethlings, as sons of the King were known –

Opposite: Cnut and Emma.

Edward the Confessor as depicted in the Bayeux Tapestry.

opposed the succession of the step-father, realising that Emma and Cnut wanted to have children who would cut them out of the succession. They remained across the Channel in Normandy with their uncle, Duke Richard II. In the reign of Richard's son Duke Robert (1028–35), relations between England and Normandy went into decline, and the Normans gave active support to the aethlings.

Cnut's death in 1035 did not solve any of the problems. There was a whole collection of successors. The aethlings were ready, Cnut's son by another marriage was on the spot, but the chosen heir Harthacnut, the son of Cnut and the aethlings' mother Emma, was abroad. The ambitious Earl Godwin of Wessex, allied with Emma, attempted to prevent the regency of Harold Harefoot, Cnut's other son, but failed. To get rid of one of the other claimants, Godwin disposed of the Wessex heir by handing Alfred the aethling over to Harefoot, who then murdered him. Emma was sent abroad and Harefoot took the throne to

himself. On his death a mere three years later, the heir Cnut and Emma had wanted at last came to the throne. Harthacnut was far from being the man his father had been. His two-year reign was marked not by great achievement but instead by brutal tax collection in Worcestershire and by his order that Harefoot should be removed from his grave and cast into a fen. The *Anglo-Saxon Chronicle* made clear his worth in the brief notice of his death: 'While he reigned he did nothing worthy of his power' and 'as he stood at his drink, suddenly fell to the earth, terribly convulsed. And they who were bye took hold on him. But after that he spake not a word ere he died.'

EDWARD THE CONFESSOR

THE SUCCESSION was made a little easier this time, for while some of the earls – the

Work on the land as shown in a medieval book.

Left: A man scything grass in June.

Right: Harvesting corn with a hook.

men governing the regions of England – held pretensions of right, the presence of Edward, son of Aethelred II, in the country thwarted all other claims. For almost twenty-five years the country was ruled in peace by Edward whose piety earned him the title 'the Confessor'.

Pious but not powerful, Edward was unable to quell the ambitious pretensions of the great earls, Leofric of Mercia, Siward of Northumbria and the great Godwin. The latter was obnoxious to King Edward because of the foul murder of his brother, Alfred, and by 1051 the King felt strong enough to throw Godwin and his sons out of the country. This did not diminish the Godwins' power – they had a strong claim to the throne, strengthened by the Confessor's lack of an heir. However, the King was determined to push the Godwins to the side and by 1051 he had promised the throne to the Norman Duke William, son of Robert and grand-nephew of Emma. The Godwin family could not accept this without a challenge. In 1052, the earl with his sons, Harold and Leofwine, landed in the country with an army. Edward did not possess the power to defeat Earl Godwin and the Crown was forced to submit to his wishes.

HAROLD GODWINSON

GODWIN DIED in the following year, but the family was strengthened by the work of the formidable heir, Harold. He defeated the Welsh, and secured the succession of his brother, Tostig, to the Northumbrian earldom. With the Norman connection broken, it became accepted that Harold would probably succeed to the throne. He was a popular figure in England, and had shown some degree of statesmanship: he was not willing to support Tostig when the latter's harsh rule in the North provoked a rebellion which drove him out of the country. Only one blemish marred Harold's own position as heir apparent. It is possible that he had promised to support Duke William's succession. After a shipwreck in 1064 Harold was stranded in Normandy. William made him welcome and facilitated his return to England. However, William and later the Bayeux Tapestry claimed that Harold swore to support William over the sacred bones of a saint at Bonneville-sur-Touques. This was perhaps true, as it is also possible that this oath was obtained under

Harold, son of Godwin. This likeness is taken from one of his coins.

August: threshing.

duress or by trickery. Tostig was another fly in the ointment. He had fled abroad — to the side of the King of Norway, Harald Hardrada. Jealous of his brother's power, Tostig was prepared to support the rival claim of the Norwegian in the event of the Confessor's death. In all there were four claimants: Harold Godwinson, Harald Hardrada, Duke William and finally, the King of Denmark, Sweyn Estrithsson. When the old King died there was going to be a scramble for the throne.

ANGLO-SAXON SOCIETY

A MAN'S WORTH had a very different and a very real meaning in Saxon England. The legal difference between the social classes was a measure of value — the compensation due for the slaying of one of the members of a class. Although the worth of a shilling was somewhat different (a Kentish shilling, for example had twenty pennies in it, whilst a Wessex shilling had only four), the valuations were roughly similar throughout the country. Apart from Kent, the wergild or value of an earl was set at six times that of the churl — the lowest class. Thus in Wessex all of the people could be referred to as 'of twelve hundred and

the two hundred': that is, the earls at twelve hundred shillings each and the rest at two hundred. This measure of worth also applied to injuries received: a churl would not be paid as much compensation for an inflicted wound as would an earl, for instance. On the other hand, earls paid higher fines for the same crime than would a churl.

The nobility in Saxon England was marked by its relative freedom from taxes. A thane, the word which replaced the earlier general term 'earl' which took on an air of title to an office of state, held land with only three duties owed to the King — military service, the construction of fortifications and the repair of bridges. The thane could leave his lands to whomsoever he wished. Rising to the status of thane was theoretically open to the industrious churl family. If a churl raised for himself a good estate of five hides extent (a hide was the amount of land which was reckoned to support a family, though it varied with soil quality and could measure between 60 and 180 acres), he could be worth a thane's wergild at his death. The family was, however, still considered as churls until a further two heads of the family had lived at such a level of wealth. Thanes lived usually in the large wooden halls described in the last chapter. A

September: treading grapes.

few of the wealthier ones may well have possessed stone-built homes, but this was rare.

The nobility was beginning to take on the air of later generations of aristocrats. They had estates in many counties, one of the prime examples being Wulfric Spott who held seventy-two estates which are definitely identified, and more in the Wirral and south Lancashire. His identified estates were spread over Derbyshire, Staffordshire, where he founded the monastery at Burton-on-Trent, Warwickshire, Shropshire, Leicestershire, Worcestershire, Lincolnshire, Yorkshire and Gloucestershire. Women in the thane class could be just as wealthy: Aelfgifu of Buckinghamshire left fifteen estates when she died. Earl Brihtnoth's widow died in possession of thirty-six estates, chiefly her own, rather than her dead husband's property.

The work of the thane had passed from the toil of manual labour to that of an administrator. Not only did he oversee the work of his paid staff, the stewards who managed his estates and the lesser workers, dairy staff and herders, as well as the tenant farmers, but he had legal duties too. Legally he was accountable for the actions of all of those in his employ, and he also dealt with matters in the local courts. He was responsible for the apprehension of criminals by calling out staff and companions – the lesser satellite nobles – and mounting a chase. If he was a man of importance he may well have attended the King's court.

The women of this class are harder to pin down. Within a marriage the noblewomen would have probably held responsibility for the management of the domestic economy. It was not an easy task for it required great administrative skills. The women would have needed knowledge of dairying, and baking and brewing as well as of the processes of spinning and weaving. All of this vital work was under female supervision, but the view of women received through verse shows them only as the servants of their men. At the great feasts or upon the entertainment of an honoured guest, the women, wives and daughters, were responsible for the large-scale logistical arrangements. In verse, and in memoir, women are shown as the cup-bearers to the guests, and to their lords. This was only a part of their duties at feasts, but the most symbolic; testimony, not to their skill, which passes largely unnoticed, but to the domination in law of their lords and husbands.

These were of course the tiny minority of the people of England. The labours and tragedies of the majority are no less hard nor great, but they are generally unrecorded. The Bardic tradition of eulogising the lords was still strong. There were perhaps some 1,200,000 to 1,600,000 people living in the British Isles, of which only 95,000 dwelt in the whole of Norfolk, the most densely populated county. Nine-tenths of the people lived in villages in rural areas, and those that lived in towns were, with the exception of Londoners, not part of great conurbations. York, the second city of the kingdom, had only 9,000 inhabitants. The great number of British people in the three countries were peasants, farming at subsistence level – growing crops and tending only enough animals for their family's needs.

The peasantry, like their overlords, came in ranks. In some of the northern counties of Danelaw, where the Scandinavians had settled, were sokemen – freemen. They owned the land which they farmed and thereby avoided the duties imposed upon those who were tenants. Between a third and a half of the people in most counties were veilleins. Villeins

rented land, perhaps as much as sixty acres or as little as ten. Below them came the cottars and bordars who had only the cottage which they rented and a small parcel of land to provide some of the food they required. Most of these would have to work on somebody else's land in order to survive. Below them came the serfs. These unfortunates were actually slaves. The numbers had declined over the centuries, but still ten per cent of the people of England had no place of their own, rented or otherwise, and no rights over themselves or over any property. They could be and were sold along with land and other property, they could not marry without their overlord's permission and they could not move off the estates where they dwelt. They ate, slept, bred and all but breathed at the will of the thane. Even the link of the common language was about to be lost to them.

WILLIAM THE CONQUEROR

IT WAS A COLD JANUARY DAY in 1066 when Edward the Confessor died and the competition to succeed him began. The obvious early winner was Harold Godwinson: he had the advantage of being in the country and enjoying the support of the nobility and the council known as the Witangemot. King Harold II was duly crowned at Westminster Abbey. For many of the European observers it was to be only a matter of time before one of the rival claimants landed on the English shore – but which one? Duke William spent the summer of 1066 building up an army on the coast of Normandy. He also staged a diplomatic effort to secure his own lands from attack and to gain military support from his neighbours. He succeeded in gaining papal support for his attempt on England, promising to bring the English Church under the firm control of Rome. By acquiring the aura of a crusade, William further secured the approval of Europe and the safety of his own country. When autumn came, the Normans had a fleet of up to 3,000 vessels and an army of men drawn from their own country, Brittany and France. There were also contingents from Flanders, Italy and Sicily. Despite an appearance of Halley's comet, which could be taken as a good omen, the winds were against

Pevensey Castle, East Sussex. William occupied this former Roman fort on landing at Pevensey Bay and subsequently transformed it into a strong Norman castle.

Duke William and throughout late August and early September the winds from the north kept the invasion fleet in the harbours around St Valéry.

The ill winds blew in the favour of the English, or so Harold thought. The troops which he had amassed on the south coast throughout the summer, stood down. However, the winds from the north were doing more good for the vengeful Tostig and Harald Hardrada than they were for King Harold. With 300 ships and 12,000 men they crossed the North Sea and sailed into the Humber, up the River Ouse and docked at Riccall, south of York. Tostig launched the campaign with an attempt to retake his earldom. He was opposed at Fulford, outside York, by the northern earls, Edwin of Northumbria and his brother Morcar of

Battle Abbey, East Sussex.

Mercia on 20 September. The battle was long and bloody, and in the end Tostig drove the earls into York and negotiations began for the surrender of the city.

In the meantime, the King gathered his forces and on the day of the battle of Fulford, he set out from London. On 24 September, Harold reached Tadcaster and on the following day passed through York and on to Stamford Bridge where the invaders were awaiting the surrender of Morcar and Edwin. The resulting battle saw the deaths of both Tostig and Hardrada and the Vikings were defeated. The few survivors of the disaster at Stamford Bridge were allowed to sail home: they needed only twenty-four of the ships they had brought with them.

The next claimant landed on the southern coast just after the battle of Stamford Bridge had been fought and won. Duke William's fleet, aided at last by favourable winds, had reached Pevensey Bay on 27 September. They constructed the pre-fabricated fort which had been shipped from Normandy and then, to get Harold to attack them as soon as possible, they began to ravage the countryside around Hastings. Every day they stayed increased the chances of losing men, whilst at the same time allowing opposition to grow. By wreaking havoc the Normans were ensuring that the King would have to do his duty by the people and defend them. It worked. Harold raced down from the North and reached London on 6 October. With only a part of his victorious army, King Harold left London on 11 October and in two days marched to Battle, near Hastings.

THE BATTLE OF HASTINGS

ON THE MORNING of 14 October, Duke William moved against Harold, who had established himself on Senlac Hill. It was an excellent position, a spur with steeply sloping sides which prevented the chance of a flank attack. The Normans had to advance upon Harold's forces across a marsh-covered valley from their position on Telham Hill. All day the battle raged, as Harold's foot forces drove off the attacks from the Norman, French, Flemish and Breton horse and infantry. The Saxon equivalent of guards — the well trained Huscarls, assisted by the levied Fyrd — drove back the attacks with great slaughter and the Bretons on William's left began to retreat. Some of the less disciplined Fyrd men chased them and were caught unprotected in the valley bottom. It was a risky moment. After a rumour that William was dead, the Normans, too, began to give way. By removing his helmet and holding it aloft, the Duke reassured his forces and led them in an all-out assault. A barrage of arrows preceded the attack, and the toll which they took on the tired Saxons allowed the Norman pressure to succeed. The impenetrable position thus weakened, the Saxon line broke: Harold and his brothers were killed at the foot of the Standards of the Dragon and of the Fighting Man. Some of the Huscarls fought on, retreating a short distance and trapping a collection of careless Norman soldiers, but the battle was over.

WILLIAM IS CROWNED

WILLIAM had to tread warily. There were still forces loyal to the dead King and it was late in November when he entered

The Battle of Hastings. Saxon forces defending their hill position from Norman cavalry, as depicted in the Bayeux Tapestry.

London, and then only after Morcar and Edwin and the aethling Edgar offered submission. On Christmas Day 1066, Duke William was crowned King of England at Westminster. England was hit by a culture shock. Although the other invasions of the country had involved cultural change, and this had been absorbed often over centuries, this time, almost at one stroke, the old order changed: the language of the government became foreign to the vast majority of people, the ownership of all land altered, and even the numbering of the kings began afresh. Yet whilst the perfidious lords and the 'prince' succumbed, not all of the people were pleased to submit to the entirety of the changes.

It was akin to a commercial takeover: new managers were assigned and it was their job to make the country profitable for the King. That also meant making it profitable and manageable for themselves too. Wales was similarly marked out for this process, and within a year, powerful Norman barons were established at Shrewsbury, Hereford and Chester. Their aim was to take over the borderlands, and to colonise them. Before the end of the century there were Norman castles erected at prominent sites in Wales, including Caerleon and Caernarvon. Many things were changed in the borderlands – the Marches: Hywel Dda's laws underwent alteration, the feudal system was introduced and partible inheritance ended. Partible inheritance allowed for the estates to be divided up between the heirs: the Normans knew it as gavelkind and probably also realised it resulted in a collection of tiny estates, farms which were not viable economic units. Most importantly, these lands now passed to Normans or the multi-racial groups which they introduced as colonists.

The Welsh kings were driven into hiding. Two of them, Gruffydd ap Cynan of Gwynedd and Rhys ap Tewdwr of

Chepstow Castle — a bastion of Norman power on the borders of Wales.

Welsh Resurgence

When Henry I died in 1135, England fell into a civil war as Stephen of Blois, Henry's nephew, battled for the throne against Henry's daughter, Matilda. The Welsh took their cue and launched a programme of reconstruction. Gwynedd was rebuilt and extended and Powys, too, went onto the offensive. The accession of Henry II, Matilda's son, in 1154 brought a temporary recession in this growth when a massive campaign on sea and land drove Owain Gwynedd, son of Gruffydd ap Cynan, back into the northern hills, and Rhys ap Gruffydd was pushed back to Dinefwr behind the river Twyi. Briefly in the 1160s the Welsh kings set out again to drive the Normans out of their country. Henry II launched a massive attack on them in 1165 only to see it defeated by weather and the Welsh. By 1172, however, the sons of Owain were fighting each other and Rhys ap Gruffydd had acknowledged the English king. By the end of the century all of the Welsh kings and princes had sworn fealty to the King of England and Archbishop Baldwin coursed the country gaining support for the crusades in 1188. Out of this defeat came a peace, even if there was still a great deal of tension in the country as not all of the people were happy about Norman rule.

Nevertheless, there was a cultural upsurge. The great classical works of Welsh literature were created at this time. Some of the writings were heavily nostalgic, like the *Lives of the Saints* which was an attempt to reassert the Celtic Church heritage against the domination of the Norman Church, which had imposed itself throughout England and then Wales, in order to justify the papal blessing of the conquest. Similar assertions about Welsh history were made in *Lives of the Princes*. International links were forged by Welsh friars who travelled throughout Europe visiting the universities; indeed many of them ended up at Oxford, which was founded as an offshoot of the University of Paris. Poetry, too, underwent a period of growth, the courts of the petty kings all had one or two poets amongst the officials at court, one to educate the heir, another to entertain the court. Celtic poems were accepted into the Norman courts too, and translated into Norman French. The *Four Branches of the Mabinogi* were written in the period of the conquest and translated across Europe.

Deheubarth were driven into the hills and guerilla warfare. After fleeing to Ireland, they were allowed to return to their realms only for Rhys to be murdered and his lands opened up for the barons of Norman England. At the end of the century, Henry I (King of England, 1100–35) extended his power into Wales, superimposing himself over the barons and the Welsh kings and princes. The King took over parts of the Marches personally and began to extend the colonisation process into South Wales.

Duke William as depicted in the Bayeux Tapestry.

THE NORMAN CONQUEST OF SCOTLAND

THE SCOTTISH KINGS were considered by William I to be of little more importance than the warring Welsh monarchs. Certainly, they too had sworn fealty to the kings of England and indeed Malcolm III's position on the throne had been largely secured with English aid. When the north of England turned against William and declared support for the aethling Edgar, the Conqueror went into the North and caused widespread devastation and erected a number of castles, like the dual towers at York, on the Ouse, to keep the population in check. In defeat the northern rebels fled with the aethling into Scotland. King Malcolm fell in love with Edgar's sister Margaret and married her – it was not a move likely to endear a man already suspicious in the Conqueror's eyes.

Malcolm was not a man to rest under the threat. In 1070 he raided far into the west of England to try and secure his hold on Lothian and Cumbria. William responded by pursuing Malcolm's forces through the Lowlands to the Tay and there receiving the King of Scotland's homage to the King of England. It was only seven years before Malcolm tried again, invading Northumberland. This time William sent his eldest son Robert, backed with a large army, to negotiate with the Scots. The talks failed and Robert seemed to acknowledge some powerlessness: on his way south he constructed a new castle on the north side of the Tyne. Malcolm went on to invade England once more before he was killed by the Earl of Northumberland near Alnwick.

His son Duncan, educated whilst held as a hostage for his father's behaviour by the Normans, was bypassed and Donald Ban, Malcolm's brother, succeeded to the throne. The English King William II – Rufus – supported Duncan's claim and put him on the throne by force, only to see him murdered and Donald Ban restored. William Rufus then placed Edgar, the eldest son of Margaret and Malcolm III's marriage, on the throne: he was clearly an English vassal. He was succeeded by his brother Alexander I, who began to introduce feudal tenure into the Lowlands of Scotland.

This process was continued and extended in the reign of David I, who also organised his county government along Norman lines. Nevertheless, although David has been seen as the man who completed the Norman conquest of Scotland, he did foster native culture and continue to revere the traditional saints of the country, which the Normans were generally trying, as part of their mission, to eradicate in the British Isles. David also tried during the civil war in England between Matilda and Stephen to repudiate the status of client king, and sided with Matilda on condition that she accept this. For his help to her and her son, later Henry II, David was granted power over Cumbria and Northumberland. This did not last. Henry soon repudiated the promises after gaining the throne of England and control over the Angevin Empire.

Scotland's independence was short-lived. David died in 1153 and was succeeded by his grandson as Malcolm IV while still a minor. Being young he was not comparable with David nor his father, Prince Henry, who had both contrived to make the Scottish monarchy rich and powerful. In the absence of the strong hand of David, northern England fell into the grasp of the ambitious Henry II, who again asserted the subordination of the Scottish kings to England. He imperiously commanded Malcolm and his brother William to join him in Aquitaine in the attempt to put down the rebellion of his other vassal, the Count of Touraine.

When Malcolm died, William – 'the Lion' – succeeded him. Again a different man, he set about strengthening Scotland's position in the relationship with England. As with many people who attempt to compete against or oppose others, William ensured that his kingdom acquired many of the traits of the rival England. The feudal system was extended into the area north of the River Tay and thus the King's power and wealth increased. William was a warlike and amorous man, unmarried but with a whole host of bastards to his credit before he was forty. One of his ambitions was to regain Northumberland, held by his father Henry and, going further back, by his great-great-grandfather Siward.

In an attempt to gain the territory, King William led his army into Northumberland in 1174. He was captured at the siege of Alnwick and sent south with his feet tied underneath his horse. He was locked up in Falaise Castle in Normandy until Henry II extracted fealty from him and from the Scottish church. It was an unequivocal statement of the King of England's attitude to the King of the Scots: in brief the Scottish kings were subordinate minor kings. Garrisons were placed by Henry in Edinburgh, Berwick and Roxburgh and only Edinburgh was returned to the Scottish king as a 'wedding present' when Henry chose a wife for William.

Much Scottish dignity was regained when William successfully forced Richard I to return Roxburgh and Berwick and repudiate Henry's other conditions made at Falaise. By the turn of the century, Scotland was heading for a new period of greatness.

Opposite: Battle scene from a twelfth century psalter.

SVDSEXE

[Facsimile of a page of Domesday Book, Sussex. Medieval abbreviated Latin text in two columns.]

Left column

Ipsi ht̄ .iiii. car̄ in dn̄io. 7 .iii. uillos 7 .x. bord̄ h̄ntes una
car̄ 7 dimid̄. 7 eccl̄a 7 pbr̄ ibi. 7 ii. serui. 7 i. haga de .vii.
denar̄. Totū T.R.E. ualeb. ccc. lib̄. 7 post. L. lib̄.
Modo .xvi. lib̄ 7 .x. sol̄ qd eps̄ ten̄. 7 tam ho de firma
.xx. sol̄ plus. 7 Walger̄ ten̄. .vi. lib̄ ual. 7 tam ho
.L. sol̄ plus. 7 alii tenent .iiii. lib̄ 7 .xv. sol̄ ual.
Decima eccl̄e clerici tenent. 7 ual̄ .xl. solid̄.
T.R.E. ptinebat huic M una hida in Icenore. Modo
ten̄ Warin̄ ho Rogerii comitis. In Hauresford hd̄.

Ipse eps̄ ten̄ HALESTEDE. 7 de rege .E. tenuit. 7 ē
p .xiii. hid̄ se defd̄. m̄ p .v. hid̄ 7 dimid̄. Tra ē.
In dn̄io sunt .ii. car̄. 7 vii. uilli cū .xx.iii. bord̄ h̄nt
.ii. car̄. Ibi .ii. serui. 7 un̄ molin de .iiii. sol̄. 7 eccl̄a ibi.
Silua .x. porc̄. Herbagiū de .vii. porcis .i.
De hoc M ten̄ Ricard̄ .i. hida. Osbn̄ clericꝰ dim̄ hid̄.
Radulf̄ pbr̄ .i. bida. que p̄ius ad eccl̄am.
Totū M T.R.E. 7 post. 7 modo .ual̄ xv. lib̄.

Durand̄ ten̄ de epo PRESTETONE In Stletone hd̄.
T.R.E. 7 m̄ se defd̄ p .iii. hid̄. Tra ē. In dn̄io
una car̄ 7 dimid̄. 7 ii. uilli cū .iiii. bord̄ h̄nt dimid̄
car̄. Ibi .vi. ac̄ p̄a. 7 parua silua ad clausuram.
T.R.E. ualeb .iiii. lib̄. 7 post 7 modo .iii. lib̄.

Ricard̄ ten̄ de epo LEVITONE In Redresbrige hd̄.
Goduin̄ tenuit de rege .E. in elemosina. 7 ta 7 m̄
se defd̄ p .vi. hid̄. Tra ē. In dn̄io sunt .ii. car̄.
7 xi. uilli cū .vii. bord̄ h̄nt .iiii. car̄.
Ibi eccl̄a. 7 in cicestre una haga de .iii. den̄. 7 xii. ac̄
p̄a. Silua .x. porc̄. 7 de .vii. porc̄ unū.
T.R.E. ualeb .x. lib̄. 7 post .vi. lib̄. Modo .x. lib̄.
Omnes hii qui p̄nueꝰ 7 p̄t eccl̄e de Boseha in elem.

TERRA SCI PETRI DE WINTONIA.

Abbas Sci petri Wintonie. ten̄ SVESSE. Sep
fuit in monasterio. T.R.E. se defd̄ p .xxviii. hid̄.
7 m̄ p .xx.vii. hid̄. Tra ē .xxviii. car̄.
In dn̄io est una car̄. 7 xl. vi. uilli cū .iiii. bord̄ h̄nt
.xxi. car̄. Ibi eccl̄a. 7 c.xxx. ac̄ p̄a.
In Lewes .x. burgeses de .ii. denar̄. 7 de uillanis
.xxx.viii. mel allecii 7 augent. p̄ marsuins .iiii. lib̄.
p forisfactura uillanoꝝ .x. lib̄. 7 iii. sūmas de pisci.
In tota ualentia T.R.E. 7 post .ualuit .xx. lib̄.
Modo ꝩ̄al̄ appciat̄ sed tam redd̄ .xx.viii. lib̄.
In Estocbrige hd̄.

Ipse abb̄ ten̄ CLOVINCTVNE. T.R.E. tenuit abbatia
M 7 m̄ p .v. hid̄ se defd̄. Tra ē. In dn̄io
est una car̄. 7 xv. uilli cū .iiii. bord̄ h̄nt .vi. car̄ 7 dim̄.
Ibi .ii. serui. 7 xx.v. ac̄ p̄a. 7 silua ad clausuram.
In Cicestre una haga de .iiii. den̄. De pasnagio
un̄ porc̄ 7 dimid̄.
T.R.E. ualeb .iiii. lib̄. 7 x. sol̄ 7 un̄ den̄. Modo .vi. lib̄.
In Benestede hd̄.

Right column

TERRA ECCLE DE LABATAILGE. In Waildelonestrac hd̄.

Abbas Sci Martini de Labatailge ten̄ ALOISTONE
de rege. Alnod tenuit de rege .E. 7 tc defd̄ se p .L. hid̄
7 m̄ p .xl. iiii. hid̄ 7 dim̄. Tra ē .xx.viii. car̄.
De his hid̄ iacent .iii. hid̄ 7 dimid̄ in Rap de Hastinges.
7 vii. hid̄ in Rap de Lewes. 7 vii. burgenses.
In dn̄io ht̄ abb̄ .iiii. car̄. 7 lx.v. uilli cū .vii. bord̄ h̄nt
.xxi. car̄ 7 dimid̄. Ibi .xii. serui. 7 L. ac̄ p̄a. Silua .iiii. porc̄.
de pasnaḡ. 7 vi. porc̄ de herbago.
De .v. hid̄ supdicas. ten̄ Rob̄t .i. hid̄ 7 iii. uirḡ de abbe
Reinberḡ .v. uirḡ. Goisfrid̄ dimid̄ hid̄. Alured̄ iii. uirḡ.
Ipsi ht̄ in dn̄io .iiii. car̄. 7 v. uillos 7 un̄ bord̄ cū .i. car̄
7 dimid̄.
Totū M T.R.E. ualeb .xl.viii. lib̄. 7 post .xxx. lib̄. Modo
xxx.vi. lib̄. qd abb̄ ten̄. 7 de hoc eī .iiii. lib̄. 7 v. sol̄.
Ipse abb̄ ten̄ de rege .iiii. hid̄ In Totenore hund.
Alnod tenuit de rege .E. 7 tc 7 m̄ se defd̄ p .iiii. hidis.
Ibi ht̄ abb̄ .vi. uillos cū .iiii. car̄. Appciat̄ est in alio M.

Ipse abb̄ ht̄ in suo rapo .vi. hid̄ 7 dimid̄. 7 tra p .vi. hid̄ se
defd̄. 7 dimid̄ funt geta. quia foris rap.
In his hid̄ ten̄ ide abb̄ in dn̄io Bocheha. Olbote tenuit de Go
duino com̄. Tc 7 m̄ se defd̄ p dim̄ hida. modo .ē una ꝩ̄ in rapo
comitis de Ow. In dn̄io ht̄ abb̄ .i. car̄. 7 iiii. bord̄ cū una car̄.
Ibi .iii. ac̄ p̄a. 7 silua .ii. porc̄. T.R.E. 7 m̄. ual̄ .xx. sol̄.
In Bece q̄ ten̄ Osbn̄ de com̄ de Ow ht̄ abb̄ .iii. ꝩ̄ 7 tc̄e. 7 ibi sunt
.iii. uilli cū .i. car̄. Val .vi. sol̄.
In Wasingate q̄ ten̄ Reinb̄ ht̄ abb̄ una ꝩ̄ 7 tc̄e. cū un̄ uillo
7 dimid̄ car̄. Ibi silua .ii. porc̄. Val .iiii. sol̄.
In Wilacinte q̄ ten̄ com̄ morton̄. ht̄ abb̄ vi. uirḡ 7 tc̄e. 7 ibi
sunt .vi. uilli cū .iiii. car̄. 7 silua .ii. porc̄. Val .xv. sol̄.
In Nibefeld q̄ ten̄ com̄ de Ow. ht̄ abb̄ vi. uirḡ 7 tc̄e. Ibi sunt
vi. uilli 7 un̄ bord̄ cū .iii. car̄. Val .x. solid̄.
In Penehest q̄ ten̄ Osbn̄ de com̄ de Ow ht̄ abb̄ dim̄ hid̄. 7 ibi
.ii. uilli sunt cū .ii. car̄. 7 una ac̄ p̄a. 7 silua .ii. porc̄. Val .xx. sol̄.
In manerio bou q̄ ten̄ com̄ de Ow ht̄ abb̄ dim̄ hid̄. 7 ibi sunt
.ii. uilli cū una car̄. Val .v. sol̄ 7 c̄ar̄ 7 una ac̄ p̄a. Val .iiii. sol̄.
In Pilesha q̄ ten̄ com̄ de Ow ht̄ abb̄ una ꝩ̄. 7 un̄ uillm cū una
In Cedesfeld q̄ ten̄ Wernec de com̄ de Ow ht̄ abb̄ .iii. ꝩ̄ in dn̄io.
In Bollinturi q̄ ten̄ com̄ de Ow ht̄ abb̄ .ii. hid̄ una ꝩ̄ min.
7 ibi sunt .vii. uilli cū .v. car̄. Val .xx. sol̄. 7 cū .i. uillo. Val xx. sol̄.
In Caohest q̄ ten̄ Walter̄ de com̄ de Ow ht̄ abb̄ una ꝩ̄ tc̄e.
In Winiges q̄ ten̄ Ingelrann̄ de com̄ ht̄ abb̄ .i. uirḡ tc̄e. Wasta.
In Holinton q̄ ten̄ com̄ de Ow ht̄ abb̄ una ꝩ̄ tc̄e. Wasta.
Adhuc .ē una silua foris rap de .v. porc̄.
De omni hac tra ht̄ abb̄ in dn̄io .ii. hid̄ 7 dim̄. 7 ibi .i. car̄.
cū .xxi. bord̄. 7 ii. molinos sine censu. Val .xl. sol̄.
He hide n̄ geld auer̄ in rapo.

TERRA SCI EDWARDI.

Abbatia de S. Edwardo ten̄ 7 tenuit T.R.E. Faleha. Tc se defd̄
p .xxvi. hida. Modo p .xv. hid̄ 7 dim̄. Tra ē .xii. car̄. In dn̄io est una car̄. 7 xl.viii. uilli 7 xvi. cot̄ cū .xv. car̄. Ibi eccl̄a. 7 piscaria de .v. solid̄. In cicestre .iii. burgenses.
de .vii. solid̄. Ibi .viii. ac̄ p̄a. Silua de .xxx. porc̄. T.R.E. ualeb .x. lib̄. modo .xx. lib̄.

Above: Kilpeck Church, Herefordshire, is a rich example of a small parish church, built in the second half of the twelfth century. The stone carving of the portel over the south door, seen here, is particularly fine.

Opposite: A page from the Domesday Book — the beginning of the entry for Sussex.

THE DOMESDAY BOOK

IN 1086 WILLIAM I instituted the greatest survey of England conducted to date. It was an expression of the colonial relationship which he, as conqueror, had with England, and also a means of assessing the wealth of the nation. England was, at the conquest, a much richer place than William's Normandy. She was already an exporter of wool to the Continent and this was making her rich, especially in the days of peace under the Confessor. A claim to the throne was just one of the reasons why William had been keen to take control of the country; in addition, the wealth of it tempted him, just as it had tempted Caesar a thousand years earlier. Twenty years later, after wars in the North, in the Marches and with Scotland, William still had not adequately acquired the facts about England's wealth. Nor had he given the new landowners, the knights and relations who had been rewarded for their service in 1066 with parcels of England, a firm record of their ownership. The great survey, decided upon in Gloucester at Christmas 1085, was to do this. It would inform William about the wealth of the country so he could assess the possible income from the geld (tax); further, it would give him an idea of the manpower that was eligible for military service, and finally it would provide evidence of tenure for the tenants-in-chief.

To conduct the survey of the country south of the Westmorland fells and the River Tees, seven areas were established, each with an enquiry team. These groups were to tour the counties and assemble the courts in each hundred, Rape or Wapentake (division within the county). There they asked the same questions of every village. The enquiry wished to discover the owner of the land, who had owned it in the reign of the Confessor, and how many men of each category, sokemen,

William II 'Rufus' (c. 1056–1100).

the aethling – and also the effects of the years of dearth such as the 'great famine' of 1082.

The Great Survey was seen as unavoidable in its thoroughness and acquired the reputation of being akin to the Day of Judgement. From the 1170s onward it was named in writing as the Book of Judgement or the Domesday Book. The information when compiled was bound together into two sets, the Great Domesday, which contained most of the country, and the Little Domesday, which had the information for East Anglia which was not incorporated into the final abbreviated survey. William never saw the final version. In 1086 he left England to die the following year in France after a damaging fall from his horse.

We can learn a lot about England from the Domesday book. It lists a total of 290,000 men in the country representing roughly the number of households. If this is multiplied by four or five, the total rural population can be estimated at 1,450,000 with a further 111,500 in the 112 urban centres – 25,000 in London.

THE FEUDAL SYSTEM

WHAT THE DOMESDAY BOOK also contained, was the record of the feudal system. The legal record of the ownership of the land was evidence of the extent of the changes which the conquest had brought to the people and the land of England. In a feudal system, the king owned all the land, being given it by God. In return for services, in this case support in 1066, the king gave out parcels of land called fiefs to his knights. They were only tenants and in return for the land they provided the king with services – loyalty, legal service at the courts, military service and some taxes. Each of these chief tenants had lesser tenants, the mesne, who were given land in return for similar duties, and villeins or sokemen who had to perform labour duties on the chief tenant's estate.

Land meant power and William was too shrewd to let his tenants-in-chief get too powerful. The estates he shared out among his followers were spread around the country. As a result, no single baron would acquire too much power in any one district. Furthermore William adjusted the system of loyalty. In continental Europe, the first call on a tenant's

freeman, villeins, cottars and slaves, lived in the village. The survey required to know the size of the village lands and how they were divided up between pasture, wood and fish ponds: how many ploughs were employed on the lord of the manor's demesne – the 'home' farms estate – and how many were used by the rest of the village. The inquiry also wanted to know the value of the land in King Edward's time, at the time of the conquest and at the time of the survey, which was conducted between 1086 and 1087. Some of this latter information is interesting; it reveals the extent of the damage done in the North during the 'harrying' – the war with the northerners and

loyalty was the immediate superior. A mesne tenant was expected to owe his or her loyalty to the local landlord. In a rebellion the tenants would be expected to fight for the landlord, not the king. William, instead, made the first duty of the tenant loyalty to the king – rebellious barons were not guaranteed automatic support from their tenants. William kept large tracts of the country to himself, to provide him with money and men and to issue as rewards to loyal supporters if necessary. He kept a close watch on the tenants-in-chief by a series of officials and appointed sheriffs in the counties to collect the taxes and handle the local courts.

As a result many of the parts of England and the Marcher counties, and later Lowland Scotland were owned by absentee landlords, who may well have toured the richer of their possessions during the year. Each individual estate took the form of one or more manors; there were somewhat over 900 in England during the eleventh century. The centre of each was the manor house and the church. These were the substantial buildings which by the twelfth century would probably have been made of stone. The majority of the people would have had smaller timber-framed structures with walls of wattle and daub, a wicker panel covered in clay or earth, smoothed and dried. In the rich-soil areas the manor would have been surrounded by three fields, in which each tenant would have had strips of land; the greater the tenant the more strips he or she would have. Crops were grown in rotation, with one field being left fallow each year to allow the soil to regenerate. In addition, there would have been common land for grazing livestock and rights to keep pigs in woodland where there were acorns to be found. The manor would have had its own lands where the villeins and others would serve their boon work, the labour done for the lord as part of the conditions of tenancy. Luxury food would be produced too. Each of the villages would have fish pools and coneries for the breeding of rabbits (or conies) in purpose-built burrows.

The residue of these manors can still be traced in street or even field names of our day. The large unfenced or 'open' fields were often named after their geographical position – west field, north field and the like. Land set aside for the upkeep of the church incumbent

Henry I (1068–1135).

was known as a glebe. Coneries have left their names to streets too. Manor houses built in the two centuries after the conquest can still be seen (there is a fine example at Donington le Heath in Leicestershire) and Norman churches can be found too, with their handsome decorated arches. There is a simple one at Heath in Shropshire, and a grander although still austere one at Stow in Lincolnshire where a Saxon building was completed after the conquest in Norman style. At Winterborne Tomson in Dorset there is a lovely simple single-cell church with an apsed east end and a fine attendant manor house.

In some places, especially when there is a light snow on the ground we can still observe the strip-field system where the strips have

The Strip-field System

This system is still evident on some common, or 'Lammas', meadows, like the Lugg meadows near Hereford in the picture above. In the foreground is a small enclosed field; beyond it is the large flat area on which hay has been harvested in strips (the light green areas) by

strip-owners. The strips do not necessarily run parallel to each other, and their position is marked by stones like the one on the left. Once the hay has been cut, the meadow is opened to commoners to graze their livestock on it — generally on Lammas Day, August 1.

been left undisturbed on lands subsequently used for pasture. There the strips were not ploughed out, but later field divisions often cut across the line of the old fields. At Laxton in Nottinghamshire the manor is still farmed in the open system with village officials still administering the farming. Not all of the country was organised into this type of manor. In hilly areas or forested lands, the ground was unsuitable to arable use and the fields were enclosed for pasture to a greater extent. In others small parcels of ground supplemented incomes derived from mining, charcoal-burning or other industries. In large parts of the country, two-thirds of which was wild and untamed, there were no manors of the type mentioned here. When communities developed there in later centuries, the feudal system and its vassals were in decline.

WILLIAM'S SUCCESSORS

WHEN WILLIAM I DIED in 1087 he left three sons. Robert became Duke of Normandy, William (known as Rufus because of his red hair) became King of England and Henry had ambitions for one or both places. Normandy was generally regarded as the centre of the Norman empire; William the Conqueror had spent most of his time there after the defeat of the northern earls' rebellion and the subsequent harrying of the North in 1072. Behind him he left an England irrevocably changed. There were still about 250 people who owned and controlled the country, but after the rebellions proved that the English were not to be fully trusted and that the Danish English harboured ambitions to make the country part of the Scandinavian Empire, most of these men were now Norman or other Continental newcomers. English was rapidly passing from being the language of law and of the court, and Latin was superseding the written word, French the spoken. The Anglo-Saxons and Danish Saxons retained their own language and its variations, but their masters spoke French.

William Rufus took up the mantle of King of England, but he also wanted to wrest Normandy from his brother and when Robert went off on the crusade to the Holy Land in 1096, he claimed it in return for supporting

The crowning of the young King Henry II, whose father serves him at table.

Robert financially and with manpower. The King was a violent, militaristic man, trained for war and delighting in that skill. England under him was prepared for military action, a feat requiring money and incurring the wrath of the Church. When, in the New Forest in 1100 he was killed, to the Church his unshriven death was just reward for wickedness; to others it was merely sad accident. In fact, the King may have been murdered. This cannot be proved, but the lightning stroke of the younger brother, Henry, who was also in the New Forest that day, is noteworthy. He seized the treasury at Winchester within hours and three days later was crowned by the Bishop of London – not by either of the primates, York or Canterbury. Conveniently Robert was still away, returning from the crusade. Henry moved fast, declaring that he would govern fairly, abolishing some of Rufus's financial chicanery and freeing the knights – the second rank of landowners after the barons – from non-military levies.

Henry I's reign was not for him a happy one. His brother Robert was an early problem, but by 1106 Normandy had been seized from him. Following this, however, Robert's son, with the help of the King of France and the Count of Anjou, tried to wrest from Henry lands on the Continent. For much of the time Henry had to stay in Normandy defending himself against his enemies and his fickle friends. England was itself mainly at peace, but Henry's severity, bred perhaps of fear and certainly not of the promise shown in his coronation declarations, left him tarnished. Criminals could be and were blinded and castrated, and moneyers – the minters of coins – were castrated and had their right hands cut off in 1125. In 1120 the son and heir to the throne drowned in the wreck of the royal White Ship and this seems to have only increased the King's fear. A king without an heir was a more likely prospect for murder than one who would be succeeded straightaway. In short, Henry could never lie down to sleep without first looking behind him (this was advice given by his contemporary, Vladimir of Russia, to his own sons).

When Henry died in 1135 the succession was a problem of a proportion unseen for a hundred years. He wished his daughter, Matilda, married to his erstwhile enemy the Count of Anjou, to succeed, but there were few precedents for this and many of the barons refused to accept it, choosing instead Stephen of Blois, Henry I's nephew, who won the race to be crowned. Whilst it may have been possible that Henry intended Matilda's husband, Geoffery of Anjou, to rule with her and unite Anjou with England and Normandy, Geoffery showed little inclin-

ation. Geoffery had gained Anjou only in 1129 when his father became King of Jerusalem and went out to Outremer that year. As a result Matilda alone gained the oath of loyalty from the English barons at Northampton in 1131.

Matilda was an arrogant woman. As the widow of the Holy Roman Emperor, Henry V, she kept the title Empress all her life, which was perhaps galling to Geoffery as it did indicate that her marriage to him was of little importance. When she did go to England, after leaving Geoffery to regain control of Normandy following Stephen's invasion attempts of 1137 and 1138, she annoyed more people through her arrogance than she won to her side; she defeated Stephen at Lincoln in 1141, and yet he still managed to gain support. In the event, she could neither win England nor her husband's full support over the Channel. Stephen reigned until 1154 in a country torn by civil war and anarchy as barons increased their wealth, and both Stephen and Matilda bought support by creating new barons and trebling the number of earls. In 1153 Stephen recognised Matilda's son Henry as his heir and in the following year when he died, the young man became Henry II, Duke of Normandy, Count of Anjou and the head of a cross-Channel empire – the Angevin Empire. He established a royal house which was to last until the Battle of Bosworth in 1485: the Plantagenets.

Henry attempted to restore order, mercenary armies were disposed of and castles built in Stephen's reign were demolished. The Scottish overlordship of the North, granted by Stephen and sanctioned by Matilda, when both were seeking support, was also ended. He

The defeat of the Christians by Saladin at the battle of Hattin, from Matthew Paris's *Chronica Majora*.

The Crusades

The Crusades were a series of military expeditions undertaken between 1096 and 1270 by the powers of Western Europe to reclaim the Holy Land and Jerusalem for Christianity. Richard I of England was one of the leaders of the third Crusade (1189–92), which was launched after Saladin, Sultan of Egypt and Syria, had captured Jerusalem in 1187. Richard managed to capture the port of Acre and gained rights for pilgrims to visit Jerusalem, but these were temporary successes in a long and doomed enterprise. By the end of the thirteenth century, the Holy Land was under the control of Moslems.

gained the loyalty of the Scots and Welsh and, with papal support, began to colonise Ireland. Henry intended to be King of all the British Isles and the master of his own Church. This latter point overshadowed the whole reign. To gain this control, Henry installed his friend and loyal supporter, the Chancellor of the Exchequer, Thomas Becket, as Archbishop of Canterbury in 1162. Becket was too honest a man to succumb to Henry's pressure. Relations between the two declined from that point, and although patched up at various times, the friendship and loyalty of Becket had switched to a greater master. Henry was not able to dominate his Church. Driven desperate by Becket's success at defending the Church, in 1170 the king fell into a fit of some form calling out 'who will rid me of this turbulent priest?' Overheard by four knights, Henry's question was answered and Becket was slain at the altar of Canterbury Cathedral, his brain pan emptied across the floor. Henry underwent paroxysms of grief and made atonement for Becket's death, but he was irrevocably stained. Despite the praise of the Pope for his 'work' in Ireland – the effects of which are not yet worked through – Henry remained tarred.

In 1189 Henry died and was succeeded by Richard I – 'The Lionheart'. His reign lasted ten years, but he was only in England for six months. His coronation sparked racist attacks throughout the country on the resident Jewish population. For some time they had lived in England as traders and merchants, and expressed their loyalty to the regime by turning out to celebrate Richard's coronation. In London they were attacked and this aggression spread throughout the country. In 1190 the Jews in York were driven into the castle by rioters, and were then besieged there by the mob and the city officials. Several of the leading families committed suicide in the castle tower rather than submit to the barbarities of the mob. Not only did York lose a valuable section of the trading population and the castle, which was burnt to the ground in a bodged attempt to cremate the bodies, but it gained a perpetual stain – this pogrom is commemorated at the foot of Clifford's Tower in York. Continued oppression of the Jewish community over the next century resulted in it being expelled totally in 1290.

Richard sold offices to finance his part in the

Above: Clifford's Tower, York.

Opposite: The monastic scribes enhanced their manuscripts with illuminated letters such as this copy of an eleventh century example.

third Crusade, and his capture by Leopold of Austria in 1193 can be seen as a disaster: England had to pay a massive ransom and suffered the indignity of becoming a fiefdom of the Holy Roman Emperor. On the other hand, the necessity of gathering the large sum demanded as a ransom strengthened the administrative system of the country, and London became the heart of the nation when it became the site of opposition to the government of William Longchamp, whom Richard appointed to govern. Richard fared better later on. From 1193 he had the able Hubert Walter heading the Government at home with his brother John in the role of Rector of England. Richard died as he had lived, as a soldier during the siege of Chalus in south-west France in 1199 and the country bent to the rule of the 'wicked King John'.

5. NATIONS

OUT OF

JOINT

THE LATE MIDDLE AGES
1200–1500

KING JOHN has received a bad press ever since the Victorian age. His poor reputation is the result of several features of his reign. He fought for the inheritance of his lands in northern France against Prince Arthur of Brittany, the son of one of his elder brothers who was judged by some to have a stronger claim to the throne. The Prince was supported in this claim by the King of France who lent military aid, but John managed to capture Arthur and there is strong suspicion that he was responsible for his murder in 1203 in Rouen. John's position in France was, however, becoming less and less defensible. Disaffected barons were surrendering their castles to the French King, Philip II; John withdrew to England and by the summer of 1204 Philip had seized Normandy, Anjou, Maine, Touraine and most of Poitou. An expedition to Poitou in 1214 to try to regain these lands ended disastrously when his allies were routed at the battle of Bouvines in Flanders.

In England, too, John stirred up resentment. In 1205 he opposed the selection of Simon Langton for the see of Canterbury and refused to allow him into the kingdom. By 1209, the Pope was so angered by the action of the King that he placed England under an Interdict; no burial or marriage was considered sanctified during the period. The pressure on John to yield was so great that in 1213 he had to submit to the Pope's command and England actually became a fiefdom of Rome.

The barons of England were similarly unimpressed with the King, whose wars were expensive, of long duration and, moreover, a failure. Their opposition was eventually

The Magna Carta issued in 1215 at Runnymede by King John under pressure from the barons.

TIME CHART

1199	King John comes to the throne of England.
1215	Magna Carta.
1216	Death of John: accession of Henry III.
1240	Llywelyn the Great dies.
1255	Llywelyn ap Gruffyd takes power in Wales.
1258	Commune of England created.
1264	Battle of Lewes; Simon de Montfort defeats Henry III.
1265	De Montfort and the Confederates defeated at the battle of Evesham.
1272	Henry III dies; accession of Edward I.
1277	Edward I defeats Llywelyn.
1282	Llywelyn killed in the second invasion of Wales.
1294	War with France.
1301	The first English Prince of Wales proclaimed.
1306	Robert Bruce becomes King of Scotland.
1307	Death of Edward I: accession of Edward II.
1314	Scottish victory at the battle of Bannockburn.
1321–2	Civil war in England.
1327	Edward II murdered: accession of Edward III.
1337	Hundred Years War begins.
1346	English victory at the battle of Crécy.
1348–9	Black Death comes to England, then Wales and Scotland.
1356	English victory at the battle of Poitiers.
1377	Death of Edward III: accession of Richard II.
1381	The Peasants' Revolt.
1399	Henry IV deposes Richard II, who dies the following year.
1400–8	Rebellion of Owain Glyn Dwr.
1413	Death of Henry IV: accession of Henry V.
1415	English victory at the battle of Agincourt.
1419–20	English conquest of Normandy.
1420	Anglo-French Treaty of Troyes.
1422	Death of Henry V: accession of Edward IV.
1429	Joan of Arc leads the French in the relief of the siege of Orleans.
1449–50	Normandy overrun by the French.
By 1453	All English lands in France except Calais and the Channel Islands conquered by the French.
1455–85	Dynastic struggle between the Yorkists and the Lancastrians (the 'Wars of the Roses').
1461	Henry VI deposed: accession of Edward IV.
1470–1	Henry VI restored to the throne but is defeated by Edward at the battle of Tewkesbury (1471) and murdered.
1477	William Caxton's first printed book.
1483	Death of Edward IV. Princes in the Tower murdered: Richard III made king.
1485	Death of Richard III at the battle of Bosworth: accession of Henry VII.

expressed through force of arms and they forced the King into signing the Magna Carta, the Great Charter, in 1215 at Runnymede. Much of the Charter dealt with specifics, such as the building of weirs on the Thames and the rights of the barons, but through the provisions of clause thirty-nine, which stressed that no person could be fined, killed, or in any other way imprisoned or ruined, without trial by his peers or the use of the law, its meaning became extended. As a result, it was issued several times during the reign of Henry III to emphasise the limitation of his power; centuries later it was used against other over-mighty monarchs and developed into the touchstone of radical politics.

It did not have such an auspicious beginning. John signed it but as soon as he considered himself strong again, he ignored it. The barons as a result signed away his throne. They called in the King of France who invaded the south of England. It was the second major invasion from across the Channel and could have been as momentous as the first had not John died in 1216. The young Henry, John's son, was crowned at Gloucester, not by an archbishop, nor with the proper regalia, but it was a coronation all the same. Despite the fact that the French held London and the South-east (except for Dover), the idea of a new King put heart into the English. The French forces were defeated on land at Lincoln and at sea near Dover, and in 1217 came to terms with the King's party. In 1220 the young King was crowned again, this time by the Archbishop with the correct regalia and at Westminster.

Opposite: Four English kings illustrated in The Chronicle of Matthew Paris of St. Albans (d. 1259). Above are Henry II and Richard I, below are John and Henry III.

d gignen
do dictū
em dir
uatum
nomen
e tra. ex q̄
omnia gig
nuntur;
se enim ꝶa
tra dr: ꝗ
ta dc̄a ꝕ
uigorem
ut q̄ uim
teneat naf
cendi atq̄;
crescendi
ꝯ ꝯ arbo
res uitam
br̄e dūr;
ꝗ gignūt
ꝯ crescunt,
Homo dicꝺ
quia ex hu

mo. ē factus sic in genesi dicitur. Et creauit deus
hominem de humo ꝶe; Abusiue enim pnūciat.
ex utq̄; suba totus homo. i. ex societate anime ꝯ corpis.
Nam ꝑe homo ab humo. Greci enim antropum ap
pellauerunt. eo q̄ sursum aspectat. subleuatis ab humo.
ad contemplationem artificis sui. Quod ouidius poe
ta designat cum dicit; ꝓnaq̄; conspectant animalia

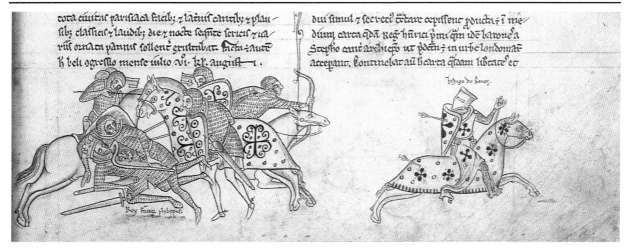

The battle of Bouvines, 1214. The French King, Philip, is unhorsed, but the battle was a crushing defeat for John and his armies. In an age where a king was judged by his military success, John was deemed a failure for the loss of most of his Angevine lands.

HENRY III

Henry took the responsibility of government onto his own shoulders at the age of sixteen, but was unable to undo the damage done in France. The King's reign was long, but he was not always a popular ruler. In the 1250s the barons of England felt the strain of warfare on their pockets. Seven of them formed a confederacy under the guidance of Simon de Montfort, Earl of Leicester. They forced the King to sign the reforming Provisions of Oxford in 1258, making Henry in effect the figure-head of the Commune of England. Government was conducted through a Parliament, small at first, with only twenty-five members, but nevertheless the start of the institution which became fundamental to the government of the country.

THE BARON'S WAR

Like his father, Henry attempted to avoid the consequences of his actions and, as John had tried to circumvent Magna Carta, Henry wanted to avoid the strictures of the Commune. He went abroad for two years and sought the aid of the King of France, from whom he gained a hearing of the case, to be judged by the French monarch. Both sides presented their arguments, but the case went in favour of Henry. King Louis was naturally

concerned that such a Commune might one day be forced on him if he showed any sympathy for the idea. In England there was resistance to the decision, but the stomach for a fight had gone from the confederates and in any case the Parliament had become a selection of people chosen largely by de Montfort. As such, it was just as autocratic as the King, and a lot of support drifted away. Henry went to war with the confederates and in 1264 was defeated and captured at Lewes. Nevertheless his supporters fought on and de Montfort was killed and mutilated at the battle of Evesham the following year. Henry was now ageing and the rest of his reign saw government pass into the hands of his heir, Lord Edward. As King, Edward I was ambitious, keen to extend his control over Wales and if possible Scotland; his reign was marked by this ambition and so were the three nations.

CASTLES

It was during the period covered by this chapter that many of the great historical features of the landscape were created. They now nestle behind skyscrapers, sit in ruins astride hills, or lie gracefully decaying in lonely vales; some even lie buried beneath fields or cityscapes. The two centuries after the Norman conquest had seen the construction of many castles, mostly built of wood. They were of a simple motte and bailey design. At their core lay a towering keep built on an

Opposite: A monk at work. Learning and the recording of history were largely in the hands of the Church.

Goodrich Castle, Herefordshire, built by William Marshal, Earl of Pembroke, to control the raids of the Welsh chieftains. William was one of King John's most able lieutenants.

artificial mound known as a motte. Adjoining this was a bailey or courtyard.

Some castles contained massive square keeps, like the White Tower in London, begun in 1086, which became the heart of the complex Tower of London. These were huge structures, self-contained in case of attack yet including offices and living-quarters for the inhabitants. Fine examples of these can be seen at Scarborough, Knaresborough — now in ruins — and at Rochester and Dover where they still tower in all their majesty. The design of castles altered in many ways. The crusades gave British people the chance of seeing the Middle Eastern castles, and their pattern was copied in some of the concentric designs shown, for example, at Beaumaris on Anglesey. These castles consisted of two walls, one inside the other, following roughly the same plan. The inner walls were higher, allowing defenders on them to dominate the outer wall if it should fall into enemy hands. The gatehouses of these great fortresses were massive affairs, strengthening the weak spot which was the entrance. The gatehouses contained many of the features of the old keeps and actually replaced them. Edward I

was the last monarch to engage in castle building on any great scale, especially in Wales where he sought to dominate the Principality. The great fortifications of Caernarfon, Conway and Aberystwyth were built at this time.

In the following century there was a parallel development: the fortified manor house. This was built chiefly for comfort but contained defensive towers and walls. Good examples are at Stokesay in Shropshire and Littlecote in Warwickshire. The building of these often picturesque forts continued throughout the unstable fifteenth century. One such is Tattershall castle in Lincolnshire which was built between 1430 and 1480, largely out of brick. Another is Ashby de la Zouch's manor house which was added to by Sir William Hastings, the favourite of Edward IV, in the 1480s. A soaring tower was constructed, capable of independent defence but designed for sumptuous living. The 'castle' was designed for the display of wealth; in particular the chapel, superfluous to needs, was ostentatious in the extreme.

Many of the castles were allowed to go to ruin. One of the twin mottes of York Castle was abandoned during the thirteenth century,

Stokesay Castle, Shropshire — not a castle, in fact, but the best preserved and oldest fortified manor house in England.

and other castles went into decay later. Castles like Warwick saw many changes of use and design. Ashby only remained a fully defensive structure for a short time. In the sixteenth century the south-west wall was demolished and replaced with a brick 'garden wall' turning the place into the palace of a major landowner.

WALES

THE OPENING of the thirteenth century seemed full of promise for Wales. The attempts of King John to extend his control over the Marches and over the Principality itself came to nothing and the country came to a new prominence. The responsibility for this falls to one man, Llywelyn ab Iorworth, known as Llywelyn Fawr — the Great. In 1200 he had become the master of Gwynedd, in 1215 his rights over Wales had been recognised in the Magna Carta and by 1234 he had come to terms with the English in the border lands. In Wales, the Norman conquest had been adapted to suit the local way of life. Wales still had its own legal system and laws, and furthermore the Marcher lords had also

built for themselves a power structure of their own. The counties of the Marches had their own law courts too and they resented interference from Westminster as much as the Welsh themselves.

Llywelyn Fawr was attempting to modernise Wales, trying to give it the stamp of a feudal state with status abroad. Castles were built as centres of administration and to control the areas of Wales which Llywelyn absorbed into his control. Towns were given charters which enabled them to govern themselves through elected councils. The law was codified, using the principle of the laws of Hywel Dda but adapting them to the needs of the modern feudal state. Taxation was systematically overhauled and the central government was conducted as that in England. Prince Llywelyn had a great seal and privy seals to authorise the acts of his government.

This did not go without notice in England where King Henry III was keen to restate the relationship between him and the Welsh princes. Llywelyn considered that he as the superior prince in Wales was top of the feudal pyramid in the country. All of the barons and other princes there would do homage to him

111

Above: Grosmont Castle, Gwent, one of the Monmouthshire 'trilateral' – Grosmont, Skenfrith and White Castles – built in the twelfth and thirteenth centuries to check the Welsh.

Below: Skenfrith Castle, Gwent.

and he to the King of England. To Henry this was not the case. He held that Llywelyn was only *primus inter pares* – the first amongst equals. All of the barons and princes of Wales should therefore owe their first allegiance to the King of England, not to any Welsh prince, even if he were Prince of Aberffraw and Lord of Snowdon. However, the reign of Llywelyn Fawr saw Wales so strong and its prince so powerful that Henry III was unable to impose his view.

By the rights of inheritance in Wales, Llywelyn's two sons, Gruffydd and David, would have jointly inherited their father's power. Instead Llywelyn persuaded Henry III and the Welsh barons and princes to agree to accept David as the sole heir. Thus Wales was in 1240 passed on intact to one person. However, when the Prince presented himself at Gloucester to do homage to the English king, Henry refused to allow him to receive the homage of the Welsh lords. Five years later the English took over the lands between Chester and Conway as Henry III pushed

David back into central Wales. David was the first prince to call himself Prince of Wales. This was part of his attempt to gain independence from England, but at his death in 1246 the achievement of his father which had made the assumption of the title possible looked as if it were in ruins. Furthermore David died childless and the country fell to his two nephews, Owain and Llywelyn ap Gruffydd, sons of Gruffydd the man set aside by Llwelyn Fawr in favour of David. For ten years these men struggled with each other before Llywelyn ap Gruffydd imprisoned Owain and became sole ruler, adopting the title Prince of Wales and, in 1263, going on the offensive against recent English gains in the Principality. In 1264 he sided with Simon de Montfort in the war against the English King. Even though the confederates lost in the following year after the battle of Evesham, Llywelyn scored a success. Anxious for stability, Henry III was generous to the Welsh Prince and accepted his position and title.

There were fatal flaws. The Marcher lords were jealous of the Prince's power and independence; they also feared him and the Lord Edward, heir to Henry, was not so sanguine about the status of this supposed vassal. When he came to the throne as Edward I, Llywelyn's younger brother, David, had gone into revolt and sought the King of England's aid. Llywelyn was concerned about the form of homage that the new King would want of him. Edward was unlikely to accept the Prince of Wales as anything more then *primus inter pares*. As a result, Llywelyn delayed his visit to the new King, wanting the relationship between the two to be sorted out first. Edward could not wait for ever and he went on the offensive in 1276, declaring Llywelyn a disturber of the peace and a rebel.

The war was brief. The South fell quickly to the English and the King himself drove into the north forcing the Welsh back into Snowdonia. There they hoped to live out the winter on the crops grown on Anglesey, but a naval attack on the island succeeded and the English fed off them instead. In such circumstances, resistance was impossible and Llywelyn had to come to terms. He lost all but central Wales, and his rebellious brother was rewarded for his work with lands given to him by the grateful English King. Llywelyn tried to exist as best he could under the humiliating terms which had set back all he and his grandfather had achieved, but it was David who grew restless. It was not enough that he had helped undo all that work: he now felt cheated. He gained the support of the Welsh living under English rule in the annexed territories, and in 1272 he went into open revolt seizing some of the English-occupied castles. The southern princes joined in and the Prince of Wales was obliged to take the lead. Again, Edward's forces crushed the resistance in the South, and again drove Llywelyn back into Snowdonia, but this time the planned seizure of Anglesey failed. With his northern forces thus supplied from Anglesey, Llywelyn made a dash to the South to encourage resistance. Disaster struck the Welsh at this point. Llywelyn's party was attacked near Builth and a squire ran him though not knowing who he was. The great Prince's head was carried to London and displayed as if it were that of a traitor on a spike at the Tower. His body was bured at Abbey Cwm Hyr, and the site of the tragedy is marked near Builth Wells. As for the unworthy David, he too was taken to London alive – and was brutally done to death.

Edward now thoroughly imposed his foreign rule on the Principality. He built castles to house the Englishmen who administered the country. What now pass for glories of architecture in Wales were built at this time. Yet the great castles of Conway, Caernarfon and Harlech, as well as Beaumaris were also symbols of the oppression of the foreign invader. The country was broken up and recast as shires on the English model, so that it was in effect ruled from Carmarthen by the Justice of the South, from Caernarfon by the Justice of the North, and from Chester by the Justice of the Marches. Further, Edward ordered the supposed grave of King Arthur, the only truly accepted ruler of all Britain, to be opened. The bodies of the King and Guinevere were wrapped in silk and reburied at the altar of Glastonbury. It was a statement. Arthur is dead, he is buried on English soil, he will not return and the kingdom is now ruled from England by an English king. To emphasise the control of the English monarch, the eldest son of Edward was made Prince of Wales in 1301.

Many of the Welsh people tried to find places for themselves in the new order. The

number of native Welsh barons and princes was being whittled down in order to break up any potentially powerful group, but others joined in the government of the Principality. They learned law in England and practised it there and in Wales; they became rich and they aped the conquerors. The surname prefix *ap*, meaning 'son of' was dropped, or as in the case of the ap Rhys, combined into one word – Pryce or Price. From the other end of the social spectrum, many Welshmen offered their services to the English army. Llywelyn's army had been modern and efficient and the most effective part had been the archers using the longbow. A good archer could have three arrows in the air at once, dealing a withering blow to the enemy. True, the Welsh seemed to misunderstand the English manner of capturing the opponent nobility to claim ransoms, instead the Welsh soldier killed all and sundry, but at the battles of Crécy in 1346 and at Agincourt in 1415 they won glowing praise for their ability to wipe out large sections of the French nobility. So impressed were the English that they conferred upon the Welsh bowmen the highest honour which they could think of: they called them English

(a misnomer of surprising longevity, for this trend continued: the valiant English army at Waterloo, a battle won largely because the Prussians arrived to the rescue, was in fact chiefly composed of soldiers from the Celtic fringe of the British Isles, not Englishmen).

For a century the Welsh suffered under the English rule, but at its end there arose a hero, a prince again to lead them out of it. Owain Glyn Dwr had been one of those men educated in England (he had been a colleague of Chaucer at one point in his life). He grew dissatisfied with the treatment of his native country and could not accept the usurpation of Henry IV and the murder of Richard II in 1399. He declared himself Prince of Wales after taking over Gwynedd and expanding his power outwards. Glyn Dwr worked with the English rebels, the Earl of Northumberland and Edmund Mortimer. Together they planned a division of England and Wales which would in effect create a new Wales, stretching from the Severn to the Mersey. Whilst this failed, the reorganisation of Wales went on apace. Owain was crowned Prince before envoys from France, Castile and Scotland, he held parliaments at Machynlleth

The gate-tower on the Monnow Bridge at Monmouth, Gwent, built as a defensive structure against the Welsh.

York Minster

Cathedrals

The monasteries of Britain were at the fore-front of the cultivation of the land. In their escape from the secular world, they unwittingly dragged part of it after them. The great churches, with their educational establish-ments, required a series of support services beyond the ability of the monks or nuns themselves. Labourers built the churches, tilled the fields belonging to the religious establishments and communities grew up on the monastic lands around them. Some of the monasteries grew rich on the income from these lands and from the tithes of those living there. This was reflected in the glorious architecture of some of these places, and later, in the sixteenth century, in the eagerness with which the lands were snatched up by purchasers at the Dissolution.

Some of the country's cathedrals, like York and Canterbury, are the latest manifestations of buildings on traditional sites of worship. Others are the remains of the monastic establishments destroyed in the sixteenth century. A great range of design can be seen, from the Norse architecture of Kirkwall, through the Norman at Durham, and on through to the Minster at York. The Minster took 250 years to build; it was initially constructed in the early English fashion, later in the perpendicular style. Cathedrals were built to the glory of God and man's wealth by the sweat and often lives of ordinary men and women; it is perhaps the magnificence of their achievement which is most signified by the beauty of these temples.

Edward I receiving the homage of John Balliol.

and planned two universities.

The aid of France was ephemeral. When they sent forces to help defeat England, they marched to Worcester, helped Glyn Dwr face the King, and then slipped away. Wales on its own could not challenge the English for long. When Henry gained full control of his country he sent his son, the future Henry V, to deal with Owain. In 1408 the big cannons of the English army battered down the Welsh castles and the new Wales fell again to the envious England. Owain went into hiding – perhaps in Herefordshire with his relatives, the Scudamores. In myth he was supposed to have gone, Arthur-like, into subterranean slumber awaiting a call. The abbot of Valle

Crucis is supposed to have told him that he had arisen too early – by a hundred years. In a way the support for the Earl of Richmond, in 1485, was the continuation of support for the last Prince of Wales.

SCOTLAND

As the thirteenth century dawned, Scotland was more concerned with the aggression of the Norwegians as they attempted again to expand their empire. The Scottish offensive against the Norsemen reached the west coast by the 1220s, after

campaigns led by Alexander II and his heir Alexander III. In 1263 King Haakon of Norway made an attack on the Scottish mainland from the islands off the north and west coast which still belonged to Norway. After reaching Loch Lomond, the Norwegians were defeated at the Battle of Largs and from there driven back to the sea. Haakon died before returning home. His son Magnus attempted to keep some of the islands, but in 1266 the Treaty of Perth ended the Norse hold on all of the western isles except Orkney and Shetland. The Norse who lived on the isles and on the mainland were given the choice of returning to their ancestral homeland or staying in their new home. Many stayed. Their cultural links with their Norse forebears were strong, they had a distinct social structure and their lifestyle was different from the Scots around them. They left us the cathedral of Kirkwall. The existence of this community with its own customs and way of life is another example of the multicultural tradition of the British Isles, where quite separate groups of people were able to live in close proximity, without sacrificing their own cultural identity, contributing to the nation's development and history.

After the death of Alexander II the English attempted to gain further control over the Scottish lands by proposing that the young heir, Margaret, marry the heir to the English throne, the future English Prince of Wales. The throne of Scotland would by this arrangement fall into English hands unless the marriage was childless. However, before the arrangements were completed, Margaret died at Orkney on the way to Scotland. King Edward I lost no time in asserting his right to oversee the choice of a successor, given that he was the suzerain – the higher king. He forced all nine of the main contenders to agree to his arbitration. He chose the weakest, John Balliol: the man with so little about him that the Scots called him Toom Tabard – the empty coat. Once he had been stood on the stone (the kings of Scotland were not crowned, instead they were stood on the Stone of Scone which seems to have had origins in Spain), Edward humiliated the new King. King John was called to England on every trivial matter and his country was charged with contributing to the English wars on the Continent. John reluctantly endured it; his

Robert I, 'the Bruce' (1274–1329).

people could not.

In 1296 John was forced by his people to declare independence. In response Edward attacked, crossing the Border, captured John and his son Edward Balliol and marched as far north as Elgin. On the return trip he took the Stone of Scone with him. Edward desired to rule Scotland himself without even the weakest of puppets to work for him. It was to little avail. The Scots rebelled under the leadership of William Wallace who drove the English across the border. It was a short-lived success as Wallace was defeated at Falkirk on 22 July 1298. Wallace fled abroad but the revolt smouldered on. The two prominent leaders, John Comyn and Robert Bruce, were unable to work together successfully, and Bruce soon sided with the English. Resistance collapsed after Comyn was defeated and Wallace, who had returned, was captured and executed in 1305.

ROBERT BRUCE

AS THE ENGLISH KING attempted to influence the succession again in 1306, Bruce entered Scotland, murdered Comyn and had himself made King at Scone. His early campaign against the English met with ill luck,

Edward III (1312–77).

and when he died in 1329 he passed the country on to his five-year-old son David.

David almost lost everything. Shortly after his accession, Edward, son of John Balliol, landed in the country, declared himself King and forced David into exile. Edward Balliol gave large chunks of land to the English King, but the supporters of David solicited French aid and stopped the English invasion of 1338 when Black Agnes, Countess of March, kept them out of Dunbar for five months. When David returned in 1341 he wanted revenge, but his country was tired and ruined after years of war. Nevertheless, in 1346 he crossed the border and invaded England, only to be defeated at Neville's Cross near Bishop Auckland. He was captured and held in England until 1357. In the end he mortgaged his country by agreeing to pay a 100,000 marks ransom. When he returned, Scotland found it impossible to pay the money and the taxation imposed on the country by the King was ruinous to many. On the other hand, during the long period of his absence the country developed the constitutional position of the Edinburgh Parliament.

This continued during the next century due to a series of weak and ill-fated monarchs. The next two kings, Robert II and III, came to the throne late in life, after which the three James' succeeded when minors. James I was only eleven at his accession in 1406 and was at the time a prisoner of the English who released him only in 1424. James II succeeded in 1437 at the age of six and died when a gun blew up in 1460. James III was murdered in 1480 after coming to the throne at the age of nine. Fortunately, the English were so preoccupied with their own unstable succession that the question of suzerainty went into abeyance for much of the period. There had been an invasion in 1385 which cost some border towns but many of these were restored in the following century. Berwick was given to Scotland by Queen Margaret when the Yorkist force pressed northwards. In 1482 the future Richard III invaded Scotland intending to depose James III. Despite occupying Edinburgh the plan was never carried out, but Berwick was re-taken by the English. There was some Scottish support for Henry Tudor's claim to the throne of England in 1485, but it was to be one hundred and eighteen years before Scotland sent its own candidate.

for he could not find much support amongst the people after the murder of the popular Comyn. Driven to the coast he went into hiding and is supposed to have taken notice of the example of a dogged spider building his web. Despite failure in the initial stages of the renewed campaign when two of his brothers were killed at Loch Ryan in Galloway, Bruce was blessed with success after Edward I – the Hammer of the Scots – died. His new opponent, Edward II, was not as capable of military action as his father and began to succumb to Bruce's campaign which was a gradual affair. By 1310, despite the English's periodic invasions, Scottish control of the Lowlands was increased. Edinburgh was captured in 1314. Edward II launched a massive invasion in the spring of that year. He was defeated at Bannockburn on 23 June. It was a signal defeat, marking the end of the crisis begun in 1296. Bruce went on to consolidate the political strength of Scotland

The Clergy House, Alfriston, East Sussex, dates from 1350 and is a rare example of a small house of this period. It was the home of the parish priest, and in 1895 became the first building to be acquired by the National Trust — for £10.

EDWARD II

THE HIGH MIDDLE AGES had seen England attempting to exert its control over the other parts of mainland Britain. To do this it exploited problems of succession, such as when Queen Margaret of Scotland died in 1290 or when the Welsh princes fell out amongst themselves. But England was not immune from these problems. When Edward I died in 1307, there was no legal difficulty about the succession, but the son had few of the qualities of the father.

Edward II was a weak and inept ruler and, although he married Isabella of France, there was suspicion of a homosexual relationship with his favourite, Peter Gaveston. The barons were concerned about his weakness and the influence of Gaveston; in 1311 they drew up a set of ordinances to place some control on the King, and in 1312 murdered Gaveston. The battle of Bannockburn in 1314 (see opposite) was a disaster and continuing dissatisfaction led to civil war in 1321–2.

Edward repudiated the barons' ordinances and fell once more under the influence of favourites – Hugh le Despenser and his son, who were killed in 1326. But the remedy for the nation's ills had to be administered to the cause. Isabella, who had fled to France, returned with her son and heir to the throne; Edward was deposed and in 1327, put to death at Berkeley Castle in a most foul manner.

THE HUNDRED YEARS WAR

EDWARD III was a more warlike man: he fought the Scots, attempted to control their king and, further, launched into the wars against the French, which became known as the Hundred Years War, in an attempt to gain control of their throne too. He defeated the fleet of Philip VI in the battle of Sluis off the coast of the Netherlands in 1340. In 1346 the battle of Crécy was won by defensive tactics and the faster firing-rate of the British

longbows against the French crossbows. Edward then laid siege to Calais, which would provide him with a valuable Channel port and staging-post into France. The siege lasted over a year. Eventually, the governor of the town and its chief burghers surrendered the town; they expected to be hanged but were spared, it is recorded, after Edward's Queen Philippa pleaded for their lives. In 1356 Edward's son, Edward the Black Prince, fought another brilliant defensive battle against a larger force at Poitiers, but by 1373 many of Edward's gains in France had been lost. The Black Prince died in 1376, a year before his father, and his son came to the throne at the age of ten as Richard II.

RICHARD II

WHILST RICHARD was a minor, the government of the country was in the hands of his uncle, John of Gaunt, third son of Edward III, who had already taken on this role during his father's old age. Richard became a capricious king, extravagant and arbitrary in dealing with friends and enemies. In 1387, after appeals against his conduct by five 'lords appellant', his army was involved in a skirmish and put to flight at Radcot Bridge in Oxfordshire. During the following year he was forced to submit to the guidance of the lords, but in 1397–8 he eliminated all five by

The Siege of Calais, 1346, from the Froissart Chronicles.

exile or murder. Another exile, Henry Bolingbroke, son of John of Gaunt, returned to England in July 1399 whilst Richard was in Ireland. His aim was to recover the Lancastrian estates Richard had seized on the death of his father, but he found wider support amongst many nobles who were outraged by Richard's tyrannous rule and was able to arrest the King on his return. Henry forced Richard to abdicate and imprisoned him in Pontefract Castle; by the following year he was dead — probably murdered.

THE BLACK DEATH

G REAT WEALTH can bring with it great sorrow. Whilst England was growing rich, largely through its wool trade, exemplified by the use of the woolsack as the seat of the Lord Chancellor in the House of Lords, trade expanded through Europe to the Middle East. As the King of England fought in France to gain the French throne, disease broke out at the eastern end of the Mediterranean. It spread westwards along the trade routes, carried by fleas on the ships' rats and by the sailors they accompanied. Finally it crossed the Channel as previous invaders had done. Through the ports at Bristol and Southampton it came into England in 1348, passing on into Wales in the following year and on into Scotland. Wherever it struck, it did so with ferocity. Nine out of ten victims died and it struck all grades of society for it came as a leveller of rank. Three archbishops died within a year. In the huge diocese of Lincoln it killed two out of five of the clergy and in the fields the peasants died too.

In some villages all the villeins died, in others there were too few left to till the fields. Some landowners turned their manors into parks because they could no longer be farmed. Villages around the country were deserted, like Ambion in Leicestershire; others were resettled away from their old core as the villagers tried to flee the 'great mortality'. Many people could not hope to escape it. Around a million and a half people died in the epidemic which was called the Black Death by 1351; that represented between one third and one half of the entire population.

The high mortality rate almost spelled the

John of Gaunt (1340–99).

Richard II (1367–1400).

121

Medieval agricultural scene by Sebastian Brant.

end of the the feudal system. Wage labour became more and more common after the plague caused a labour shortage in many areas. Desperate to get their lands tilled, landowners were paying higher and higher wages to attract a work force. This destabilisation of the system caused great concern: it could threaten the whole fabric of society. To stem this, Parliament issued the Statute of Labourers in 1351 to limit the wages paid to the whole gamut of the English work force. It kept the rates low – economic would be the phrase used now – economic for those who paid, not those who received.

THE PEASANTS' REVOLT

To cover the cost of the expensive wars in France – later the Hundred Years War – the government imposed a blanket tax of four pence per head of the population over the age of fourteen. At that time four pence represented four days wages for a dairywoman or a shepherd or carter. Any tax which is at the same rate for everyone is in fact iniquitous as it always falls more heavily on the poorer members of society because the sum represents a larger proportion of their income. In 1377 the Poll Tax was levied on everyone but beggars who could prove that they were licensed. The tax was hard on the peasantry, but in 1381 a new levy, a shilling this time, was levied on everyone over the age of fifteen. To the peasants this was unbearable.

In the South-east, as the tax was collected whole communities began to provide false information to the assessors. When the collector Thomas Bampton rode into Brent-

Geoffrey Chaucer c. 1343–1400

Born the son of a London vintner, Chaucer rose, through a legal education, to be an experienced diplomat, using his spare time to further his reading of the works of foreign authors. He served with King Edward III's army in France just after the Battle of Poitiers when he was captured and ransomed. In the 1370s he went on a diplomatic mission to Italy where he read the works of Petrarch and Boccaccio, whom he may have met. His legacy to posterity rests not with his diplomatic arts nor with his membership of Parliament for Kent but with his writing.

Chaucer absorbed the influences of the French authors and displayed this in his work *The Book of the Duchess*, but *Triolus and Criseyde* showed definite Italian influence. His most famous work, *The Canterbury Tales*, was written in a language which is recognisably a forerunner of modern English. It was derived from the dialect spoken in the East Midlands and London and can be read with a little practice today. *The Canterbury Tales* owes something to Boccaccio's *Decameron*, being a collection of stories which a group of pilgrims tell to each other on the road to Canterbury as they travel to the shrine of Thomas Becket. Its opening lines are famous:

> Whan that Aprille with his shoures soote,
> The droughte of March hath perced to the roote.

Twenty-four tales are narrated, and one is begun by Chaucer, who includes himself in the group. He portrays himself as a bumbling storyteller who is cut short by the innkeeper who tells him 'Thy drasty rymyng is nat worth a toord'.

The *Tales* contain excellent, timeless characterisations and stories which have remained fresh and authentic throughout the passing centuries. Even in his own time Chaucer was recognised as a great poet, and when he died he was buried in Westminster Abbey in the future Poets' Corner.

Opposite: Chaucer reading his work to an audience, from an edition of his *Troilus and Criseyde*, c.1400.

Above: John Ball, leader of the peasants' revolt, preaching.

wood to find out why collection was slow in Barnstaple, Fobbing Corrigham and Stanford, he and his followers were attacked. The action spread throughout the region. Behind spontaneous events like this, and there were others, were ideas binding the people together in their action. Such notions were expressed in William Langland's poem *Piers Plowman* which had stressed the holiness of the simple life of the peasant over the '... tricherye of tresoun and of gyle' in the form of a dream of Piers. This image, and that of the Christ in labourer's clothes were adopted by the peasants. Their leader John Ball suggested that God had not created a society of strata and inequality. 'When Adam delved and Eve span, who then was the Gentleman?' was one piece of doggerel which was repeated by the rioters and rebels.

The localised riots spread and eventually two large armies of people, each of 30,000 or

so, advanced on London; one from Kent and the other from Essex. By 12 June the Essex army had reached Mile End and the Kentish army arrived at Blackheath. Other county bands arrived to consult with the leaders, Wat Tyler and John Ball with the southern army and Jack Straw with that from the North. On the fourteenth, the young King Richard II, who had succeeded to the throne in 1377, went out to meet them, and agreed to their demands. The peasants wanted the end of the Poll Tax and the execution of many of the King's advisers who were felt to be responsible. Further, they wanted the end of feudalism and demanded the right of self-government in the villages. For their time these were profound political points. An entire restructuring of society was desired: peasant participation in local government was entirely alien in the England of the fourteenth century.

As the King's heralds drafted the proclamations, the gates of the Tower of London were left open to the people. The Archbishop and treasurer were dragged out and executed at Tower Hill. Some of the peasants began to drift home, believing the revolution was over. It was what the King wanted. When he rode out to see the people's army at Smithfield on the day following the original meeting he went armed, but Tyler rode out as to a rendezvous. When Tyler repeated the demands of the people, he was attacked and wounded by the Mayor of London. The peasants retreated from the field carrying the wounded Tyler with them. Later in the evening armed and armoured men rode into the rebel camps, captured Tyler and executed him in the usual barbarous manner. From then on reaction reigned. Soldiers hounded the rebels from village to village and the towns through which they passed stank of the corpses of the people who had challenged the feudal system. John Ball was executed in St Albans in July. A salutary lesson had been learned: a king's word was not his bond.

HENRY IV AND HENRY V

Henry, the first Lancastrian King, faced a formidable array of enemies, including Owain Glyn Dwr and the Earl of Northumberland. With the help of his son, he quashed several rebellions during the first years of the new century, and when that son succeeded to the throne in 1413 he felt powerful enough to reopen the Hundred Years War and claim the throne of France. At the battle of Agincourt in 1415 the British longbowmen again proved their worth; the French suffered a large number of casualties and 1,000 were taken prisoner, whilst British losses were comparatively slight. Henry then went on to conquer Normandy. In 1420 he signed the Treaty of Troyes with Charles VI of France, who thereby acknowledged Henry as Regent of France and heir to the French throne. A condition of the treaty was the marriage of Henry to Charles' daughter, Catherine of Valois, who bore him a son the following year — heir to both the thrones of

The coronation of Henry IV, Froissart MS.

125

The battle of Agincourt, 1415.

England and France.

Henry V died in 1422 (as did Charles VI), and his son, Henry VI, was indeed crowned King of France in Paris in 1431, but a resurgence of French nationalism had already begun and it was led by a young peasant girl called Joan of Arc. She had managed to convince the French heir to the throne, the dauphin, that she had heard saints' voices urging her to help him and free the country of the English. At the head of a large army she managed to raise the siege of Orleans in 1429 and then had the dauphin crowned King in Rheims. When the Burgundians, allies of the English, captured her she was arraigned as a witch and burnt at the stake in 1431.

There was a great need for peace. The English Parliament felt the costs of the wars in France as a heavy burden, but any negotiations would mean conceding territory that had been paid for with blood, and many English magnates now regarded such territory as their land. The French gained in strength while the English failed to formulate proposals for a permanent peace. In 1449 the French lost patience and invaded Normandy; by 1453 they had conquered all the English lands in France save Calais and the Channel Islands — even Gascony which had been English since the twelfth century.

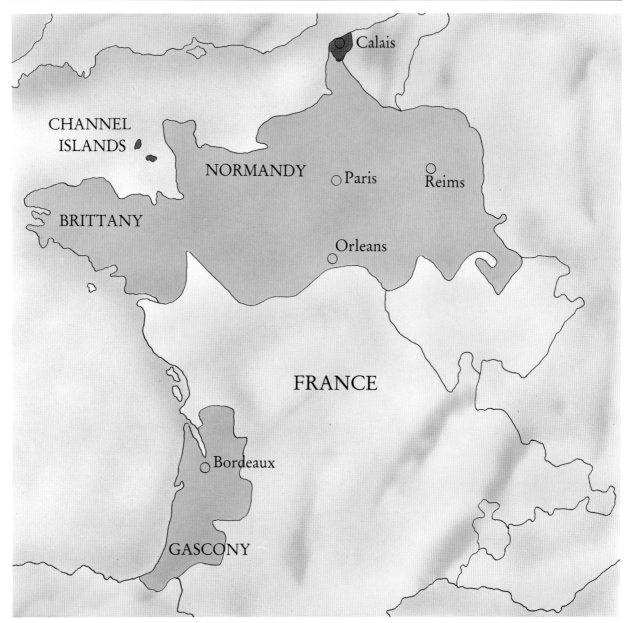

English territories in France lost by Henry VI. Only the Channel Islands and Calais remained English.

THE WARS OF THE ROSES

IN 1450 DISCONTENT at Henry's inability to maintain the peace at home or to secure his father's gains in France, manifested itself in the rebellion of Jack Cade who led a rebel people's army from Kent to London. The King and the government fled. One of the demands of the rebels was the recall of the King's cousin, the Duke of York, from virtual exile as Lieutenant of Ireland. When the duke did return, it was to impose his control on the country with the aid of the Commons in Parliament, but the people who had followed Cade were not all ready to

follow York into war against the King. For a year he was isolated but when Henry had a catatonic fit which left him paralysed York came to office as chief member of the Privy Council. When the King recovered, the Queen and her supporters turned on York and forced him into armed revolt. He defeated their army in St Albans and captured the King. For four years, York prospered as the Constable of England with the Earl of Warwick his chief ally as captain of the Calais garrison. In 1459 as the King's party gained support, the Yorkists were defeated at Blore Heath, but the following year Yorkists captured the King

after the battle of Northampton. The Queen, stronger and more politically astute than her husband could ever hope to be, gathered an army and defeated the Duke of York at Wakefield (1460). York and his son, the Earl of Rutland, were killed. Soon after, York's other son, the Earl of March, defeated the Lancastrian Earls of Wiltshire and Pembroke as they marched into England from their landing sites in Wales, at the battle of Mortimer's Cross. However, Warwick was defeated by the Queen at St Albans on 17 February 1461, and as a result the King was released and restored to the throne. It was a short-lived restoration: March reached London and was proclaimed King. Then he turned north and went after the retreating Queen and her forces.

At the bloody battle of Towton on 29 March 1461 the Yorkists won and Henry and his Queen fled northwards. March returned to London where he was crowned King Edward IV. The Wars of the Roses — so called because of the white rose emblem of the Yorkists and the red rose supposedly adopted by Henry's Lancastrians — were now well underway.

Fighting in 1464 at Hedgeley Moor and Hexham saw the Yorkists extend their control over the North. Henry was captured again and imprisoned in the Tower. In 1469 Warwick, with Edward's brother Duke of Clarence, dissatisfied with his gains, rebelled against King Edward. In 1470 their revolt drove Edward and his friend William Hastings abroad. It was only a year before they returned, gathered their forces, deposed the restored Henry VI and defeated Warwick at Tewkesbury. Henry VI was murdered in the Tower, Warwick was killed in battle and Clarence was drowned in a butt of malmsey. The Queen was imprisoned and eventually ransomed to her brother the King of France.

Paradoxically, despite the turmoil that led to his gaining the throne, the latter years of Edward's reign were secure and popular. When he died, in 1483, it seemed that England should continue in a period of stability, for there was an heir, albeit another minor of twelve years of age, Edward V. This boy and his younger brother were, however, placed under the protection of an ambitious uncle, Richard Duke of Gloucester. Edward V and

The Wars of the Roses.

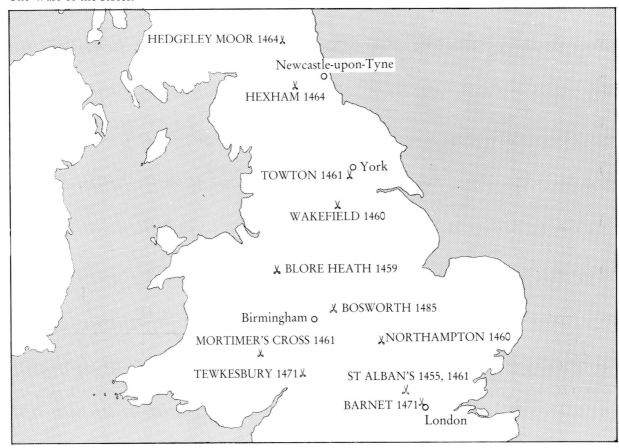

Anthony Woodville, Earl Rivers, presenting a book printed by Caxton to Edward IV.

William Caxton

In the 1430s a German printer, Johannes Gutenberg, invented a system of movable type which would allow books to be produced quickly and in quantity. William Caxton was the first Englishman to master this new craft. He won the patronage of Edward IV and between 1477–91 he printed approximately eighty books in his Westminster printing works, including Chaucer's *Canterbury Tales*.

his brother were murdered in the Tower, and whether or not Richard had any hand in it, he benefited. Richard was crowned King in the face of opposition – one opponent, Lord Hastings, was executed.

Richard III had been a popular man in the North when he administered the provinces, and as high admiral, but as King he was disliked partly because of the method of his accession. He was soon to be challenged. In 1485 the son of Margaret Beaufort, landed in Wales. He was Henry Earl of Richmond and is said to have harvested the support owed once to Owain Glyn Dwr. Richard marched to meet him. In the fields near, but probably not on those comprising the battlefields centre, the battle of Bosworth was fought near Market Bosworth in Leicestershire. Richard was slain, his body was carried into Leicester strapped to a horse. His heels kicked the bridge upon which an old woman had predicted his fall. On the field of battle the first Tudor was crowned with the circlet pulled out from a thornbush.

6. TUDOR TRAGEDIES

THE SIXTEENTH CENTURY

HENRY VII

HENRY VII'S POSITION as king was not secured on his accession in 1485 after the battle of Bosworth Field. In 1486 he married Elizabeth of York, daughter of Edward IV, but he still faced Yorkist claims for some years. Henry was not automatically entitled to the throne. There were two candidates with better claims: the Earl of Warwick, a youngster aged ten, and the Earl of Lincoln — both of these were nephews of Edward IV. It was Lincoln who struck first. Involved in a failed rising in 1846, he led a serious rebellion in the following year. Lincoln collected mercenaries in Germany and in Ireland where there was much support for the Yorkists and led them to England. He was fighting not for his own right to the throne, but for the Earl of Warwick, or at least an impersonator, Lambert Simnel, who was playing the role of Warwick who was actually in the Tower of London. Lincoln was defeated at East Stoke near Newark on 16 June 1487. Lincoln died, and with him the real military threat to the Tudor regime.

Pretenders abounded however. Lambert Simnel, the pseudo-Warwick, was taken into the King's household as a servant, but in the next decade another pretender arose. This time it was not so easy to dispute his authenticity. Henry had simply produced

Opposite: Henry VII (1457–1509) by Michael Sittow, painted in 1505.

Below: View of the Tower of London — an eighteenth century print.

TIME CHART

1485 Henry VII ascends the throne.
1487 Rebellion of Lambert Simnel.
1501 Prince Arthur dies.
1509 Henry VIII succeeds to the throne.
1513 King James IV of Scotland dies in the war with England. Battles of Flodden and of the Spurs.
1515 Wolsey appointed Lord Chancellor
1527 Beginning of Henry's divorce crisis.
1530 Wolsey disgraced and dies. Sir Thomas More succeeds as Lord Chancellor.
1532 Resignation of More.
1533 England leaves Church of Rome. Henry VIII marries Anne Boleyn. Birth of Princess Elizabeth.
1535 Sir Thomas More executed.
1536 Act of Union of England and Wales. Dissolution of the monasteries begins.
1542 James V dies during the war with Henry VIII. The Reformation begins in Scotland in the absence of the Queen, Mary Stuart.
1547 Henry VIII dies; accession of Edward VI.
1549 First Book of Common Prayer.
1553 The year of two Queens. After the usurpation of the throne by Lady Jane Grey, Mary I succeeds and the Reformation is reversed.
1554 Wyatt's rebellion.
1557 War with France.
1558 Mary I dies: accession of Elizabeth I.
1561 Mary Stuart (Mary I of Scotland) returns to her country.
1564 William Shakespeare born.
1568 Mary Stuart driven out of Scotland and flees to England.
1570 Papal bull declares that Elizabeth is excommunicated and deposed.
1587 Mary Stuart executed.
1588 The Spanish Armada is defeated.
1603 Elizabeth dies and James VI of Scotland crowned King James I of England.

Greenwich Palace, a favourite residence of the Tudors and birthplace of Henry VIII.

Perkin Warbeck (c. 1474–99).

Warwick from the Tower to reveal Simnel's imposture, but the new pretender, Perkin Warbeck, a man of Flemish origin, paraded around the courts of Europe, purporting to be Richard IV, the younger of the two sons of Edward IV who had been murdered in 1483. The real Prince's body could not be produced. When his charade came to England in September 1487, Warbeck was caught and later, after an attempt to escape, he was placed in the Tower in 1498. Sadly for the real Warwick, Warbeck inveigled him into an escape plan which failed. This, coupled with yet another impersonation of Warwick, this time by Ralph Wilford, convinced Henry VII that the earl was too dangerous to keep alive. The young man, now twenty-four, was tried and executed for treason. So Warbeck's days of impersonation came to an end. As he was not allowed to impersonate a noble's death, he, a mere commoner, was swung from a rope. There were other Yorkist plots, which kept the Tudor King busy securing his position, but not one of them matured into a serious military threat.

THE KING'S PEACE

HENRY DEVELOPED a county-based defence force, skilled in bowmanship and in the handling of the heavy-infantry weapon, the pike. These were part-time forces, supposedly in receipt of regular training and maintained at the expense of the village communities each of which contributed a man or two to the county regiments. The private armies which had in the fifteenth century been the foundation of the armies of Yorkists and Lancastrians, were abolished. Instead, the notable figures in the counties were given power, as commissioners, to raise the county forces when and if there was an emergency. The year of 1497 saw these Commissions of Array being put to use. Henry raised an army to invade Scotland using the commissions, but the cost of this enterprise angered the people of the South-west who went into revolt and marched from Cornwall to Blackheath near London. The people of Kent did not rise with them, and the rebels were defeated. Only their leaders, the lawyer Flamank, the blacksmith Joseph, and Lord Audley were executed, whilst the rest of the rebels were allowed to return home. This was followed quickly by the rising of Warbeck's personification of Richard IV. This was a short-lived revolt which again showed the power of the country's loyalty to Henry, for his county notables once more led their part-time forces against the disturber of the king's peace.

The king's peace was to be kept even in times when military force was not necessary. The counties had held quarter sessions to deal with minor breaches of the peace, thefts of goods under the value of a shilling, riots, non-payment of taxes and breaches of community responsibility – failure to take care of the local roads or bridges and the like. These courts, held every three months, had been instituted in the fourteenth century and had been presided over by Justices of the Peace drawn from the upper echelons of the county gentry and empowered to act as Commissioners of the Peace. More difficult cases – major thefts, felonies, murders and treason – were passed on to the annual or bi-annual assize courts held by judges who toured a circuit of counties. Under Henry VII the justices gained more and more responsibilities. They were empowered to watch over the activities of the village constables who were the holders of a multi-faceted office, responsible for village affairs, but also for the administration of the law, taxation policy or military duties on behalf of the king. Justices also watched over the activities of the military forces in peace time and controlled the legal

133

Ludlow Castle, Shropshire. Ludlow became the centre of government for Wales and the Marches in Henry VII's reign.

duties of the sheriff. The JPs additionally had to regulate the alehouses of the county and check on the weights and measures used.

And who governed the governors? Henry developed a council, not in itself new, but formalised and with clearly defined powers and responsibility, which drew not so much upon the wealthiest members of the nobility, but upon the lesser, reckoning that they were more dependent upon the King for favour and for their position than the richer and more powerful. Henry's use of the latter in government depended upon their loyalty to him. As an adjunct to the council and to give it legal power, Henry created the Court of the Star Chamber named after the room where it met, which overlooked, and if thought necessary, over-rode the courts in counties and the courts of common law in Westminster.

Henry VII built up uncommon wealth for an English king. The long peace enabled him to collect taxes and income in excess of the expense of government. He also amassed personal wealth consisting of plate. By the time of his death his meticulous attention to detail – he checked every column of figures produced by the exchequer – had made him a millionaire. In old age Henry, partially disillusioned by the death of his son Arthur some eight years earlier, had become a tired, toothless, wizened figure. On the day that he died, 21 April 1509, there was beside him an eighteen-year old lusty youth – perhaps one of the most striking figures of British history.

was this support which he rewarded: his uncle, Jasper Tudor, became Duke of Bedford and Justicar of South Wales, four Welsh men became bishops, Welsh sheriffs began to be appointed in the Welsh counties and Henry's Welsh nurse received a handsome pension. One family entered into royal service for the first time under Henry VIII in the guise of Dafydd Seisyllt who was in the King's bodyguard. Two generations later the family was represented at court with an anglicised name by William Cecil, the great Lord Burleigh.

In Wales itself and the English border country, Henry VII had to resurrect the courts of the Marches. In the violence of the fifteenth century these had fallen somewhat into abeyance and Henry had to reconstruct them to give them stability and an outward look of great importance. He sent the heir, Prince Arthur, to take control. This young lad, named, no doubt, as an expression of Henry's concern for the Welshness of his being, had recently married Catherine of Aragon. For him to be sent to hold court at Bewdley was a mark of the importance of the mission to restore social order in the country. Sadly for Henry VII's hopes and for the fifteen-year-old and his wife, the Prince died in 1501, six months after arriving in the Marches. The council, however, did not fail, and after the death of the Prince it moved to Ludlow, which for the next two hundred years or so was considered the capital of the region. Lawyers, ambitious for place, went to Ludlow to further political and legal careers if they could not find a position in London.

Henry VIII, succeeded in 1509 to his father, just as he in his turn had succeeded eight years earlier to Prince Arthur's position and to his wife. He had little of his father's affinity for Wales, and his reign saw two drastic impositions which were to last long in Welsh memory. Wales, like England, saw its monasteries dissolved at the end of the 1530s, whilst the land belonging to them passed through the hands of the King into the possession of the gentry who were able to build up large estates and wealth. At the same time plans were made for full political union of Wales and England and in 1536 Henry's Act of Union declared '. . . that Wales shall for ever, from henceforth, be united and annexed to and with his realm of England'. The 'i's

THE TUDORS AND WALES

HENRY TUDOR was of Welsh blood and had received strong support in his claim to the English throne from the Principality. As a consequence, for the first time since before Owain Glyn Dwr, Welshmen held major office. Henry had been brought up in Wales as the son of Edmund Tudor, half-brother of Henry VI. He was part French, part English, and lived abroad from the age of fourteen onwards, but he carried the name Tudor and that linked him to the Welsh princes; he may not have had a command of the Welsh language, but in 1485, he could command the loyalty of many Welsh men and women. It

135

Catherine of Aragon (1486–1536) married Prince Arthur in 1501 and his brother, Henry VIII, in 1509.

At the same time, there was another crusade to be undertaken in Wales, which was the dissolution of the monasteries. This was not an isolated event related solely to the King of England's pocket. It was an integral part of the Reformation in England, begun as much for reasons of sexual politics as for theological purposes. Henry VIII realised that the control of the Pope over English and Welsh affairs meant more than the passage of money from England to Rome, when he wished to rid himself of his loving and loyal wife, Catherine of Aragon. Despite the base reason for this momentous act, the break from Rome allowed the religious ferment imported from the Continent to continue almost unfettered in England. Those who sought to bring Protestant worship to the parishes of England and Wales carried out an evangelical mission. The first Protestant bishop of St David's, William Barlow, placed a burden on his fellow clergy by requiring them to introduce Protestantism into the Principality despite their own and their parishioners' conservatism.

In Wales, as elsewhere, theological reorganisation was only a part of the story. There was money to be made and wanton destruction could appear in the guise of religious zeal. Lands and religious plate passed into secular hands and brought wealth to a portion of the Welsh gentry who were able to participate in the carving up of religious estates. A more brutal force was left to others. The religious images which had adorned churches, acting as religious/educational visual-aids for the illiterate masses as well as replacing the pre-Christian god images, were now to be destroyed. Classed as graven images which replaced the true majesty and oneness of tripartite god with false idols, they were to be destroyed, smashed or defaced. Walls were white-washed, altars were desanctified and the Holy Communion, the transubstantiation of the bread and wine into the body and blood of Christ was gone. It was replaced by the more communal affair of sharing in God's name a representation of the Last Supper. The shock, and in some cases, revulsion, that this inspired was felt throughout Wales and England, but in

were dotted and the 't's crossed in the second Act in 1542.

Welsh identity was denied; instead of acknowledging the different cultures the Welsh people were termed backward and their separate language was described as being 'nothing like or consonent with their mother tongue'. English was established as the one language, speaking Welsh was ascribed to mere ignorance. The purpose of the Act was the complete subordination of Wales, to which end the Principality was to be submerged into greater England. The shire system was extended over the whole of Wales and the legal system was reorganised in step with England, although there were to be separate circuits of counties, four in all, and a high court independent of Westminster. There were some advantages however, Welshmen were held to be equal to Englishmen in English courts and they no longer had to possess certificates of worthiness before they could take part in town affairs. Wales also gained representation in Parliament. In effect, being Welsh was henceforth to be a state of mind, for the English wished to extirpate the country and its customs.

Opposite: Llantony Abbey, Gwent. The Dissolution of the Monasteries affected Wales as well as England.

Crathes Castle, Grampian, Scotland, is one of the finest examples of the true Scots style of architecture which, in its height and mastery of stone, can be traced back to the brochs of the first century. It was built for Alexander Burnet, one of whose ancestors had been a key supporter of King Robert the Bruce. The building of the castle was begun in 1553 although it does not appear to have been inhabited until 1594. In Scotland the first half of the sixteenth century was a sad time that included the battle of Flodden, in which the Scots king James IV was killed, and closed with the battle of Solway Moss and the death of James V in 1542; he was succeeded by his new-born daughter, Mary Queen of Scots. However, the Reformation did not have the destructive effect that was apparent in England, nor was there any dissolution of the monasteries.

Wales it had the added sting of being imposed by the English and it became tangled in minds as being a part of the unification process.

HENRY VIII

ON TO THE STAGE of England's and Wales' history strode Henry VIII. Often symbolic of England, Henry was a virile man, standing tall by contemporary standards. He was active, a lover of sport, performing very well in the tournaments. In his youth he had a muscular body, the form of which can still be seen in the suits of armour in the Tower of London. Certainly he showed characteristics which can be reviled, such as his callous attitude towards women; these he used not only for sexual gratification but for the production of children after which he would dispose of them, by divorce or the axe. Such an attitude was not particularly unusual: it was untypical only in the extreme to which it was taken. In explanation, Henry could also claim

Opposite: Henry VIII (1491–1547) after Holbein.

political necessity. He was determined to assert the stability of the regime and would have always had at the back of his mind the chaos of the past century and was probably determined to do his uttermost to prevent the country falling into such turbulence again. To do this he wanted a secure succession and he saw a male heir as the answer. It is ironic, for him, that the greatest monarch the countries of Wales and England were to see was a woman: his daughter.

Henry brought to the throne not only his prowess and love of martial spectacle; he also brought a desire to turn England into a centre of culture comparable with the rest of Europe. Henry began actively to involve England in the renaissance of learning and art, which Europe was experiencing. To foster the development of an English school of art, Henry introduced artists from the Continent. In his very first year on the throne he brought in Torrigano from Italy to produce the tombs for Henry VII and the Queen in Westminster Abbey.

The most famous appointment, and the one to which we are the most indebted, was that of Hans Holbein who came over from

Maximilian I (1459–1519), Holy Roman Emperor and Henry VIII's ally in his attempts to regain some of the French lands lost in the previous century.

was associated with the most powerful royal and imperial family in Europe, the Hapsburgs. It was with the imperial branch of this family, the Holy Roman Emperor Maximilian, that Henry launched into his first war with France. He was with Maximilian in France during the war of 1512–14 and was present at the battle of the Spurs on 16 August 1513. At the same time Henry built up the English fleet and demonstrated mastery of the Channel, something his father had not achieved. His commander in the North, the Earl of Surrey, defeated the Scots army which was allied to the French, at the battle of Flodden, three weeks after the battle of the Spurs.

These victories seemed promising but were not followed by good fortune. The war of 1522 with France saw all the honours go to Maximilian's successor, Charles, whilst the English, for their vast expenditure, got little return. This time the Scots pressured the English and there was no second Flodden. The war placed a heavy burden on the people of England. The benevolences, taxes usually garnered from the wealthy alone, were levied on the poor peasants and the urban peoples. There was a threat of rebellion given edge by the Peasants Revolt in the Germanic states. The Government turned to the mighty lords, who preserved the peace, but at the same time counselled the withdrawal of the tax. This was done and the campaigns, dependent upon the revenue from it, were abandoned too. It was not only the people who baulked at the cost of these wars. Parliament, too, having disliked the costs of the first war, was less than enthusiastic about contributing to the second. Nothing is more odious than the costs of unsuccessful wars. Whilst there were some rich pickings to be had from the earlier conflict, the second brought nothing at all. Further, the war at the end of the 1520s (this time with France as an ally against the Emperor), brought only expense and no gain at all.

Switzerland. Because of this we have an unparalleled record of the people in the court of the English King in paintings, like those of Henry himself, and *The Ambassadors*, and sketches such as the one of Anne Boleyn or that of Sir Thomas Wyatt.

Yet the reign of Henry VIII is sadly perhaps best remembered by his ruthless search for the stability of the succession. When he came to the throne he was not a man perturbed by the restlessness of the Yorkist ambition, as his father had been at his coronation. Instead 'Bluff King Hal' was able to look not to securing his place in England, but to carving a niche in Europe. Using his marriage to the widow of his brother Arthur as his lever, he

THOMAS WOLSEY

THE END OF THIS WAR coincided with the end of the career of Thomas Wolsey, the Lord Chancellor. Wolsey had astutely mastered that which Henry VIII could not be bothered to do

— manage the financial government of England. He taught the great men to respect the law courts; he encouraged the lesser to use them. He gave the less wealthy access to justice through the relatively cheap Court of Requests and he set his face solidly against the large-scale enclosure of lands. This was causing hardship in the communities where it was occurring: lands and commons were lost to the peasantry and some were entirely dispossessed as their manors became converted to pasture for the creature which Thomas More described as devouring all, the sheep.

Wolsey projected much in the way of government reform but in the end achieved less in this sphere. He was torn between three masters: Henry VIII, because he was his chief minister, the Pope because he was a cardinal, and God, whom they all served in their way. There was a cataclysm approaching Wolsey which he could not avoid and from which he probably could never have escaped.

Thomas Wolsey (1475–1530), cardinal and Henry VIII's Lord Chancellor.

THE SUCCESSION

In europe, fired by the objections of Martin Luther to the excesses of the Catholic church, there was a reformation of religious thought and life. Some of the German states, influenced by those protesting the purity of the Church when freed from Rome's control, were sweeping away the trappings and ties of papal authority. At first England, led by Henry VIII himself, stood firm to the mother Church. Henry attacked the doctrines of Luther and a grateful Pope gave him the title *Fidei Defensor* — defender of the faith.

Yet Henry was more fickle than his title suggested. From 1527 onwards, Henry wanted a divorce. His faithful wife Catherine had borne many children, but most were to die in infancy; only one survived and she was not the male heir Henry wanted. His prejudice, crafted and nurtured by the long-held belief that it was difficult to secure the loyalty of the nobility and people to a woman, made him strive for new conjugal relations. His eye had turned to Anne Buleyn or Boleyn and he wanted Wolsey to make arrangements for him. Naturally the Pope would not give him a divorce, seeing through the sham set up by Henry. Wolsey arranged to have the case tried

Anne Boleyn (1507–36).

Overleaf: The Field of the Cloth of Gold. In June 1520 Henry met the French King, Francis I, near Calais to confirm Wolsey's plan for peace between France and Britain. It was a sumptuous display of pageantry and power. Henry and Wolsey can be seen in the left foreground, and the kings meet at the top right. Within two years Henry had resumed his war to try and gain French territory.

141

Sir Thomas More (1478–1535).

Thomas Cranmer (1489–1556).

position as Chancellor, and retired to his Archbishopric of York. Henry originally wanted him to stay in reach in case he was of use later and he fended off Parliament's attacks on Wolsey. Nevertheless, in late October he was arrested in York and escorted to London. At Leicester Abbey he stopped his journey. He informed the abbot that he came into his community to lay his bones amongst them. On that very night, 9 November 1530, the richest man in England died. The abbey has largely gone, but Wolsey still lies among its ruins, his tomb exposed to the air.

Without Wolsey, the King turned to Parliament instead and the first session of the Reformation Parliament sat before Wolsey's death. Henry was to use the Parliament to reform the Church, and his new Chancellor, Sir Thomas More, began to continue the work promised by Wolsey. The money sent to Rome was drastically reduced. It was a cold war between the King of England and the Pope, aimed at forcing the latter's acquiescence to a divorce. In the end Henry was compelled to move on regardless. His lover, Anne Boleyn, became pregnant. He had to divorce Catherine and marry Anne before the child was born. The futile negotiations in Rome ended and in January 1533 Henry secretly married Anne. At the same time Thomas Cranmer was recalled from Rome to become Archbishop of Canterbury. On 23 May the marriage of Henry and Catherine was declared to have been null from its very start. Thus, conveniently, the secret marriage of January ceased to be bigamous. On 1 June Anne was crowned.

Her child, England's greatest queen, was born on 7 September. To her foolish father she was not what was wanted. To Rome she was illegitimate. Cranmer was excommunicated. The Pope threatened Henry with the same. It was the final straw. Henry, Defender of the Catholic faith, broke all links with Rome and became supreme head of the Church of England. More did not last long either; he refused to accept Henry's position as head of the Church and was executed in 1535. He was replaced by Thomas Cromwell and it was his responsibility to continue the reformation with the dissolution of the monasteries of England and Wales. On the pretext that they were corrupt dens of sin and, moreover, loyal to the Pope, monasteries, abbeys and priories

before the Church in London at the Legatine court under his charge. The Pope revoked the court and ordered the hearing to Rome. Henry was to attend. The failure destroyed Wolsey. Arraigned by the courts he lost his

were dissolved and their inhabitants pensioned off. Centuries of tradition disappeared and vast tracts of land changed hands rapidly as the King sold off the estates which had once been farmed by the clergy and their tenants. Between 1537 and 1540 there began the process by which some of the most beautiful buildings of the country fell into ruins or were dismantled and their remains used to construct secular buildings. The poor were left without their benefactors as the almshouses of the monasteries disappeared with their monasteries. Many of the people of England and Wales lost their only pathway to education – and for what? The production of a series of ruins in desolate places – future tourist traps of faded glory; the increase in wealth of those who already had more than most or the temporary solvency of a monarchy which had failed to keep up the standards of financial management set by Henry VII. The shackles of Rome may well have been broken but for many the advantages of this were very difficult to perceive. Fortunately not all of the monasteries or abbeys disappeared. Some became minsters or cathedrals, others became mansions, and more humble ones such as the Priory at Bridlington were only partly demolished and gained new life as parish churches.

In the meantime, Henry disposed of Anne Boleyn. He claimed that she had committed adultery, but it was a case of wounded pride and frustrated ambition, for Anne had failed to produce a boy. She was beheaded like many of the other people Henry rejected. He had already spotted a successor. This time it was Jane Seymour, and in 1537 a male heir was born – the future Edward VI. Again, Henry's drive for an heir cost a life, for Jane died in childbirth. His next marriage was short-lived and a failure: Anne of Cleves did not live up to the King's expectation of a bride and was 'set aside'.

At the same time Cromwell fell from grace. The reform of the Church was going further than Henry had ever wanted. The Protestant party was growing in influence, the Bible was printed in English, the northern rebellion against the destruction of the monasteries had been crushed. Cromwell had made many enemies, and the reform programme in the King's name was making Henry look foolish by its very speed and direction. Henry for

Thomas Cromwell (*c.* 1485–1540).

consolation turned to the charms of the young Catherine Howard. He was not her only conquest and this told against her though it would never have counted against any man. When details of her sexual promiscuity became known, she too was sacrificed on the block. One final wife, Catherine Parr, was taken by the now corpulent and lame King. She was as loyal as his first wife, but had the luck to outlive him. Henry died in 1548, with his country in a state of economic hardship: the state itself was constantly staving off bankruptcy by selling the monastic properties at below the market price, the coinage itself was devalued and the people on the areas once owned by the monasteries were at the mercies of the agricultural entrepreneurs who replaced them with the all-devouring sheep.

EDWARD VI

THERE FOLLOWED an almost anarchic period. Henry was succeeded by the weakling Edward VI whose rule was undertaken first by the Duke of Somerset and then by the Duke of Northumberland. In the 'reign' of the

Edward VI (1537–53).

Edward Seymour, Duke of Somerset (c.1506–52), Protector of England (1547–51) during the minority of Edward VI. He was overthrown by John Dudley, Duke of Northumberland.

first, the people of England rose up again partly to express their disapproval of the enclosure system which put sheep in the place of people. But in the South-west, they protested against the Protestant prayer book which had replaced the Catholic service beloved by the people who understood no Latin but trusted in the intermediary qualities of their priest.

Ket's rebellion in Norfolk during 1549 was another example of the disturbances. The landowner, Robert Ket, sympathised with the peasants who objected to his enclosures, and he not only helped to pull them down but led the people to destroy other enclosures as well. A commune was established outside Norwich and the rebels governed themselves, just as the upper classes feared that they might be able to do. The peasants were not supposed to be able to organise themselves – but of course they could, for self-government when not couched in Latin is straighforward enough. Inevitably Somerset could not permit this and the rebellion was put down fiercely by German mercenaries. The other rebellion, which took place in the West, was quelled by Italians. It spelt the end for Somerset. He was displaced by the Duke of Northumberland and executed. But Northumberland had enemies and as the life of Edward slipped away, he sought to strengthen his position. At the end of the sad boy's life, Northumberland married his youngest son to Lady Jane Grey of Bradgate in Leicestershire, daughter of his ally the Duke of Suffolk.

MARY TUDOR

THE LAST PART of the Tudor Age was dominated by women, three of them Queens: two Marys, one Elizabeth; two English, one Scot; two Catholics, determined to set back the clock, one a religious pragmatist. The first to come on centre stage was Queen Mary of England, fresh on the wave of support which defeated Northumberland. She came with a mission. Her mother Catherine, herself born of a Catholic mother and a father who was also of the Roman faith, had not been a party to any of the machinations of the Protestant party. She came to save the souls of her people by leading them back to the mother Church.

The Execution of Lady Jane Grey by Paul Delaroche (1797–1856). This depiction may not be historically accurate, but it evokes the tragedy of the 'nine-day queen'. (Reproduced by courtesy of the Trustees, The National Gallery, London.)

Lady Jane Grey (1537–54)

Edward died in 1553 on 4 July. Jane, through the line of her grandmother, Henry VIII's sister, was proclaimed queen by the council. Mary, the daughter of Henry and Catherine of Aragon and the presumed heir, fled to Norfolk where she raised an army which Northumberland failed to defeat. Jane was abandoned just as shabbily as she had been used. And sacrificed. A young woman more intelligent than those who abused her, she was imprisoned by Mary, but her father's ambition drove him into joining a revolt after Mary's assumption of the throne. Jane was executed after the failure of the revolt and the death of her father. Northumberland was dead, and both Jane and her husband Guildford Dudley were sacrificed on the altars of their fathers' ambition.

Lady Jane Grey.

The councillors who had surrounded Edward VI and the churchmen who had led the Protestant reformation in the reign of Henry VIII were disposed of. Cranmer, Latimer and Ridley were burned at the stake, the last two hoping to light a candle which would never be put out. They were to become two of the chief characters in the history of the English Church written by Foxe. This book, generally known by its short title, Foxe's *Book of Martyrs*, was a descriptive account, illustrated with woodcuts of the sufferings of the Englishmen and women who had died for the Protestant faith. It served as an inspiration and, after Mary's death, a reminder of the perils attendant upon Catholicism in England. Many did die, at the stake or in the damp, dangerous prisons, in order to satisfy the spiritual hopes of the sad Queen. Her popularity did not last. The acrid smoke of martyrdom burned harshly in the throats of her people and her marriage to King Philip of Spain, England's enemy, did nothing to endear her to her subjects.

Sir Thomas Wyatt took advantage of this feeling and led the most threatening of the Tudor rebellions. In fact his rebellion in Kent was only part of the planned series of risings in 1554. Whilst relatively untroubled by the religious strife, Wyatt could not abide the Spanish King. He led his army to the very walls of London, first to Southwark bridge and then round through Kingston, over the Thames and up to the walls of London at Ludgate Hill. The city held firm, inspired by the courage displayed by the Queen as much as anything else. Wyatt was penned in and surrendered. It was his failure which secured the death of the young Jane Grey and her husband Guildford Dudley. Before the end of the year, Philip had come to England to be married at Winchester Cathedral in June and four months later England re-entered the Roman fold. Her parliaments proved less amenable than Mary desired: although one actually agreed to the establishment of the Catholic Church, none would permit restoration of the monastic lands to the Church.

War with France, entered into at Mary's insistence, resulted in a defeat which cost the last of the English hold on France. Calais, which Mary asserted would be found engraved upon her heart, was lost. The support for her disappeared; this and the loneliness of life without Philip, whose stay had been brief, together with her frustration at her childlessness threatened her sanity. In November 1558, Mary died.

Opposite: Mary I (1516–58).

Below: The martyrdom of Bishops Latimer and Ridley at Oxford in 1555.

Pitchford Hall, Shropshire, one of the finest timber-frame houses surviving from the late sixteenth century. Houses of this kind were pre-fabricated structures, the timbers being sawn and jointed at the builder's yard before erection on site.

ELIZABETH I

LADY ELIZABETH was brought out of comfortable obscurity and proclaimed Queen. Politically astute, Elizabeth realised that marriage would end her control over the country as the male would take precedence. She proved a finer monarch than any of her suitors would have been and, although she stated that she had only the weak and feeble body of a women, she could never be considered less than resolute. Her reign was to be regarded as a golden age. She stabilised the throne, the nation and the religion. In defence of the first she incarcerated and then executed the chief threat, Mary Queen of Scots: she also ensured that the position of Lord President of the Council of the North, conferred upon the Earl of Huntingdon, a man with a claim to the throne, involved so much expenditure that he was impoverished by a small allowance for carrying out his duties. In defence of the

nation she presided over the defeat of the Spanish threat. Thirdly, in defence of her religion, Elizabeth established a settlement which put her at the head of the Church as Governor. It was a Protestant settlement which was to be applied with relative gentleness by coercion. This was flawed by the fact that all of the Marian bishops stayed loyal to the Roman Church and left the country. In their place, men, determined to establish the new Church on solid foundations, set about implanting an educated ministry in the country. The problem was great: of the 9,000 parishes only about 600 had viable livings. Lecturers were placed in prominent towns and in Wales, ministers toured several parishes to make good the shortages. The process was slow, but throughout the long reign of Elizabeth the Protestant faith was established and, alongside it, the people were fed on the horror stories of Foxe.

MARY, QUEEN OF SCOTS

THREE YEARS after Elizabeth ascended the throne of England, Mary, Queen of Scots and widow of the dauphin, returned to her native land. It had changed since the death of her father in 1542. In the absence of a monarch, it had fallen under the influence of Henry VIII, and from that developed a Scottish reformation thrust forward by John Knox, the founder of Scottish Presbyterianism. Mary's return as a Catholic went against the grain of the past decade. It was a return which owed much to international politics. The Catholic world refused to acknowledge Elizabeth: technically she was illegitimate in Catholic eyes and, therefore, Mary of Scotland had more right to the English throne. Thus Mary returned not only as Queen of Scotland but Queen of England too.

This she played down, attempting to remain on good terms with the English Queen until relations became strained when Elizabeth suggested that Mary marry the Earl of Leicester. It was an insult and Mary responded by marrying Lord Darnley, whom Elizabeth disapproved of. Darnley had a claim to the English throne, which added to Elizabeth's discomfort. He was very young; after all, we must remember he died before the age of twenty-two. He was also arrogant which gained him no allies. The couple had a son, James, born in 1566. Darnley was soon seemingly displaced as a lover to Mary by David Riccio, the secretary for French affairs and papal spy. He was murdered with Darnley's connivance. This was the last blow and Darnley too was murdered, probably with his wife's connivance, as she soon married the Earl of Bothwell who had planned the murder. The Scottish earls turned on the pair and their recourse to arms failed. Mary was imprisoned on an island in Loch Leven — the place can be seen, a beautiful sight, on the road north from Edinburgh. The infant James was crowned James VI at the end of 1567. Mary escaped the following year and raised an army only to be beaten at Langside near Glasgow, after only eleven days' freedom. The ex-Queen fled to England to claim kinship and friendship of Elizabeth. It was not a success.

To Elizabeth, Mary was a threat and to the English Catholics, a promise. Instead of receiving a welcome, Mary was accorded the

Mary Stuart, Queen of Scots (1542–87).

Sir Francis Drake (*c.*1540–96).

Philip II of Spain (1527–98).

status of a prisoner, an honoured and high-born one, but a prisoner all the same. For eighteen years Mary was moved around the north Midlands and south Yorkshire, ever more restricted in freedom as she became implicated in rumours of plots against Elizabeth.

The plots against Elizabeth were not only internal moves: the Catholic world did not accord her legitimacy, even less acknowledge her crown. Philip of Spain still reckoned himself King through his marriage to Mary. Relations between Spain and England were never stable after the succession. Moreover the interception in 1577 of the Spanish gold ships, returning from the West Indies, with the sanction of Elizabeth, was coupled with Francis Drake's attacks on the Spanish colonies. Mary was implicated in the Ridolfi plot of 1572, partly inspired by Elizabeth's excommunication which had almost made it open season on the reigning English monarch. This only resulted in the Scottish Queen being yet further confined in her freedom. She was moved around the north Midlands and south Yorkshire, to such places as Wingfield and Hardwick in Derbyshire, and Ashby de la Zouch in Leicestershire as well as Sheffield Castle.

WAR WITH SPAIN

B Y 1580, with attacks on the Spanish Main and on the treasure fleets plying the wide Atlantic, continued relentlessly by Elizabeth, relations with the Spanish declined yet further. In that year the Pope blessed a Spanish invasion force which landed in Ireland, but the triple-crowned patriarch's infallibility was not sound enough to ensure victory and the army was defeated and massacred by English and Irish-English troops. On the other hand the Spanish were strengthening their power. Portugal was annexed by Philip and although the Spanish Netherlands went into revolt against Philip the tyrant, French attempts to capture the Azores were defeated. In 1583 the Marguis di Santa Cruz advised the King of Spain that he had the sea-power necessary to add England to his dominions.

For five years the operation against England was almost left in abeyance, but the attacks on the Spanish Main by Francis Drake forced Philip to act. At first the attempts to overcome England centred upon Mary Stuart, but in 1586, she was caught out, enmeshed in Thomas Babington's plot to overthrow Elizabeth. A massive invasion fleet was

Fire ships attacking the Spanish Armada, 7 August 1588.

assembled in the Mediterranean and on the Spanish and Portuguese coast, but Mary was executed, early in 1587, by an exasperated, saddened Elizabeth who quickly sought to shift the blame onto other shoulders. Philip had a claim to the English throne and, to wreck his plans, Drake was sent out with a fleet to deal with the threat. At Cadiz harbour he singed the King of Spain's beard, destroying a large number of the Spanish ships in April. It dented and delayed the plans, but did not destroy them.

A year later a great Armada assembled at Lisbon and progressed to Corunna, where more ships joined it, giving a total of sixty-eight battleships and over sixty troop and supply vessels. The fleet was to pick up soldiers from the Spanish forces fighting in the Netherlands and then move on England. It arrived in the Channel on 19 July. For five days there was a running battle as the English

fleet, under Lord Howard, Drake and John Hawkins tried unsuccessfully to break the powerful crescent-shaped flotilla of the Armada. Elizabeth rallied her troops at Tilbury in case a landing was achieved, but the success at Calais when fire ships were floated into the middle of the harboured Spanish, scattered the Armada on 7 August. The following day there was a battle at Gravelines which saw the Spanish fleet unable to re-form and it moved into the North Sea. They had failed to pick up the Duke of Parma's forces from the Netherlands, and in any case they were stricken with plagues and their effectiveness was in question.

The English fleet had to call off its chase through lack of supplies as the Armada was driven by storms towards the Scottish seas. But there was nothing to fear. The storms drove the remains of the Armada onwards around the coast of Scotland and Ireland,

wrecking ships and drowning many of the poor frightened conscripted sailors and noble captains in the cold Atlantic sea. Only half the fleet returned to Spain. It was the British weather which ensured the safety of England. Elizabeth owed a lot to the fleet too, for it was the English sailors and the commanders who had begun the work of defeating the Armada. But servicemen are forgotten when the danger passes and within a year decommissioned, wounded and unemployed, many of the sailors of England begged on the streets of the coastal towns, swelling the numbers of the already growing poor.

THE VIRGIN QUEEN

THE CENTURY ENDED with England secure under an aging successful monarch. Her achievement of stability in the realm had been completed in the face of great religious struggle, growing poverty, rising inflation and numerous internal and external threats. The name Virgin Queen, suggesting then in some way failure or later a superficial purity, is a singularly inappropriate way to remember perhaps the greatest of the monarchs of England: a woman who achieved far more lasting success than the vain wars and contentions of her father who had perpetuated the tragedies of the country for little gain.

Less to her credit is the continued incursion into Ireland, grabbing yet more and more from the native population often in the name of a 'crusade' against the Catholic people. Many of the English latter-day crusaders fell victim to disease in the wild lands of Eire. During this a one-time favourite also fell from grace. The Earl of Essex, with hopes of marriage dashed, still attempted to take power, but his coup failed and he died on Tower Hill.

In Scotland too, there was stability. The young James VI had grown up in a world dominated by the Presbyterian faction in the country. He was bred a Protestant and he became the heir to the English throne. The Welsh blood of the Tudors gave way to the Scottish Stuarts when Elizabeth died in 1603 after a reign of forty-five years.

Opposite: Elizabeth I (1533–1603).

William Shakespeare (1564–1616)

The end of the century saw, too, the development of the career of the country's most gifted and celebrated man, William Shakespeare. Born at Stratford-upon-Avon he was educated in one of the grammar schools established in the century to undo the harm caused by the destruction of the monasteries and their schools. He may even have taught at a school in his early life. However at some time he moved to London and trod the boards, becoming in time a writer of the plays he appeared in. By 1594 he had produced comedies, several history plays, one Roman play and most of the parts of the dramas dealing with the Yorkist and Lancastrian wars. He grew prosperous on the success of the company of players, The Lord Chamberlain's, for whom he wrote and performed. At the end of the decade he wrote more tragedies and in the following century produced *Hamlet, Macbeth, Troilus and Cressida, Anthony and Cleopatra, Coriolanus,* and *Timon of Athens.* His final play, written perhaps for the fated marriage of King James's daughter, Elizabeth, to the Elector Palatine, was *The Tempest,* generally, but rather simplistically perhaps, assumed to be his farewell to the stage.

7. REBELLIONS AND REVOLUTIONS

THE SEVENTEENTH CENTURY

WHEN JAMES VI travelled south to become the first James, King of England, he came into possession of a stable nation. There was little if any trouble at the time of his accession; the JPs of the counties may have been alert, but there was not much for them to watch out for. James was a Protestant, and probably a Calvinist who believed that God had ordained that certain souls, the elect, would go to heaven, and that the mass of the rest, the reprobate, were damned. He was not attracted to the Presbyterian system which had become the most powerful Church, or Kirk, in Scotland. Indeed he was gratified to become the head of the Church of England, which was Episcopalian having bishops appointed by the monarch, not elders elected from within the Kirk and beyond the King's control. Puritans in England, people who saw the Elizabethan settlement as only a stepping-stone on the way to a reformed or pure Church, were to be disappointed in James. They hoped for a reform of the English Church, based on that in Scotland, but James did not comply. The most he would accept was a compromise, but here the Anglican bishops were able to draw a line and the reform plans came to little in 1604.

THE GUNPOWDER PLOT

NEVERTHELESS, not all of the people in England were happy to accept James and his Protestantism. There was still a significant number of Catholics in the country, often concentrated in the more remote areas, such as north Yorkshire and the North, the Peak District and the neighbouring areas of Staffordshire or even the south of the county. Their opposition to James was usually shown only by their adherence to the old Church, but some of them were more politically active. Two years after the accession of James a gang of men including Guy Fawkes, a York man, and others hatched a plot to destroy James, and his Parliament as it sat for the opening session of 1605. The plot was discovered on 5 November, the perpetrators cruelly butchered as was the norm with such people, and the day of celebration joined the others on which bonfires were lit.

Below: The conspirators in the Gunpowder Plot.

Opposite: James I of England and VI of Scotland (1566–1625).

156

IACOBUS I. DEI GRATIA MAGNÆ BRITANNIÆ FRANCIÆ ET HIBERNIÆ REX DEFENSOR FIDEI.

Hic, verus Geryon, tria regna ex orbe Britanno,
  Sanguinis ignarus, sanguine composuit.
Huic pax, huic Themis, huic refluunt Parnassides undæ,
  Regiaq; huic pietas sceptra decorā facit.

u a

TIME CHART

1603	James VI of Scotland succeeds to the English throne as James I.
1605	The Gunpowder Plot.
1607	Midland Revolt.
1610	Failure of the Great Contract (reform of royal finance).
1611	Publication of the Authorised Version of the Bible.
1614	The Addled Parliament.
1620	Migration of the Pilgrim Fathers to New England.
1621	James forced to call an English Parliament.
1623	The failure of the Spanish Match.
1625	Death of James I: Charles I ascends the throne and marries Henrietta Maria, sister of Louis XIII of France.
1626–9	War with France.
1629	Charles dispenses with Parliament and begins the period of Personal Rule.
1633	William Laud becomes Archbishop of Canterbury.
1635	Ship Money levied throughout England and Wales.
1637	Scotland, forced into rebellion by the religious intolerance of Charles, sees the signing of the Covenant defending the Kirk.
1639	First Bishops' War.
1640	Second Bishops' War and the calling of the English Parliament.
1642–6	First Civil War.
1648	Second Civil War.
1649	The King executed and England declared a republic.
1649–50	Oliver Cromwell conquers Ireland.
1650–1	Third Civil War.
1653–4	The Protectorate of Oliver Cromwell formed.
1658–9	Following Cromwell's death the Protectorate falls.
1660	The restoration of Charles II as king.
1665	The Great Plague.
1665–7	War with the Netherlands. Dutch fleet enters the Thames.
1666	The Great Fire of London.
1667	John Milton's *Paradise Lost* published.
1678	The Titus Oates Plot. Publication of John Bunyan's *Pilgrim's Progress, Part I.*
1683	The Rye House Plot.
1685	Charles II dies: accession of James II and VII, though known to have Catholic sympathies. Rebellion of the Duke of Monmouth (Charles II's Protestant bastard son).
1687	Publication of Isaac Newton's *Principia Mathematica.*
1688	The Glorious Revolution. James II flees. The Protestant William of Orange and his wife, Mary, daughter of James II, are invited to assume the throne.
1689	William III is proclaimed joint sovereign with Mary II.
1690	William defeats James II's attempt to regain the throne at the battle of the Boyne.

MIDLAND REVOLT

THERE WERE OTHERS who were not happy. To many the change of dynasty had meant little. The great land deals which had followed the selling of the monastic lands had continued throughout the century and so too had the depopulation and the loss of grazing rights on common lands in the villages once owned by the Church. In the Midlands the rate of enclosure, the process of fencing in the former arable fields in order to make them suitable for grazing, had gone on apace. The scars are still there: the fields which were thus converted still show the observer the ridges and furrows of the old strips. At the time, many of the people living in the Midlands expressed their disapproval by breaking down the fences and hedges surrounding the fields. Men and women, in teams of three and under, to escape the charge of riot, dismantled a section of fence and then retired as another team replaced them. When they claimed that they were actually restoring access to lands over which they had rights, the Star Chamber took the incidents seriously. Officially the government frowned upon enclosure, but since the death of Thomas More there had been little done to ease the situation. The Poor Law of 1601 was a response to the situation partly caused by the enclosures. The numbers of poor people had increased and after the Dissolution the number of almshouses had declined. Private donations made in wills were not enough to cope with the problem; there were beggars and homeless in every town, and a number of masterless people wandering the roads of the country. The Poor Law placed heavy penalties on the vagrants. It was feared that they were part of an anti-society and village constables were given the power – even the obligation – to whip the ones who passed through their villages if they were able-bodied. Villages were

London in 1616. Shakespeare's Globe Theatre can be seen in the foreground on the right. The skyline is dominated by old St. Paul's, destroyed by fire fifty years later.

obliged to provide for their own poor, giving money to the aged and infirm and work for the able-bodied, paid for out of parish rate.

The laws did not do anything about the causes, only the symptoms. In 1607 the largest rebellion for years broke out in the Midlands. The cause was undoubtedly enclosure and depopulation. The June of 1607 saw tens of thousands of men and women go into revolt in the area where the counties of Leicestershire, Northamptonshire and Warwickshire meet. Rioters came from miles around. Over seventy people from Leicester marched out of the town to join in the revolt at Cotesbach in the south of the county, despite the town's erection of gallows as a warning to the citizens. James's reaction was tough. The Lords Lieutenant, the men in the counties responsible for the militia, were ordered to call out the Trained Bands and apprehend the rebels and

their leader Captain Pouch. Pouch, really called John Raynold, had an eponymous sack filled, it was supposed, with a document signed by the King, giving him power to destroy enclosures, and magical potions capable of curing injuries. It was actually filled with cheese. James was keen to use the civil courts to try the rioters once the rebellion was ended, which resulted in the sympathetic juries letting a lot of the rioters off completely and reducing the charges of others. James was also keen to investigate the causes. In some ways he justified the rioters expectations of him. Commissions were sent into the affected counties of the Midlands and enclosing landlords were called to appear before them and provide evidence of the enclosures carried out. The government intended to make it more difficult to enclose and aimed to increase the penalties on the enclosers who

159

depopulated farms and encroached upon common land. Unfortunately the process was faulty from the start. The landowners who had enclosed were related to and associated with the very people who were to investigate their activities and prevent them continuing. In the 1630s fines on enclosers simply became a part of government finance and not a punishment.

James and his Parliament were not always on the best of terms, for problems of finance tended to dog the relationship after 1605. Attempts to arrive at a compromise, giving the King a set amount of income in return for his surrender of rights to collect taxes over which Parliament had no control, were all failures. In 1610, James dismissed Parliament with no agreement reached. He did not accord to the Parliament the status which it felt it deserved. Parliament had grown in importance in government during the past century, it had been central to Henry's break with Rome and pivotal in Elizabeth's religious policy at the commencement of her reign. James however had a different view. Kings were the appointees of God, they were little gods themselves and their rights – prerogatives – were paramount to Parliament. In practical terms James knew that this view was generally untenable, but nevertheless, after seven years of dispute, he determined to manage without Parliament. For most of the next eleven years, James ruled with only the Privy Council to assist him. A Parliament in 1614 was soon dismissed when it refused to provide him with money; it became known as 'the Addled Parliament'.

HENRY, PRINCE OF WALES

JAMES'S ELDEST SON, Henry Prince of Wales, was hailed as a paragon of the Renaissance man. All hope turned to him as the future glory of England, Wales and Scotland. His martial skill was held to be estimable, his love of learning and of the arts marked him as exceptional. How different was the second son. Charles had been born a sickly child and for much of the time he was ignored, very much in Henry's shadow. Partly because of his stutter, he seems to have found relationships with all but his brother difficult. Henry was

Entry of Prince Charles into Madrid in March 1623.

exceptional in the friendship which he showed to the young prince. The two developed their knowledge of warfare with model cannons and the like. Charles shared Henry's love of the arts but never achieved a high level of intelligence, or tolerance. It was a great shock to the political nation when in 1611 Henry died, a young man of eighteen, thrusting the younger prince, a boy of twelve into the forefront.

James fell in love shortly after the tragedy.

His attachment to his wife, Anne of Denmark, was little more than the perfunctory fondness of a diplomatic relationship. The partner in his real love affair was the aspiring George Villiers, created Duke of Buckingham, more of an ambitious young man than the genuine lover James took him to be. As James grew older and prematurely took on the aspects of an old man – his appeal was not helped in any case by his habitual uncleanliness – Buckingham switched his attention to the rising star, Prince Charles.

This time there was no homosexual relationship, but nevertheless, Charles was deeply fond of his new companion. In the early 1620s the two were inseparable. It was in 1623 that they set off for Spain to find Charles a wife. This was part of the King's unpopular pro-Spanish policy; to seal it Charles was to marry the Infanta. The policy was incredibly out of touch with the minds of the English, Welsh and British people. Spain was the

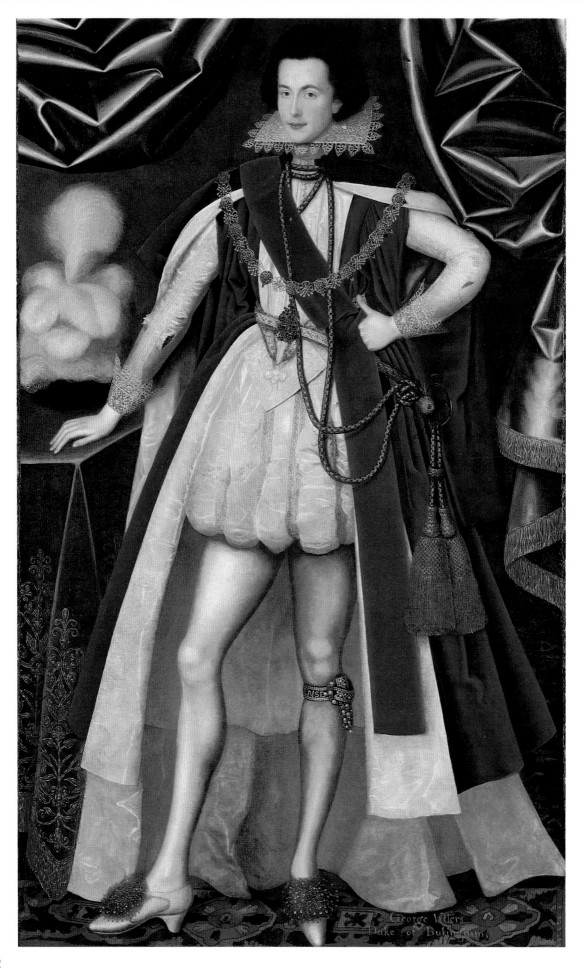

traditional enemy and friendship with her would do little to help the beleaguered Protestant Elector Palatine, Charles's brother-in-law who had been kicked from his Bohemian throne and then hounded by the Catholic forces of the Holy Roman Emperor out of the Rhineland Palatinate. James had done little to help his daughter Elizabeth whose short Bohemian reign had landed her with the epithet of Winter Queen, and any alliance with the papist Spanish monarchy was frowned upon. The marriage match failed and there was great rejoicing in London and in the country as a whole when the Prince and Buckingham came home empty-handed.

CHARLES I

J AMES had by this time, been forced to call parliaments again. His lack of resources permitted no other course, although all over Europe such bodies were falling into disuse. In France after the *Etats Généraux* met in 1614, it was not to sit again until the eve of the Revolution. In England, however, the monarchy could not survive on its own funds; government finance could not be found from the royal resources. When James died in 1625, he was succeeded by a man, Charles I, who took his views even further. He was prepared to carry out to the extremity his belief in the Divine Right to rule meted out to him by God. Parliament was not viewed by Charles as a permanent part of government, only as a council to be called when and if required by the King. This view was not shared by Parliament and in order to prevent the King managing without them as James had done, it severely curtailed the amount of income which it voted the new monarch at its first sitting.

There were other worrying traits in the new monarch. He did not espouse the same Calvinism shared by many of the Protestants in England. Moreover this brand of Protestantism, founded on the works of John Calvin, was predominant in parliamentary circles. Charles and his favourite Buckingham instead favoured Arminianism and were, from

William Laud (1573–1645).

1625, in a position to impose it upon the Church. It was to be a slow process as Charles could only place Arminian churchmen into vacant places and thus the hierarchy of the Church only altered piecemeal. Charles was fortunate in that he was able to place the prominent William Laud into the Bishopric of London early in his reign and then into the Archbishopric of Canterbury in 1633 from where Laud could exercise greater influence. In some quarters Arminianism, or at least Laud's practice of it, appealed to more people than Calvinism, which was rigid in its interpretation of the process of salvation. This was entirely in God's hands: people were chosen or elected for heaven even before birth and, do as they will, a reprobate soul condemned to hell could not alter his or her future regardless of their lifestyle. In theory a person could be selfish, disagreable and even fail to attend church at all and still enter heaven. On the other hand a person could be pious and godly yet be condemned. In the event those who thought themselves elect generally sought to justify their election or seek confirmation of their belief by living a godly and hardworking life.

On the other hand, Arminianism offered

Opposite: George Villiers, Duke of Buckingham (1592–1628), by an unknown artist.

people the chance to have some control over their fate by allowing them to ensure salvation by leading a godly life and receiving the sacraments of the Church, baptism and Communion. As a result Laud was able to control churches and ordained that the Communion tables, set in the body of the church so that the Communion was held amongst the people, should be moved to the east end and railed off as an altar. As Communion had become more important, the ceremony was to be sanctified by the conversion into an altar. Preaching, an essential part of the Calvinist service, was relegated, especially as it was well understood that those who controlled the preaching had the power to influence the people. This switch in importance, from the word of God to the representation of Christ's body and blood, was, to many, a direct throwback to Catholicism. Foxe's *Book of Martyrs* was again widely read and Calvinists were thrown into opposing the policy of a Church they had once been very much a part of. The label, Puritan, once referring simply to these who wished to reform the Church from within, continuing the work begun under Henry VIII, was gradually applied to a much wider range of people. It soon referred to any opponent of the King's religious policy, and later to any opponent of the government's actions in any sphere.

EXPEDITIONS TO NORTH AMERICA

THOUGH THE ENGLISH had discovered Newfoundland in 1497 and subsequently staked their claim, it was not until the reign of Elizabeth that they made more systematic attempts to establish a hold on North America. Then the piratical Walter Raleigh had made an abortive effort to found a colony on the eastern seaboard which, in honour of the Virgin Queen, he had named Virginia. In 1585 he had actually placed settlers on Roanoke Island (on the coast of what is now North Carolina), but Sir Francis Drake had brought them home within a year at their demand. In 1600, Raleigh's protégé, the

Charles I (1600–49) by Van Dyke.

geographer Richard Hakluyt, published his last version of *Principal Navigations, Voyages and Discoveries of the English Nation*, a cogent argument for colonisation.

It was abundantly clear that land in Virginia could mean opportunity and riches. In 1605 two companies were chartered, for London and Plymouth, with the purpose of establishing colonies in America, but it was not until 1607, after several exploratory journeys, that the London company founded a successful English plantation on the James river in Virginia. The colonists had already suffered losses on the voyage – only 105 survived of the 144 who had embarked on the three little ships to cross the Atlantic from England – but their foundation of Jamestown endured under their leader, the soldier of fortune, Captain John Smith. The settlers were dogged by disease, starvation and the Indians; hundreds died or fled back to England, but by 1643 they had thrived sufficiently for their numbers to be calculated at around 5,000.

Meanwhile, expeditions had continued to the east coast and in 1609 Sir Henry Hudson had discovered Manhattan Island and the river which carries his name. It was a region that promised a hugely rich fur trade, another argument for colonisation. Yet not all the expeditions were prompted by hope of financial gain or by the hunger of the dispossessed for land. Religious motives provided an equally powerful stimulus for other settlers.

In 1620 Puritans from Nottinghamshire and Lincolnshire, seeking freedom of worship at Leyden in Holland, decided to apply to the London merchants to settle in the New World. It was a struggle to organise the voyage but on 16 September, their ship *Mayflower* sailed from Plymouth, complete with livestock, provisions and cooking utensils. Thirty-five of her voyagers were Pilgrims. When they arrived at Cape Cod on 9 November, they planned to pause only briefly in this inhospitable region, then sail south and settle on the Hudson. They were forced back to Cape Cod and found their way in heavy snow to Plymouth Harbour where they made their first home. By 1630 the town of Plymouth had a population of about 300 and, thereafter, Puritan emigrants, urgently escaping from Archbishop Laud, followed in

quantity to Massachusetts. So many came from Lincolnshire that they called their capital Boston, after their home town. The settlers established their Separatist world under the leadership of John Winthrop, a member of the Suffolk gentry. He was both Governor of the Massachusetts Bay Company and of the colony. An ardent Puritan though no killjoy, he was a man of enormous energy, vision and purpose and had advised his first settlers: "We must consider we shall be as a City upon a Hill; the eyes of all people are upon us".

CHARLES AND PARLIAMENT

CHARLES AND HIS PARLIAMENTS did not have a happy relationship. The Commons and Lords refused to give him *carte blanche* to collect taxes, and they constantly questioned the military charges of the Duke of Buckingham who did not meet with any success in his foreign ventures against the French. The King attempted to raise money by a series of means. In 1626 after dismissing Parliament he asked his subjects for a free gift of money. Not surprisingly he received little. The Derbyshire JPs raised only £111 from the whole county and they themselves had given £91 of it. Following this failure the King demanded a forced loan instead and made the JPs responsible as commissioners for the loan. There was some resistance to this with people up and down the country demanding that a parliament be called to discuss the King's need for money. In some areas of the country like Leicestershire, people refused to pay their assessment. Five knights were arrested and held in prison and many people were summoned to appear in front of the Privy Council before the majority of the loan was paid in.

This was only one of the King's means of gaining an income. He began to drain some of the lands in the Isle of Axeholme and in the neighbouring Hatfield Chase in order to produce more corn and generate a higher return. In doing so he ruined the economy of the local villages which had pastured animals for leather production and grown hemp on the newly drained ground. Charles also had lists of gentlemen considered eligible to have received

The Departure of the Pilgrim Fathers from Plymouth 1620 by Bernard Finegan Gribble (1873–1962).

knighthoods at his coronation. By an old law, such men should have presented themselves at the time. If they failed they were liable to a fine of ten pounds. The financial qualification for knighthood had long been eroded by inflation and now a large number of men unknowingly fitted the bill. A commission was established in each county to seek these men out and extract the required ten pounds.

Successive parliaments were dissolved by Charles, one to save Buckingham from impeachment. When Buckingham was murdered by one, Felton, who blamed him for his seafaring brother's death, Parliament could hardly contain its delight. This further soured relations with the King. Charles was also interfering with trade by creating monopolies. These gave the right of manufacture or import of some goods to individuals in return for a lump sum. Whilst this gave the Crown a source of money, it was disturbing well established patterns of trade and manufacture, some of which were represented in Parliament.

Finally when the King was pressurised by lack of funds into signing the Petition of Right which effectively forbade him to collect any tax without the consent of Parliament, Charles could endure it no longer and he dissolved Parliament in 1629, intending to manage alone if he could.

Naturally he needed income and he continued his search for extra parliamentary tax. To enable him to govern more effectively, he expanded the size of the Privy Council and instituted committees within it to conduct particular duties. Some business he passed on to Archbishop Laud, notably the examination of enclosure. This time the reason was not really to prevent abuses which led to depopulation; rather it was to find culprits who had encroached upon territory and who could be fined and therefore benefit the Treasury. Similarly, surveys of the royal forests were carried out to discover the people whose lands had encroached upon them over the centuries and to fine them too. The Court of Wards which administered the estates of minors was also exploited, the rights to administer the estates were sold off for lump sums and the estates were then thoroughly ravaged for profit in the short time available to the purchaser of the right.

CHURCH PROBLEMS

IT WAS IN THE 1630s that Charles' government began making demands on the people's loyalty. The changes wrought in the Church were being felt throughout the community as Communion tables were removed from the centre of the churches and replaced by altars at the east end, which were railed off. This development gave a greater importance to the delivery of the Christian message than the sermons and lectures which the people had become accustomed to. The Arminian emphasis was on the body of Christ, commemorated by the Holy Communion, rather than on the word of God as interpreted by the Calvinist ministers who had predominated hitherto. To many the altars were suggestive of papist practices, and the renewed pressure upon the clergy to wear vestments and to make the congregation bow at the name of Jesus seemed to confirm this view. Laud and the King, who after all allowed a Catholic chapel to exist in the Palace of Whitehall for his Queen, fell under suspicion. This was further linked with the reluctance of Laud to prosecute vigorously Catholic priests, even though he showed apparent fervour for punishing Protestant divines such as William Prynne and Dr John Bastwick who produced tracts criticising Arminianism. In fact, Laud and the King were not Catholic; both considered that the Roman Church had erred from the truth and that it would eventually return to the fold, but they had no intention of restoring the Church of England to Rome. However, other people had reasons for

Soldiers of the Civil War period — a pikeman, a trooper and a musketeer.

making it seem as if they were Catholic. A lot of Laud's attempts to regain some of the wealth of the Church were opposed because they involved trying to reclaim the rights to tithes which had been transferred to secular hands at the Dissolution. Of course, Laud had also been involved in getting the fines for enclosure collected. Moreover, he had trodden on the toes of the JPs by reasserting the powers of the church courts. Many of the crimes which they had taken care of had passed to the lay courts – the quarter sessions. Now the Church was reassuming the right to try cases of bastardy and fornication as well as swearing and slander.

SHIP MONEY

In 1634 Charles declared that the coastal counties were in need of defence because of the war in Europe and because the coasts of the South-west were occasionally subjected to raids of Barbary pirates who carried Cornish folk into slavery in North Africa. To combat this he issued a writ of Ship Money, an emergency tax levied on the coastal counties to build ships. In 1635 Charles expanded the collection to include the inland counties where Ship Money had never been collected before. This meant that Rutland, for example, was charged with constructing a ship and sending it to the docks in London. For the first year or so, opposition to the collection of Ship Money was muted. Just as in the days of the Forced Loan, some people demanded that Parliament be called to determine the issue, but it was not until John Hampden challenged the need for the extension of an extraordinary tax when there had been plenty of time to summon Parliament and arrange for a more usual supply of cash, that large numbers of people stopped paying.

Many of these merely suspended payment whilst the case was being examined by the twelve Judges drawn from the King's Bench, the Court of Chancery and the Court of the Common Pleas. The case went against Hampden, but only by seven to five and many people took this as a moral victory, because the pressure placed upon the judges by Charles had failed to gain him a larger majority. As a result, many people were hauled before the quarter session courts throughout the country charged with non-payment. If they were proved guilty their goods were distrained, that is taken away by the sheriff's bailiffs and sold. The courts were faced with large numbers of defaulters and it slowed business down. Defaulters in normal times rarely came before the courts; such disputes were usually sorted out by the JPs before coming to this stage. Now this was impossible as by 1639 people in growing numbers refused to pay.

WAR WITH SCOTLAND

There was yet a further set of problems heading the government's way. Charles wished to bring the Scottish Church into line with that of England. James I had weakened the Presbyterian Church, but it was still supported by large numbers of ordinary Scottish people. Charles wanted to undermine the Kirk and bring Scotland under the sway of the bishops instead. This would lead the way to introducing the Laudian innovations into that country and then uniting the churches into one. Just as in England, Charles introduced a revised Book of Common Prayer into Scotland and, whereas in England it was perhaps grudgingly and suspiciously accepted, in Scotland it was greeted with popular revulsion. In Edinburgh stools were hurled at the Bishop as he attempted to use the book in the Cathedral. Women and men leapt to the defence of their Kirk, and led by men like James Graham, later Marquis of Montrose, they signed a great petition called the Covenant binding them to uphold it by force of arms if necessary.

Charles could not accept this rejection by the people and in 1639 went to war against the Scottish people. The English trained bands, called together for the war in the North were not keen to go. They resented many of Charles's actions, including the imposition of the Prayer Book and the Book of Sports which permitted games on a Sunday to fill in the time usually taken up by a sermon or lecture, and they were understandably not willing to fight to impose such a regulation on another country. Fortunately the war of 1639 did not come to major conflict and the Pacification of Berwick ended the year's hostilities. Charles

was now broke. The people had stopped paying Ship Money in full and they further halted the payment of the tax — Coat and Conduct Money — which was to support the war. By 1640 there was a tax strike in effect. Charles quickly summoned Parliament in April expecting loyalty, but it was, after an eleven-year wait, unwilling to be a lap dog. There were great grievances to be settled and action on these was demanded before money would be forthcoming. Charles dismissed this Short Parliament and in the summer took on the Scots again.

This war, dubbed the Second Bishops' War as it was firmly laid at Laud's feet, was for Charles a fiasco. His own army made its way north reluctantly. The soldiers took courage from their numbers and destroyed new enclosures and smashed altars and rails on their way north. At Ashby de la Zouch they practised musketry on the trusting tame white deer in the Earl of Huntingdon's park and then went on to release prisoners in Derby gaol. On the other hand the Scots, reinforced by moral commitment to a cause they saw as godly and right, swept all before them and crossed the Tyne, defeated the English force in August and went on to occupy the north of England.

PARLIAMENT IS RECALLED

CHARLES'S NEW PARLIAMENT called in November was able to impose its will on the politically weakened King. The members, whom Charles had expected to be patriotic in the face of invasion, sympathised with the Scots and had been in contact with them in the summer. All the machinery of the King's personal rule — to be labelled the Eleven Year's Tyranny — was dismantled. Laud and Thomas Wentworth, Earl of Strafford, a 1620s oppositionist whom Charles had lured to his side, were arrested, and other ministers fled. By the end of the first session, Parliament had abolished Ship Money, the Star Chamber Court, the Ecclesiastical Courts, the Court of Wards and had instituted an act ensuring that a Parliament would sit every three years regardless of the King's will and had made sure that the King could not dispose of the present Parliament without its own consent. Charles

had little support in the Houses, but the execution of Strafford on ill-founded charges using a Bill of Attainder which basically ensured that you were guilty if some people believed you to be, led to some drifting towards the King's side. This was nearly messed up by a plot by army officers backed by the foolish Queen to seize the Tower and institute a military coup.

When the second session opened in the Autumn of 1641, Charles played a moderate role, convinced that he would be able to gain an upper hand later. Parliament moved slowly to the abolition of the state Church and removed the bishops from the House of Lords. Its major action was the drawing-up of the Grand Remonstrance which stated the grievances of the past years, asserted the good Parliament had achieved and laid out a series of roads for further travel. These included some say in foreign policy and over the appointment of ministers, which were both the perogative of the King. At the same time a revolt broke out in Ireland as the Catholic population rose up against the Protestant settlers and their government. This created pressure for military action, but no one trusted the King to take command of the forces in case he used them on Parliament. The fact that the Catholic rebels claimed to be acting in the King's name and even with his sanction, did nothing to ease matters.

The Grand Remonstrance was hotly contested, some thinking it unnecessary given that the King had agreed to all Parliament had wanted, even the execution of Strafford. It only just scraped through the House, but was published immediately. Then it was seen as being an appeal down to the people, not to the King, and many MPs drifted across to the King's side. Again, the effects of this were all but wrecked when Charles, as ever mis-timing his moves, stormed into the House of Commons attempting to arrest five prominent MPs and the Lord Mandeville, who led the opposition to him. As the plot was one of the worst-kept secrets, the men had all escaped into London. Charles was hounded through the streets and soon evacuated his threatened Queen to the Continent with a portion of the Crown Jewels to sell for arms. He himself went north and set up court in York.

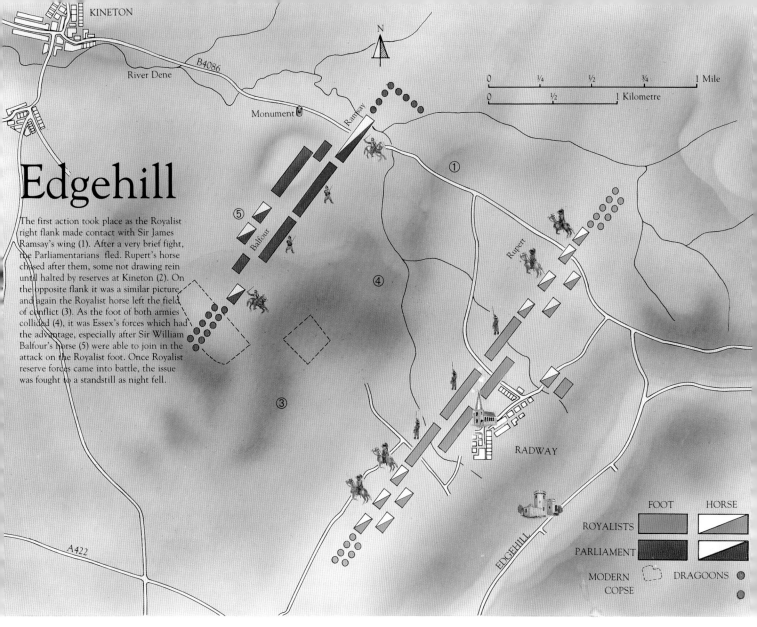

Edgehill

The first action took place as the Royalist right flank made contact with Sir James Ramsay's wing (1). After a very brief fight, the Parliamentarians fled. Rupert's horse chased after them, some not drawing rein until halted by reserves at Kineton (2). On the opposite flank it was a similar picture, and again the Royalist horse left the field of conflict (3). As the foot of both armies collided (4), it was Essex's forces which had the advantage, especially after Sir William Balfour's horse (5) were able to join in the attack on the Royalist foot. Once Royalist reserve forces came into battle, the issue was fought to a standstill as night fell.

Plan of the battle of Edgehill.

THE FIRST CIVIL WAR

THE ISSUE over the control of the trained bands dragged on and in March Parliament seized the initiative and took control, creating a whole set of new Lords Lieutenant to command the militia. In the summer Charles created his own military committees in the counties, the Commissions of Array, and attempts were made to raise forces. The Militia Ordinance men set about raising forces for the defence of Parliament in Lincolnshire and the Midlands and the King's commissioner, Henry Hastings, took the first commission to Leicestershire on 22 June. Both sides failed to raise troops in these ways and in the end active men like Hastings were issued commissions to

raise forces by themselves. Parliament centred an army of the Earl of Essex in Northamptonshire. The King failed to get the magazine at Hull and then at Leicester and Coventry, but at Nottingham declared war on 23 August. In September the two armies began their march to the Midlands, and on 23 October, the battle of Edgehill was fought. The battle, which every one had hoped would end the conflict, gave no one an outright victory. The King was able to march on London. He pushed through Parliamentarian forces at Brentford on 12 November but the following day was opposed by the Earl of Essex's forces, the London Trained Bands and

171

many of the citizens of London at Turnham Green. He had to turn back.

Charles based himself at Oxford and despite negotiations taking place over the winter, the war dragged on into the following year. Both sides organised administrative machinery to finance the war. The Royalists used their commissions of array, whilst Parliament set up committees in the counties. Both these bodies raised taxes, the chief being a weekly levy on property and perhaps income, called 'contribution' by the King's followers and 'assessment' by the Parliament. Levies were also made on the estates belonging to enemies and excises were raised on goods, all to pay for the war.

The spring of 1643 saw the Royalists attempt to strengthen their hold on parts of the country and by the summer they held Yorkshire and the South-west and much of the Midlands. They never exploited this because in the autumn the initiative passed from them when the three armies, the Earl of Newcastle's in the North, the King's in the south Midlands and Prince Maurice's in the South-west, each became involved in sieges which wasted time and manpower. Outside Hull the Earl's army wasted away. The Prince turned to Plymouth and the King attacked Gloucester. This latter siege was raised by Essex who raced over the South, took food into the town and dodged back to London avoiding defeat when the King attacked him at Newbury on 20 September.

The winter was spent in stalemate, but the initiative passed to Parliament. Successful negotiations had been conducted with the Scots who were encouraged by the Presbyterians in England to expect the creation of a Presbyterian Kirk south of the border. Thus lured, they joined in the war and in mid-January 1644 they crossed the border. The now Marquis of Newcastle marched to meet them but spent winter and spring vainly trying to bring them to battle. In the west Midlands, the Royalist hold was slipping from Lord Byron's grasp after Sir Thomas Fairfax's army had won the battle of Nantwich, and he was replaced by Prince Rupert, the heroic leader of the King's horse and a very able administrator. The attempt to seize the south Thames area failed as the Earl of Forth and

An officer of the New Model Army.

Lord Hopton were defeated by Sir William Waller at Cheriton on 18 March. In the east Midlands, Lord Loughborough's control of the region was dented by the great siege of Newark led by Sir John Meldrum and he needed the help of Rupert to relieve the town and stabilise his region. It was in Yorkshire where the first disaster occurred: the Royalists there were defeated at Selby in mid-April forcing the Marquis of Newcastle to retreat from Durham to York.

When York fell under siege from the three Parliamentarian armies of the Scots, the Earl of Manchester and the Lord Fairfax and his son Sir Thomas, Prince Rupert was sent to relieve it. This he did on 1 July, but on the following day he was beaten at Marston Moor. This resulted in the whole of the North falling into the hands of the Parliamentarians. Newcastle fled abroad and the Prince retreated via Lancashire into the west Midlands. Lord Loughborough's north Midlands was all but swamped by Parliamentarian forces. The King seemed to be of the opinion that he had redressed the balance by defeating the Earl of Essex at Lostwithiel in Cornwall at the end of August, but this was illusory as it did nothing to replace the loss of the North. In October the combined Parliamentarian forces of Essex, Manchester and Waller failed to defeat the King when they had him cornered at Newbury. This prompted a complete reorganisation of the Parliamentarian war effort.

In the following spring the New Model army was created out of the three main Parliamentarian field forces and the two earls were removed from their command to be replaced by Sir Thomas Fairfax. In May the King set out from Oxford to capitalise on the work done by his nephews, Rupert and Maurice, in the west Midlands by ending the siege of Chester. By the time he reached Staffordshire the siege was over and instead he turned east and stormed Leicester. Whilst this had gone on Fairfax had attacked Oxford, but in the second week of June he led his army north and followed the King through Northamptonshire after it had gone south to Daventry to send food on to Oxford. On 14 June the King's army of 7,000 or so rushed up hill into the New Model Army which was twice its size and was defeated in the battle of Naseby. A large amount of credit for the

Sir Thomas Fairfax, Commander-in-Chief of Parliamentary forces.

victory was due to Fairfax's second-in-command, Oliver Cromwell.

The victory at Naseby was quickly followed by the defeat of Lord Goring at Langport and in September of the King again at Chester. The war continued chiefly as a series of cleaning-up operations until the last field army was defeated at Stow-on-the-Wold in March 1646. The King surrendered to the Scots in May.

THE SECOND CIVIL WAR

DEFEATED BUT UNDAUNTED, the King still refused to come to terms hoping that his enemies would fall out amongst themselves. And they did. The Presbyterians in Parliament battled against the independents who did not want a state church at all. The latter's support in the army prompted Parliament to try and disband it. Scotland grew frustrated with the English problem and sold the King to the Parliament in return for money owed. As Parliament and the army leaders argued, a

The battle of Preston and Walton, 17 August 1648 by Charles Cattermole.

group known as the Levellers developed a power base in the army to complement their support in urban areas. The Levellers believed that the electorate in England, which was then a tiny unevenly distributed minority of the male population, should be extended. They wanted also to secure the backpay of the army and to create pensions for the war widows and orphans. In late October they and the representatives of the army high command met in Putney church to discuss the Agreement of the People, the document setting out a form of male democracy for England. The army leaders who were present, led by Oliver Cromwell and Henry Ireton, had no wish to spread power downwards to the lower classes and prevented any full-scale debate on the text, halting for much of the time at the first clause. As they talked, Charles escaped from Hampton Court and fled to the Isle of Wight. From there he negotiated with the Scots who had opposed military intervention in 1644 and persuaded them to invade England in his support.

The following spring there were several

The battlefield of Marston Moor in Yorkshire from the position known as Cromwell's Plump. The monument to the battle is visible in the distance to the right of the trees.

risings led by Royalists or discontented one-time Parliamentarians, in Wales, the South and Essex. None of these was well co-ordinated and they were defeated as was the Scottish invasion force, which was crushed by Cromwell at Preston. Attitudes to the King hardened. And while Parliament ordered the destruction of many of the castles which lie in ruins about us today, in order to prevent them being used again in renewed war, and while Cromwell besieged Pontefract which was held for the King, others planned the trial of Charles and purged Parliament of the Presbyterian faction who opposed such moves. In January 1649 Charles was brought to trial at Westminster in front of a newly created High Court of Justice.

THE EXECUTION OF THE KING

A REVOLUTION was now taking place. It was not one of the aims of Parliament in 1642 or 1646 or even of a year earlier. Yet, the refusal of the King to acknowledge his defeat and the need to secure the state of England and her people, brought them to revolution. A shrewder and wiser person would not have failed his subjects. The court needs to be judged not by the way in which the King saw

The Execution of Charles I after Weesop.

it, nor by the ways of English law hitherto, in which light it was plainly illegal. Instead it must be seen as a revolutionary body, a part of the process of forging a new state; judged therefore by its own merits. Representatives of the whole country, the counties and the towns were co-opted onto the commission, although less than half reached London. The result was determined in advance, as was inevitable to ensure any stability, any peace: Charles had to be disposed of. He died with dignity and courage and won a sympathy he never deserved in life.

'A cruel necessity' is the verdict accredited to Cromwell on the execution.

THE THIRD CIVIL WAR

Scotland did not approve of what England had done. Aside from the defeated Scots army retreating over the border, neither the Kirk nor the Parliament could sanction the execution about which they had no say. Negotiations were opened with the young Charles, Prince of Wales, effectively the King of England and Scotland since the moment of his father's death. In Ireland there was still a sizeable Royalist force, composed of English refugees and Irish Catholics united against the rule of Parliament and the newly proclaimed

Republic. At first Charles almost went there, but the disunity in the segments of opposition meant that Cromwell who shipped over to Ireland, was able to defeat the Royalists and drive down the east coast and into the South during 1649. When he left his son-in-law Henry Ireton to continue, the mass of the Royalist forces had been broken, and sundry people killed in the dreadful sieges of Drogheda and Wexford. The English soldiers suffered no less badly; many of them succumbed to appalling ravages of plague and even Ireton died of such an illness. Charles decided on Scotland and went from his exile in the United Provinces to Edinburgh, sacrificing the military expedition under the Marquis of Montrose which he had earlier commissioned. Montrose was ritually slaughtered as a traitor by the vengeful Presbyterians mindful of how he had defeated them in the campaigns of 1644−5. Charles suffered for his action, being subjected to hours of Presbyterian sermons aimed at bolstering him into adopting that form of church when he was restored to the English throne. His military ventures failed. The army under David Leslie was defeated by Cromwell at Dunbar on 3 September 1650 after a campaign which had given earlier hopes of success. This failure gave Charles an unexpected break. The floundering of the Presbyterians gained him the crown which they had held from him and the command of

the army which he enlarged with Royalists and veterans of the 1648 campaign. He dodged past Cromwell and struck into England in 1651 and marched as far south as Worcester, but expected support did not materialise and some towns refused him entry. On the anniversary of Dunbar he was defeated at the battle of Worcester and he began his series of hair-raising adventures which led to his safe landfall in France.

THE REPUBLIC OF ENGLAND

Worcester was hailed as a saving grace – a crowning mercy. God was happy with the Republic of England and things could move apace. They did not. The Republic had come into existence piecemeal. The King's execution had been held up because they had forgotten to deal with the fact that the Prince would automatically become king once the axe had fallen. Likewise the House of Lords was abolished some time later after it had become almost defunct of its own accord. Moreover the Parliament consisting of the remains of the Commons called in 1640 and with the additions of the recruiter elections of the war and the subtractions of the 1648 purges, did not seem very interested in establishing a new constitution. Nor did it have a really sympathetic attitude to the soldiers once it had given them their back pay in 1649. These payments had reduced army support for the Levellers, whose rebellion in May 1649 in support of the third draft of the Agreement was, as a result, put down by the army. Nor had the army supported the True Levellers or Diggers who had established communes on waste land in the South and Midlands. These communes had been open to men and women; they could enter them, live there and work together on the common treasury of God's earth. To landowners the social revolutionary threat posed by the suggestion that the land belonged only to God and therefore could be shared by all was too threatening and the communes were smashed up and the diggers dragged before the courts, presided over by the same 'threatened' landowners. No, the Long Parliament was not really revolutionary and its lack of sympathy for the soldiers led in April 1653 to its

Oliver Cromwell, after Walker.

expulsion. Not everyone was unexcited. Some people were convinced that God was so much on their side that the second coming was imminent.

The new legislative was more prosaic, consisting of a one-chamber Parliament which first sat in the summer of 1653 and was supposed to devise a new constitution. It was composed of people from a wide background: some supported Cromwell; others wanted the Commonwealth, destroyed in April, to be restored; another group desired a form of monarchy. The Parliament tackled some of the major issues of religion, debated establishing a new national church and the cutting of taxes. In part, the latter led to its dismissal as this would again result in the loss of army pay. The body was the first British assembly having Scots and Irish MPs as well as the usual English and Welsh representatives. Nevertheless, despite the progressive nature of the programme, Cromwell dismissed it in December 1653.

The new constitution devised by General John Lambert established the Protectorate, with a Council of State and a one-chamber Parliament. Cromwell considered that this constitution, called the Instrument of Government, was a finished work, but the

new assembly considered the relationships between the elements of government to be open for discussion and in January 1655 it, too, was dissolved.

There then followed a period of military rule following the Royalist rising in the South-west known as Penruddock's Rebellion. The country was divided into eleven districts ruled over by a major-general who had civilian as well as military duties and sat on quarter-sessions benches. The major-generals were unpopular and the next elections saw their attempts to influence the voting defeated. The new Parliament concentrated a lot of its energy on persecuting James Naylor, an associate of the Quakers who rode into Bristol on an ass in the manner of Christ. In 1657 some of the members began to draft a Humble Petition and Advice which created a second selected Chamber and proposed giving Oliver the crown. Pressure from the army led to Cromwell rejecting the crown, but other elements of the Petition were accepted.

CHARLES II

WHEN CROMWELL DIED in 1658 and was succeeded by his worthy eldest son, the Republic began to slide downwards. Able as Richard was, he had no real basis of support. The Commonwealth men in Parliament were still intent on diminishing the army's importance and in the end they and the new Protector were swept away. They were replaced by the recalled Long Parliament, but when the swordsmen discovered that the Parliament's attitude to them had not changed, it too was disposed of. The army then established a Committee of Safety which in turn proved unacceptable to the ruling elite. By the end of the year the Long Parliament, ridiculed as the Rump, was sitting again. In the early months of 1660 Parliament moved towards restoring the monarchy. General Monck brought his loyal army south from Scotland and outfaced the English army's hostility. Charles issued the Declaration of Breda, stating the conditions upon which he would return, and England accepted it and him with open arms. The traditional conservatism prevalent in the country ended the bold experiment. God turned his back, but

Charles II at a ball in the Hague after his flight from England. He is dancing with his sister Mary, watched by his mother.

before he had, Colonel Fleetwood, a stalwart of the revolution, was certain that the Lord had spat in his face.

The restoration of the monarchy was greeted with bonfires and much quaffing of ale. It was followed by a barbarous display of vengeance aimed at a few of the regicides, but generally an attempt at some compromise. Land which had changed hands as a result of the war was not automatically handed back unless it was royal, and government was made

Right: Charles's embarkation for England.

up of ex-Royalists and Parliamentarians. The Church, however, was restored with vigour. There had been hopes again of a Presbyterian established church, but the Laudians and their supporters would have none of it. There had been no national church since the Civil War and numerous churches had developed, some allowing women an equality denied in society as a whole. The most lasting of these, the Baptists and the Quakers, were able to survive underground for much of the time, but the

latter shed their commitment to women's equality and adopted pacifism in response to repression. The period of Charles's government saw the religious repression of all dissent and the Presbyterians. More people died as a result of religious persecution in his reign than in the dread days of Mary.

WOMEN IN SEVENTEENTH-CENTURY ENGLAND

WOMEN FARED BADLY in Charles's reign. The jolly licence of the court's sexuality was arguably a form of repression in itself and actresses allowed on the stage for the first time were considered fair game in the same way as prostitutes were. This was in part a backlash against the Commonwealth during which women had played a more important role in the religious affairs of the nation. The Quaker sect had seen women like Elizabeth Hooton of Skegby in Nottinghamshire preaching and contributing to the debates on the nature of the relationships between people and God. The Quakers were not the only progressive sect. Women in many other religious groups felt confident enough to deny St Paul's dictum that they should not participate in such matters except at home where they might ask explanations of their husbands. Several women had gone into print on religious matters, many apologising for entering the 'male world' and, like Mary Cary, claiming that they were passing on God's words which he had vouchsafed to them in dreams and visions. Others 'dictated' their entranced communications, like Anna Trapnel, an associate of the fifth monarchists. Upon the Restoration this freedom was curtailed partly because many of the sects were destroyed. The Quakers began to drop their earlier equality in order to avoid further censure in a period when local magistrates hunted them down.

Yet there was another strand to the writings of women. Secular publications had also appeared in the 1650s, amongst them poems and plays by Margaret Cavendish, the second Marchioness and later first Duchess of Newcastle. This remarkable woman whose very clothes flouted the rigorous restrictions

Opposite: Nell Gwyn (c.1650–87).

of Stuart society was keen to delve into the sciences, the arts and philosophy. Largely self-taught in many spheres, she had plays performed in London and visited the Royal Society, which Charles had founded to encourage the development of science in England during a period of great expansion of scientific knowledge. Whereas the enquiring minds of other nobles like Prince Rupert were accepted in society, even if seen as somewhat eccentric, Margaret Cavendish was observed as a freak. Pepys, Secretary of the Navy and one of the most notable diarists of his age, described the Duchess as 'a good comely woman' but then commented, 'her dress so antic and her deportment so unordinary, that I do not like her at all, nor did I hear her say anything that was worth hearing...' Margaret Cavendish also entered into the field of biography. Like Lucy Hutchinson who wrote a brilliant biography of her husband, the imprisoned regicide Sir John Hutchinson, trying to establish his reputation as an honourable man, Margaret Cavendish wrote about the Duke whom she felt was failed by Charles II after the sacrifices (including an estimated £900,000) he had made in the war.

Perhaps the most remarkable woman is the writer of what was probably the first novel in English, Aphra Behn. Behn was distinguished from Hutchinson and Cavendish, who had both been born into upper gentry families, in that she, like Trapnel, Cary, Susanna Parr and the prophetesses of the 1650s, came from below the gentry class. Behn was born into a yeoman family in Kent. She was a convinced monarchist and probably served Charles II as a spy following her brief marriage to a Dutchman. She wrote and had performed on the Restoration stage some fifteen plays, including *Lucky Chance* and *The Rover*. In addition she wrote poetry which she claimed was influenced by her distant relative, the poet Edmund Waller, and was helped initially by the Earl of Rochester, a poet of some note. Her prose included the first philosophical novel, a treatment of slavery which she had witnessed first hand in the Indies in the early 1660s. The book, *Oroonoko, or the History of the Royal Slave*, savaged the racism of the white settlers in the Indies and questioned the very foundations of the then assumed white supremacy in a way which prefigures the later works of Harriet Beecher Stowe. Her novel in

Samuel Pepys (1633–1703)

Pepys was Secretary to the Admiralty (1673–9 and 1684–9) and played a significant part in the administration and reform of the Navy. He was also president of the Royal Society (1684–6), chartered in 1660 by Charles II to a group of illustrious scientists whose interests also extended into trade, shipbuilding, navigation, agriculture and history. It is, however, for his effervescent and intimate personal diary that Pepys is now best remembered. Covering the period 1660–9, it provides memorable insights into the life of the Restoration. The following extract is dated 4 September 1666 during the Great Fire of London:

Saw how horridly the sky looks, all on fire in the night, was enough to put us out of our wits; and, indeed, it was extremely dreadful, for it looks as if it was at us, and the whole heaven on fire. I after supper walked in the darke down to Tower-streete, and there sawe it all on fire, at the Trinity House on that side, and the Dolphin Taverne on this side, which was very near us; and the fire with extraordinary vehemence. Now begins the practice of blowing up houses in Tower-streete, those next the tower, which at first did frighten people more than anything; but it stopped the fire where it was done, it bringing down the houses to the ground in the same places they stood, and then it was easy to quench what little fire was in it, though it kindled nothing almost.

letter form, *The Love Letters Between A Nobleman and His Sister*, foreshadows many of the novels of the next century. She was popular with the audiences who saw her play, but Behn's sex was used as a weapon against her: she and her work were described as lewd in ways to which no contemporary male playwright's works were subjected. She was also accused of plagiarism, yet she succeeded in a world in which plays like *The Country Wife* by Wycherley sought to undermine women's freedoms and confine them to the roles of wife, whore and mistress whilst ridiculing the women who 'presumed' to enter the male preserve.

The most famous of the male authors were William Wycherley and John Vanburgh, Sir George Etheridge and George Farquhar. Their plays seemed to exhibit a great release from the strictures of the theatre's repression in the 1650s. The writers felt able to present sexual matters in an open way which had never occurred in the English theatre. Many plays dealt with marital relations, like *The Country Wife*, and were bawdy. Whilst the King, Pepys and members of the court frequently attended London theatres, many of the 'respectable classes' kept away.

PLAGUE AND FIRE

LONDON WAS BESET by plague in 1665 which filled the graveyards and emptied the streets. The full horror of it can be only dimly imagined as the plague indiscriminately picked off the Londoners at an appalling rate, leaving

Londoners fleeing from the city to escape the plague.

The Great Fire of London 1666 (Dutch School).

the stench of death and the rattle of the death carts to haunt the streets of London. With this in mind the great fire of the following year which struck the town was partly a blessing. It acted as a purifier, destroying the dank streets and eradicating the conditions that encouraged the rats which carried the plague-bearing flea. It also gave Londoners the chance to rebuild, yet they adopted only a half-hearted approach; the great plans put forward for the reconstruction of the town were overlooked and instead they concentrated on the construc-

tion of the churches and the cathedral of St Paul, the magnificent monuments of Nicholas Hawksmoor and Sir Christopher Wren.

England's disasters were increased by the temerity of the Dutch, with whom England engaged in three wars. On one occasion, the Dutch Admiral Trump and the fleet sailed into the Thames in June 1667, burned ships at Chatham and towed the flagship of the Royal Navy out to sea. The unwillingness of the English to pay for the navy – witness the struggles that Pepys had to keep the finances on an even keel – was well illustrated when seamen at Chatham were hailed in their own language by their own countrymen; they were sailing with the Dutch fleet because the pay was better and regular.

England was periodically gripped by fears of a Catholic revival in the reign of Charles II. This was partly due to the knowledge that Charles's barren marriage (contrasting with the trail of bastards he left to feed off the state purse) would result in the succession to the throne of the Duke of York, who was a confirmed papist. Catholics were blamed for the Fire of London and, according to reports, some were brutally murdered at the time. With almost inevitable predictability, there

TITUS OATES.

Titus Oates was convicted of perjury and placed in the pillory.

were several plots which were linked with papists. In 1678 Titus Oates, who was more than a little deranged, denounced a supposed plot to kill the King, massacre Protestants, invade Ireland etc. Charles did not really believe Oates, but others did or pretended to, and executed Catholic opponents, while seeking to exclude James, Duke of York, from the succession. A new plot, which was named Rye House, came to light in 1683 and this time helped Charles to remove some Whig politicians who wished to exclude James by enabling him to label them as traitors. Charles dispensed with his last Parliament in 1681 and called no more.

THE 'GLORIOUS REVOLUTION'

DURING THIS PERIOD, Charles was denied the financial expedients of his father's personal rule and was forced to take money from the King of France. In effect the country's ruler was in the pocket of the great Sun King, Louis XIV. At one point even the

The defeat of Monmouth at the battle of Sedgemoor.

184

religious future was mortgaged to the French. In the secret Treaty of Dover of 1670, Charles promised to restore the Catholic religion – there were grounds for the fears of the English. It was claimed that Charles died a Catholic in 1685, but his conversion is dubious. He was very ill and in great pain when his confession was allegedly received; moreover, he was a cynic who was prepared to play with other people's consciences and may have had sport with his own.

James succeeded peacefully enough, but his short reign was marked by his efforts to restore the Catholic religion. His attempt to secure religious toleration for the dissenting Protestants was only a backdoor way of heralding in the Catholic Church. His arrest of the seven bishops in 1688 when they refused to read the Declaration of Indulgence, promising religious freedom, stirred up great opposition to him. Three years earlier, this opposition had hardly been shown when Charles's illegitimate but Protestant son, the Duke of Monmouth, had landed in the West. Denied the popular support which he had expected, Monmouth was defeated at Sedgemoor in July 1685. He spoiled the effect rather by grovelling at the feet of the King and suffered an appallingly bungled execution. It was the mistreatment meted out by the savage Judge Jefferies, who sentenced 1,400 people to death in the aftermath of the rising, which began a popular backlash against him, heightened in 1688 when the bishops were imprisoned.

This in turn inspired plotting by Whig earls who by the end of the year had succeeded in bringing the daughter and son-in-law of James, Mary and William, into England. In the attempt to fight off the invasion force, James lost his nerve and his best general, John Churchill, changed sides. Thus occurred the last of the revolutions of the seventeenth century. Its bloodlessness and seeming complete success led to it being called the Glorious Revolution. Its glory was chiefly the spoil of the Whig party who freed themselves of James II and VII and appropriated the right to choose the monarch and his or her religion. The rightful King fled and the pretenders, Mary, his daughter, and William of Orange, her husband, were crowned after a divided Parliament compromised on the King's voluntary abandonment of the throne when

James II, after Kneller.

James Scot, Duke of Monmouth.

Overleaf: The Lord Mayor's water procession on the Thames in the time of Charles II.

Above: Parliament offering the crown to William and Mary.

Opposite: The Duke of Marlborough (1650–1722).

he fled abroad. This established Parliament's right to decide the future of the throne, confirmed through the Bill of Rights in 1690, which was fundamental in pointing England and Wales and later Scotland towards a constitutional monarchy.

The reign of William and Mary was brief. Mary died childless in 1694, and it was left to William with only a thin claim to carry on as William III and IV alone. He was for much of his reign involved in foreign affairs, bringing England into the Grand Alliance against Louis XIV in 1689, when Louis supported James's claim to the English throne. William defeated James's army decisively at the battle of the Boyne (1690), but again had to face the Sun King's ambitions to dominate Europe in the War of the Spanish Succession. In 1700 Louis proclaimed his grandson Philip V of Spain and invaded the Spanish Netherlands in the following year. William, who died in 1702, did not see the spectacular victories of English forces led by John Churchill, Duke of Marlborough, and of their allies at the battles of Blenheim (1704), Ramillies, Turin (1706), Oudenarde, Lille (1708) and Malplaquet

(1709). The war ended with the Peace of Utrecht in 1713; French military supremacy had effectively been crushed.

GLENCOE

WILLIAM'S reign has forever been stained by the massacre of the Macdonalds in Glencoe in the winter of 1692. The Scots had not been as willing to accept the new King as the English. In an attempt to stabilise the country, William offered an amnesty if the clan chieftains swore an oath of loyalty by 1 January 1692. Macdonald of Glencoe was late. William was persuaded to allow a force of Campbells, traditional enemies of the Macdonalds, to deal with this apparent show of disloyalty. The Macdonalds greeted the Campbells as guests, and were then massacred by them. Though the Campbells were the instrument of murder, William was clearly recognised as the perpetrator, leading to great ill-feeling against the English.

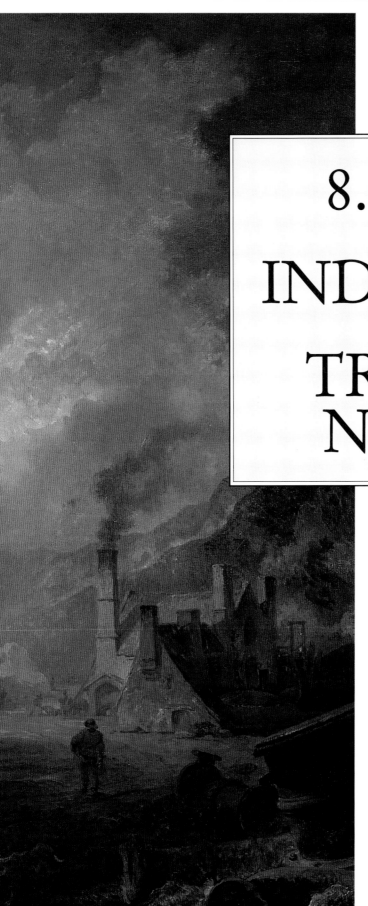

8. BIRTH
OF AN
INDUSTRIAL
AND
TRADING
NATION

BRITAIN HAD ALWAYS had industries but in the eighteenth century industry became the dominant force in the economy. Agriculture which had in its various forms brought wealth to the landowners, merchants and monarchs of Britain, was also greatly improved. More was produced; soil as a resource was exploited more rigorously. This nurtured a growing population which, in turn, drove the wheels of mechanised industry and consumed the goods produced by that industry.

Politically, too, there were great changes. A new dynasty sat on the throne. German Georges, inhabitants and rulers of Hanover, followed the last of the recognised Stuart monarchs. For much of the century the Whigs dominated Parliament and government. Britain's people, the most riotous in Europe, rattled their leaders and, at the end of the century, imbibed revolution and reason from France and, more importantly, from home-grown radicals like Mary Wollstonecraft and Thomas Paine. A new nation and a new consciousness were born.

Coalbrookdale by Night by P. J. de Loutherberg.

TIME CHART

1701	Beginning of the War of the Spanish Succession.
1702	William III dies: accession of Queen Anne.
1704	Battle of Blenheim. The British, under Marlborough, and allied forces defeat the French.
1707	Act of Union between Scotland and England.
1713	Treaty of Utrecht ends the War of the Spanish Succession. Spain cedes Gibraltar to Britain.
1714	Queen Anne dies: accession of George, Elector of Hanover, as George I.
1715	Jacobite Rebellion.
1716	The Septennial Act limits parliaments to a life of seven years.
1718	Attempted Jacobite rising in Scotland.
1720	'South Sea Bubble' bursts. Investors lose large amounts of money.
1721	Walpole becomes chief minister.
1726–9	Famine in Ireland.
1727	George I dies; accession of George II.
1733	John Kay invents flying shuttle, enabling weaving to be carried out much faster.
1738	War of the Polish succession. Britain, alone, at war with Spain.
1739	War of Jenkins' Ear: Anglo-Spanish naval war.
1739–41	Famine in Ireland kills 400,000.
1740	War of Pragmatic Sanction. Britain aids Austria.
1743	The battle of Dettingen.
1745	The battle of Fontenoy. 'Bonnie Prince Charlie', Prince Charles Edward Stuart, lands in Scotland and proclaims his father King. He marches into England and reaches Derby.
1746	Prince Charles is chased out of England and defeated in the north of Scotland at Culloden by the Duke of Cumberland.
1747	After several Continental victories for the allies, the war against France and Spain ends.
1751	George II's son, Frederick, Prince of Wales, dies.
1755	English ships attack French vessels without a declaration of war.
1756	War against France. In India, French-backed forces capture Calcutta; English residents are imprisoned in the 'Black Hole'.
1757	Bengal captured by the British after the battle of Plassey.
1759	Quebec captured by the British from the French.
1760	Death of George II: accession of George III, his grandson.

Edinburgh in 1693.

1763	The Seven Years' War with France ends with the Treaty of Paris. France cedes Canada and the Mississippi valley to Britain.
1764	The Sugar Act, placing duties on sugar exports, is imposed on the American colonies to recoup some of the cost of defending them during the war.
1765	The Stamp Act similarly imposed.
1773	The 'Boston Tea Party'.
1774	A continental congress is called in the American colonies to discuss the relationship with Britain.
1776	The colonies declare themselves independent of Britain. Adam Smith publishes his *Wealth of Nations*.
1778	The French join in the War of Independence on the side of the Americans.
1779	Compton's Mule combines Hargreaves's Spinning Jenny with Richard Arkwright's water-powered frame, speeding up the process of spinning strong cotton thread.
1781	Yorktown falls ensuring the victory of the Americans.
1783	America wins its independence. William Pitt the Younger placed into office by the King.
1789	The French Revolution.

George I (1660–1727).

The Hanoverian Succession

The origins of the Hanoverian succession go back to 1616. In that year, James I's daughter Elizabeth married the Elector Palatine. Their daughter Sophia married Ernest Augustus, first Elector of Hanover. Sophia's brothers, the Elector Charles Louis, Prince Maurice and Prince Rupert, all died before her. When the English began to search for a successor to the throne, following the failure of William and Mary and of Mary's sister Queen Anne to produce surviving children, Sophia was the last survivor of James I's progeny who was acceptable. She did not succeed herself, for when Anne died Sophia, too, was dead. The throne passed to her son, George. He was fifty-four.

Set in his ways, George never learned English and he communicated with his English and Scottish ministers in French. This meant that he was often excluded from debate as the ministers discussed matters in English and then presented the King with a summary. Thus the monarch's role in the process of government declined again, almost by accident. George was not much bothered; he found his power in Britain restricted anyway and preferred his almost absolutist rule in Hanover. Consequently, he spent as much time as he could there. His British ministers were relieved every time he departed as his absolutist tendencies were frowned on by them and by Parliament.

A NEW NATION: THE ACT OF UNION

JAMES I HAD FAILED to achieve political union between England and Scotland early in the seventeenth century. Charles I's clumsiness blighted the relationship between the two nations, and even Cromwell's domination of both did not bring about one nation. The expulsion of James II did not ease matters and, in the last years of William's reign, the decision by England to bring over the Hanoverians in succession to Anne to rule both countries did not sweeten the relationship between them. Scots were rightly angered by this Act of Settlement, especially as it was enacted without any consultation.

William saw the problem and favoured union, but England remained cool to the idea. He was concerned that Scotland might choose a Stuart, Catholic monarchy; Louis XIV of France had already recognised James VIII (of Scotland) and III (of England) as king. But when Anne came to the throne, there had been no progress. Indeed, in the Scottish Parliament there were suggestions that Scotland should become an independent nation; moreover,

Mompesson House, Salisbury, Wiltshire. Some fine domestic buildings were constructed during the reign of Queen Anne, mostly in brick or stone which had largely replaced timber-frame structures during the seventeenth century. This house in Salisbury's Cathedral Close was owned by the Mompesson family and is now a National Trust property.

with the Act anent Peace Scotland declared that it was not to be involved in a war decided upon by England without Edinburgh's consent. The Act of Security furthermore stated that when Anne died, Scotland would choose its own monarch.

England retaliated by threatening to treat Scottish commerce as alien if the Hanoverian succession was not accepted. A commission to discuss the treaty between the two nations was suggested in 1706 and, in nine weeks, a draft was presented to both Parliaments. Both countries had good reason to press for union at this time. England was at war with France, knowing that France often saw Scotland as the back door to England. The Scots desired free trade with England. In such circumstances the United Kingdom of Great Britain came into

being with one parliament, one flag and one coinage.

Although the Edinburgh Parliament passed the act, it was to prove unpopular in the country. Scotland was perceived as having been suborned by England. Only forty-five MPs were to represent the nation in the House of Commons and only sixteen nobles sat in the House of Lords. Mob violence greeted the passing of the act; Scots felt that their country was losing its identity. An independent legal system preserved the nation's integrity but, with the English being given the right to tax the Scots, many felt that England was paying its national debt at the expense of Scotland. It was a relationship in which it was often to be observed that Scotland was a junior partner.

THE SOUTH SEA BUBBLE

THE WHIGS ruled supreme under George I, and from amongst them rose the first prime minister, Robert Walpole. It was an economic crisis that threw him to the fore. In 1720, large numbers of the wealthy sections of society were carried away by investment fever, rushing to buy shares in the South Sea Company, which had prospered from a monopoly of trade in the Pacific region.

The company was soon over-subscribed. Bribery was widely used to persuade royalty and members of the government to show interest in the company, and very soon the share price ceased to have any relation to the real value of the company. Naturally, the bubble burst; royalty and gentry faced ruin and reputations followed. The whole venture had failed and only then did the bribery seem unacceptable.

As royalty and the government were execrated by the country, Walpole stepped in. Aided by a strong economy, he managed to re-assign South Sea Company stock and speculators had some of their money back. With the government stabilised and with a king unable to take an active part in government, Walpole went from strength to strength, taking a leading role in ministerial meetings – a role that was later to be called

Robert Walpole (1676–1745).

that of 'prime' minister. His was a strong ministry with low taxation, but it depended upon bribes or, more likely, the perquisites of office for much of its support. Nevertheless, its very existence ensured that Britain remained a parliamentary monarchy.

A satirical cartoon on the folly and disaster of the South Sea Bubble.

GEORGE II

W HEN GEORGE DIED in 1727, during his summer excursion to Hanover, he was succeeded by his son, George II. The two had never been close. The Prince had gathered the parliamentary opposition around him at Leicester House and the King had tried to humiliate him whenever he showed a desire for independence. However, the full majesty of the new monarch inspired Handel's coronation anthems, including 'Zadoc the Priest'. The four Biblical texts chosen for the work were on the theme of celebration, but also conveyed a highly reverential tone. They were designed not only to celebrate the occasion but also the monarchy itself. The King was appreciative; his interest in music was informed and it was through his encouragement that Handel made his home in England.

George II was in turn ruled by his wife, Caroline. Her political desire maintained Walpole in office, despite George's dislike of the man. Unlike his father, he was no mere cipher in the work of government but worked through business thoroughly and sometimes shrewdly. When Queen Caroline died, George's ministers adopted her methods of pressurising the King. He usually gave way under pressure, but his awareness of his weakness drove him into terrible rages.

George's son, Frederick, became the centre of an opposition group just as his father had been. Leicester House was again the centre of the group and, upon the death of the Prince, his widow continued to court the opposition politicians. From 1742 to 1760 the political scene was dominated by William Pitt, later Earl of Chatham, even though, because George II found him odious, he was for most of the time out of office. Nevertheless, the wars with France in the period were largely inspired by Pitt's belief that trading rights and colonies had to be won in war. When Pitt finally reached office in 1757, Britain achieved a run of military victories unparalleled in her history. At the height of all this glory, the King died whilst on the toilet.

Above left: George II (1683–1760).

Below left: William Pitt the Elder, later Earl of Chatham (1708–78).

PARLIAMENT AND ELECTIONS

THE DIVISION of the Tory party caused by the Glorious Revolution of 1688 resulted in Britain being dominated for much of the first part of the following century by the Whigs. The Tories enjoyed the sympathy of Queen Anne and devoutly wished that they could bring in James II's son (later known as the 'Old Pretender') to succeed her, but his continued adherence to Catholicism was too great a stumbling block for even the most loyal.

The Whigs eschewed the theory of Divine Right, the idea that kings derived their authority directly from God — the principle to which Tory loyalists adhered. They considered that there was a contract between ruler and ruled, as John Locke had suggested. This contract was made null and void if broken by the monarch, who could, as with James II, be removed from power. This idea of a contract was felt to be the basis of their relationship with William and Mary, Queen Anne and later George I.

The Tories were particularly unhappy about the crown being passed on to so distant a set of relations of the Stuarts as the Hanoverians; but although some flirted with the armed attempts to bring in the kings from over the water, they were largely powerless. They wanted to reform Parliament to allow a greater chance of being able to grab power from the Whigs. They suggested that elections be held every year, arguing that this made Parliament more accountable; but what they really intended was to increase their chances of seizing upon occasions when the Whigs were unpopular and coming into government. At the end of the century, these arguments were being used by the Tories' most implacable enemies — the radical reformers.

Parliament was at its most impressive at the beginning of the century. In a period punctuated by the absences of the first two Georges, Parliament was able to increase its prestige. The House of Commons was now the supreme power, but it could not match the sheer majesty of the Upper House. Both Houses were dominated by the landed classes, either directly by the great magnates or through their client gentry chosen for loyalty and usefulness. This was true not only of the county seats, of which there were eighty in the

The Election by William Hogarth. Plate III *Polling.*

House of Commons, but also of the borough seats. Each county sent up two MPs, known as the Knights of the Shires (Durham did not do so as it was a principality, represented in the House of Lords by the Prince Bishops of Durham). Each of the towns granted a representation returned two burgesses.

These seats should have — and indeed did in some cases — represent wider interests than the county seats, and men from the merchant and urban gentry classes were elected by some of these places. Nevertheless, the great and powerful were dominant — the great rebuilders, magnates like the Pelham-Holles, now Dukes of Newcastle, or the Cliffords of Castle Howard.

However, throughout the eighteenth century the wealthy were brought into contact with this unrepresented mass at election time. In front of the 'great unwashed' the candidates had to speak at the hustings. In the contested elections, which were occurring more frequently, the gentry often trembled before the crowds they were obliged to address. They could be subjected to being pelted with fruit (or worse) as well as verbal abuse. For the people it was the only opportunity to register their ideas and to give approval, or not. The successful candidates' ordeal did not end there and then. Polling took place over several days; in Devon it took no less than fifteen days. Methods of polling were varied, but most involved a head-count lavishly interspersed with copious drinking and bribery. Upon victory, the winner could be subjected to 'chairing' — being carried around the town on a chair by drunken, cheering crowds.

THE JACOBITE REBELLIONS

THE PEACE of the new kingdom was disturbed on four occasions by the dispossessed branch of the Stuart family. The old King, James VII of Scotland and II of England, who died in 1701, and his son – also James, and known as the 'Old Pretender' – had little chance of success. The support they wished for from Europe was never forthcoming to the extent they required. In Scotland there was complacency, encouraged by growing wealth, about the imposition of the daughters of James VII and II – firstly Queen Mary II and then Queen Anne – and later of the Hanoverians. Furthermore, the devout Catholicism of the two Jameses prevented them being adopted by either the Presbyterian or Episcopalian Scots.

Nevertheless, in 1708 the exiled Stuarts' interests had become identified with those of Louis XIV of France, who wanted to offset the victories of the Duke of Marlborough in Europe. A fleet of 6,000 men and the Old Pretender set sail from France. Weather came to Anne's aid and the fleet, already hampered by bad navigation, failed to land. The small rising in Scotland was mercilessly crushed.

In 1715 the Earl of Mar, representing a wide range of antagonism to the Act of Union and the Hanoverians, raised the Stuart banner on 6 September. He gathered 12,000 men of High- and Lowland extraction and took control of the east coast of Scotland, around Inverness, and awaited the French. The inland towns remained loyal to George I, and Mar was an unimaginative rebel. He did not risk attacking the government forces under the Earl of Argyll at Stirling until November. The ensuing battle of Sheriffmuir was a draw, but Mar withdrew towards Perth. The attempt to raise England failed when Mackintosh of Borlum was defeated at Preston (12–14 November). By the time the Old Pretender, son of the deposed James VII and II, arrived at Peterhead, all was lost and he and Mar left for France.

An attempt in 1719 was part of the wider European diplomacy of the Spanish. It consisted of a prolonged coastal raid, based on Eilean Donan, in the West Highlands, in an attempt to immobilise Britain, one of

The battle of Culloden.

Austria's potential allies. There was little homegrown support and the Spanish party returned home.

The '45 was a very different affair. It was led personally by the Young Pretender, Prince Charles Edward Stuart, acting as regent in his father's name. He was a dashing figure, backed once more by France as Britain and her trading rival drifted yet again towards war. The original plan for a French landing, led by Marshal Saxe, was wrecked by bad weather but, pawning his jewels, the Prince set off. He landed in July. His considerable charm won over the reluctant chiefs and, on 17 September, he took Edinburgh. Four days later he defeated loyalist forces at Prestonpans. At the end of October came the great gamble: the Scots army invaded England. Skilfully eluding the opposition, Charles Edward Stuart reached Derby. He was within striking distance of London; Welsh support was growing, and the French were victorious on the Continent.

Prince Charles Edward Stuart by Antonio David, c.1729.

However, the Prince's army was weak and, even though there was panic in London, two great armies were closing on him. A retreat began on 6 December. It was well conducted and, once across the border, new recruits were raised. He besieged Stirling and defeated a relief force attempting to reach the town. This was the last success. Instead of escaping into the Highlands, the Prince turned on his pursuers. He did battle with the Duke of Cumberland's forces at Culloden on 16 April 1746. The rash, romantic Highland charge of the Scots was cut down. A thousand men died and the gamble was lost.

A hunted man, the Prince was pushed from pillar to post by embarrassed and worried chieftains. Finally, Charles reached Skye, guided by the reluctant Flora MacDonald. There he slipped away to France and into obscure depravity. When his father died, Charles was not recognised as a king by any European leader.

AGRICULTURE

THE LARGE UNFRANCHISED POPULATION did not always wait for election times to make their views known, particularly when high prices strained their idea of economic fairness. In extreme cases, high grain prices, or the suspicion that grain was being hoarded in times of dearth for export or to force up prices, drove people to direct action. A belief that there should be or even that there was a normally 'fair' economy led rioters to seize grain or bread and to sell it at a hastily created 'market' at the more usual or 'moral' price. The money raised at the sale was then usually given to the legal owner of the stocks. The 1766 edition of the *Annual Register* reports riots at Bath, Malmesbury, Leicester and Gloucester amongst other towns. These riots followed price rises which marked the end of a period of cheap grain from plentiful harvests. In some of these instances, anger and

frustration coupled with desperation resulted in violence, and mills, shops and stores were destroyed.

There was a great distance between food rioter and landed magnate, yet all elements of British society were, in the eighteenth century, contributing to and being affected by massive social change. At the beginning of the century over 70% of the population was involved in and dependent upon agriculture. It was, in short, an agricultural nation. The wealth of the country was derived from the fields, be it the open arable lands of the South or the pastures of the North and high ground. By the end of the century the great mills of the burgeoning new industries produced a large share of the country's wealth. To some, a new wealth, a new dynamism was infectious and profitable. To many others there came only a new clock-worked day and a fixed, if low, income derived from work in large iron-framed, brick-built manufactories. It was not an easy process; indeed it was a difficult birth for this new nation. The numbers of poor rose and communities could not cope. By 1782, groups of parishes had to be banded together to enable them to afford to cater for the increasing poor with out-relief or in workhouses.

All of this change probably began with agriculture itself. There was a revolution here too. The open field system, little changed from its mediaeval origins, could not produce enough food or profit; it hampered crop experimentation and was of little use in animal husbandry. Not all of the land was open. In woodland or pasture areas of the country, like the Yorkshire Pennines or the Sherwood Forest area of Nottinghamshire, fields were enclosed for the purpose of sheep farming or for temporary husbandry of poor soils. Enclosure had been common in the late sixteenth and early seventeenth centuries in order to convert land into pasture, but in the eighteenth century enclosure was carried out for arable use. The majority of enclosure took place after the middle of the century, and some of it was pressed through in the face of opposition by an act of Parliament. The pattern of the country's fields changed dramatically, and the now familiar patchwork system appeared. As the gaps between the field strips disappeared, waste land came into cultivation. Commonland, too, was enclosed in many places and people who dwelt or squatted there were generally driven off. On the other hand, in farming terms, a whole new range of improvements could now be made 'separating dry ground from wet, or draining the latter, liming the rotten parts' (as suggested by Arthur Young in *A Six Weeks Tour through the Southern Counties of England and Wales* 1768).

Accompanying this reform of land usage was a series of improvements in machinery and methods throughout the century. The introduction of the much stronger, metal-bladed ploughs facilitated the ploughing of more difficult soils. A number of agricultural improvers altered attitudes to farming; men like Jethro Tull who invented the seed drill, the horse hoe and advocated neat, well-spaced crops producing stronger plants with higher yields. Charles Townshend introduced the cultivation of new crops such as root vegetables, giving him the nickname 'Turnip Townshend'. Thomas Coke of Holkham spread the notion of 'scientific breeding' of

Mowers by W.H. Pyne.

Ploughing by W.H. Pyne.

sheep, goats and cattle. Although it owed more to experience and judgement of the eye than to science, the idea of selective breeding changed the shape of Britain's farm animals, and wool and meat yields increased.

These improvements were publicised by the Board of Agriculture, founded in 1793, by journals such as *The Annals of Agriculture* and by the interest of gentleman farmers like George III and professional observers like Arthur Young. Young, in particular, spread the idea of the four-year Norfolk rotation, which increased yield by rotating crops – chiefly turnips, barley, clover and wheat – and by using fertilisers to maintain the quality of soils. All of this culminated in more efficient agriculture, producing greater yields and providing the food necessary to sustain a growing population, and one, moreover, that was healthier and more resistant to epidemics.

The population in England and Wales grew from around five million at the beginning of the century to nearly nine million at the end. The principle reason for this was probably good weather, which allowed for high yields. Partly because of this plentiful food, the population was not subject to any major epidemics; cheap food meant that more money was available for new, clean clothes. It also increased fertility and raised the birth rate.

Some people, of course, found new employment in the expanding farms; others were displaced by them, including many small farmers who could not afford the high costs of enclosing lands. These people became day-labourers, or sold their land or, worse, became a pool of unemployed ensuring the continuance of low wages in agriculture. The evils of low wages became yet more evident when Britain went to war with the French Republic in 1793. Prices rose and poverty increased. In Berkshire, Justices of the Peace met at Speenhamland and set a relatively generous poor rate, linking payments to the price of bread. However, because these payments could be used to supplement wages, they often encouraged farmers to pay low wages.

Above: Longleat, Wiltshire: one of Brown's great landscapes which has survived virtually intact. He started his first of four contracts here in 1757.

Opposite: Lancelot 'Capability' Brown by Richard Cosway.

Lancelot 'Capability' Brown (1716–1783)

No artist has wrought so evident an effect upon his country as the small asthmatic Lancelot 'Capability' Brown, who transformed the English landscape. A huge acreage is a monument to his work and an even larger area attributable to his vision of the English pastoral scene.

Brown began work as a gardener's boy, but by twenty-four he was appointed to the famous gardens of Stowe in Buckinghamshire. His next move was to set up in private practice at Hammersmith. Commissions followed swiftly and his illustrious clients multiplied, rivalling each other's conspicuous expenditure on their estates. It was Brown's practice to assess the suitability of these country seats for his landscaping by riding round them with their owners. The acceptable candidates had 'great capabilities' of improvement (this customary phraseology earned Brown his nickname) but others were rejected for their 'want of capabilities'.

The landscapes Brown created for most sites shared instantly recognisable characteristics. Turf swept out from the base of the house, curving and dipping to water in the middle distance and thence to rising, asymmetrical ground, punctuated by clumps of trees and rimmed by perimeter belts of woodland. The beauty was gentle but only obtainable at harsh cost on many estates, for it involved the destruction of the existing walled and avenued gardens with their structured parterres. It was partly on these grounds that Brown was censured.

Blenheim was one such example and remains his most famous and controversial labour. Here he had not only destroyed the existing formal garden, but dammed a little tributary of the River Thames to form two huge lakes, an audacious course of action which involved half-drowning Sir John Vanbrugh's palatial bridge. 'The River Thames will never forgive me for this' was Brown's shame-faced comment. Bowood is another of his creations and perhaps the most beautiful.

The secret of Brown's success and survival is threefold. He transformed rough wilderness into a landscape which was not merely beautiful but also agriculturally useful. Secondly, he used form and ingredients which were native to England – gentle hills, mostly indigenous trees and green sward. Thirdly he worked on an extended time-scale with lasting tools: trees, water and grass rather than evanescent flowers. As a result, the Brownian landscape remains – lush, undulating, green, watered and wooded, a monument to the eighteenth-century notion of beauty.

INDUSTRY

THE NEW FACTORIES, or more properly 'manufactories', were beginning to appear in certain parts of the country by the end of the century. Most of this activity had its origins in domestic industry. It was in the textile sector, dependent upon outworkers in their own homes, where many of the early changes took place. These industries were widespread in areas like the West Riding of Yorkshire, where agriculture was difficult and incapable of generating a livelihood; here domestic industry provided the solution.

Technological advances which spurred on the industrial revolution began in this sphere. By 1733 John Kay's flying shuttle was in use, allowing weavers to manufacture greater quantities of broader cloth. This in turn required a faster spinning process to increase the production of yarn demanded by the weavers. Hargreaves's Spinning Jenny, named after his wife, came in the 1760s at the same time as the wider introduction of larger flying shuttles. Where before one person had spun one thread at a time, the Jenny could spin eight and later sixty threads simultaneously. Richard Arkwright invented a water-powered frame which could make stronger cotton thread suitable for the warp threads around which the weft was woven. Crompton's Mule combined the Jenny and the water frame in 1779. These developments brought with them yet more dramatic changes. The machines needed power, first water and then steam, on a scale that demanded factory buildings. As a result, domestic industries began to decline into the next century.

The growing population increased demand for other large-scale industries. Iron was needed for household goods, for machine parts and frameworks in the new factories. Up until the middle of the century furnaces were limited in size by the need to use brittle charcoal for the smelting process. The fragility of the charcoal meant that only small amounts of iron ore could be placed on top of it during smelting. A new fuel had to be found.

Although Dudley Dudley of Dudley, a sometime Royalist officer, had claimed to have produced coke of a sufficient purity for smelting in the previous century, it was left to the ironwork magnate Abraham Darby to perfect the use of coke in the eighteenth century. Being less brittle, coke could support a greater weight of ore, thereby producing larger amounts of iron in bigger furnaces. With this breakthrough the iron industry began to produce the iron needed for the new age. Innovations improved the quality. In Henry Cort's puddling process, impurities were extracted before the iron had hardened; the iron was run into a puddle and detritus fished out as it floated to the top. This gave the

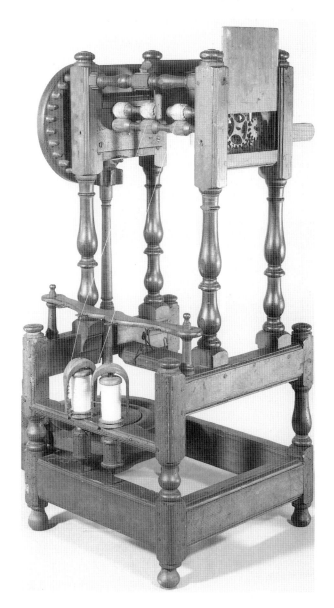

Above: Spinning machine by Richard Arkwright.

Opposite: Richard Arkwright (1732–92).

iron a greater strength, which was necessary for the construction of powerful steam engine boilers and workings, built in increasing numbers at the end of the century.

James Watt was a brilliant Scots engineer who saw the potential of improved steam engines. A primitive engine created by Newcomen at the close of the previous century had been used to drain mines. Such engines were leaky and inefficient in their use of energy. It was Watt who made the necessary adjustments to produce an engine capable of driving machinery and providing Britain's burgeoning industry with the power source it needed. It freed factories from their dependence upon fast-running rivers, from which they had hitherto drawn power through water-wheels. Watt and his partner, Matthew Boulton, opened works at Soho, Birmingham and the steam age had begun.

The Thames from Somerset House with Westminster Bridge and Westminster Abbey, painted by Canaletto c.1750.

Stage Coach by W.H. Pyne.

TRANSPORT

WHILST IT WAS to be the next century before attempts to create a mobile steam-engine succeeded, transport was also changing the face of Britain. Canals were cut in great numbers after the middle of the century by hard-drinking, hard-working gangs of labourers. Living in often appalling conditions, these men dug across Britain, linking the great rivers and the growing industrial

cities. Trade drove the canals on. Ever since the Duke of Bridgewater saw the possibilities for selling his coal more cheaply and, of course, in greater quantities in Manchester if he could only find a less expensive method of transportation than by road, other men saw the advantages of these artificial rivers. Bridgewater employed James Brindley, who built the Bridgewater Canal by 1761. At the end of the century, the Grand Trunk Canal was criss-crossing the Midlands, bringing markets closer and sources of raw materials within easy reach. It was another important factor in the great leap into industrialisation; more goods could be produced yet more cheaply because the cost of delivering raw materials fell as did the cost of delivering finished goods to more markets. Small wagons travelling on badly maintained roads were, by comparison, expensive and inefficient. Tolls were charged on some roads at turnpike gates, established by entrepreneurs who kept a piece

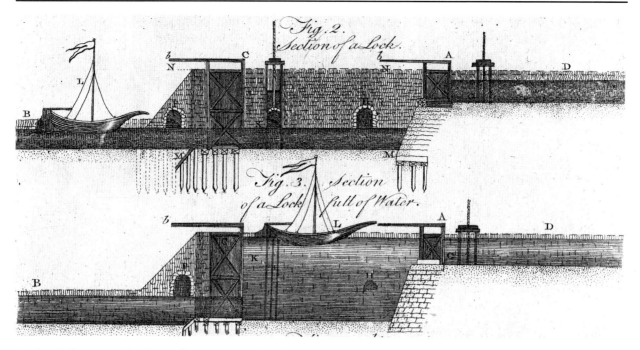

Sectional diagrams of eighteenth-century canal locks.

of road in good condition for their own use and who saw they could make a profit out of it too. Jack Telford ('Blind Jack of Knaresborough') built excellent roads in the eighteenth century, but the canals with the greater speed and carrying capacity of the barges, won the day.

THE AMERICAN WAR OF INDEPENDENCE

Britain was not short of export markets to sell its industrial products to – an empire with colonies in America, the West Indies and extensive commercial interests in India controlled by the East India Company. In all cases, colonial interests provoked international rivalry. The Seven Years' War with France (1756–63) was fought not so much on the European continent as in Canada, India and the West Indies.

The capture of Canada following the spectacular victory of General Wolfe at Quebec, secured the northern frontier of the thirteen colonies of America. These were not the jewel in the colonial crown; they did not bring in vast wealth, but they were a source of tobacco and cotton and a market for finished goods. In some ways they were a liability. It had been costly to defend them from France

and justified a belief in Britain that the cost should be borne by the colonies.

A Stamp Act imposing duties on legal documents, and a Sugar Act were the chief new levies – a fairly light burden compared with the demands made on England, Scotland, Wales and Ireland. Nowhere, with the possible exception of Virginia which had currency problems, should the new taxes have presented a problem. What angered the Americans was the fact that they had been levied without the consent of the colonies; they had not even been consulted.

Networks of clubs and societies spread across the colonies; their call was for 'no taxation without representation'. Boycotts of British products began. In Britain, the House of Commons listened to pleas from the American Benjamin Franklin and the London merchant Capel Hanbury, who argued that Virginia and Maryland did not possess enough cash to pay the new levies. Parliament repealed the Stamp Act but, in a simultaneous Declaratory Act, magisterially claimed the right to tax colonies how and when Parliament felt fit. The Stamp Act had gone but there existed still the principle under which it had been created. As if to emphasise this, Parliament passed new levies collectively known as the Townshend Acts in 1767. In response to these import duties, which drove up the price of goods imported into the

The British Atlantic Empire in the Mid-Eighteenth Century

The British Empire of the mid-eighteenth century was the envy of the world: huge, rich and greater than any dream its early proponents could have envisaged. Even its merchant navy was the largest in the world. Its Atlantic possessions stretched in a curve that ran from Newfoundland, extended down the east coast of North America, across the Caribbean colonies with their precious sugar trade to the west coast of Africa with its gold.

The empire was built by and existed for trade – sugar, rice, tobacco, cotton, fur, fish, slaves, indigo and even ships, for the New Englanders eventually supplied almost half of all British vessels in colonial trade. By 1750 this trade was worth more than £20,000,000 annually.

The thirteen colonies of North America seemed a Utopian Britain, their ranks swollen by successive waves of hopeful, dispossessed Scots and Irish who followed the English. Their population expanded rapidly, growing from 340,000 in 1700 to 1,200,000 in 1760. All this was to be lost to George III by rebellion.

A Mad King and a Fat Prince

'A worse king never left a realm undone.'
Lord Byron

George III, who reigned for sixty years (1760–1820) has borne more than his fair share of odium. The loss of America and the repression of his people during the 1790s under Pitt's government, as it attempted to stop republican ideas spreading from France, have both been levelled at him. He was labelled mad, too. In 1819, Shelley declared him 'old, mad, blind, despised'. He was right on only one count. George III was certainly old; he was probably not mad but likely to have been driven to distraction by porphyria, a disorder of the phorphyrin metabolism which can poison the whole nervous system; and he was not despised but probably pitied, if ever he crept into his subjects' minds in 1819.

It had not always been so as he was very unpopular when young. As soon as he came to the throne in 1760, his desire to end the Seven Years' War flew in the face of the Englishman's desire to crush France, the perennial enemy. It was all to get much worse. The Wilkes affair, when George and his government sought to punish John Wilkes for his attacks on the King in the journal *North Briton*, left George execrated as a tyrant. Further, the loss of America made him appear incompetent. Yet no one was more critical of the King than George himself; in the wake of the American war, he saw his failure clearly and thought of abdication.

His enemies were legion. It was not only the common people who saw George III as a threat to their liberty, such as it was: Parliament thought its own liberties under pressure. In 1780, a parliamentary committee accepted the proposition that the power of the Crown 'has increased, is increasing and ought to be diminished'. George certainly wished to play a full part in the government of Britain and this led him to persist with ministers of his choice — men like Lord Bute, Lord North and latterly Pitt the Younger — against all opposition and often against their own wishes. Even so, George held Parliament to be sovereign and did not intend to diminish its power by his actions; he only wanted to fulfil the role of an active and participatory monarch.

Above all else, George believed in the dignity of the Crown and he embodied this to the full. One has only to look at the portrait of him opposite, which came from Allan Ramsay's studio, to appreciate this. In the end it was this very dignity that saved him from all, except the satirist Gillray and his followers. The dignity of the King was in sharp contrast to the behaviour of his sons; it gave George an air which found favour. His savage bouts of illness brought him pity as he slid into the background of national affairs and the Prince of Wales became regent.

The Prince gathered the Whigs, in opposition for most of George III's reign, about him. The Prince had few of his father's talents; he appreciated architecture, but was not the fine draughtsman that George III was. He dabbled in politics, but was not loyal to his allies like his father — as regent he never placed his men in government. Moreover, he was vain and childish. Given to stamping rages and tears when thwarted, he made demands upon the loyalties and, frequently, the wallets of his friends; often, as in the case of the Earl of Moira, upon those least able to bear the cost. His debts were massive; by 1794 they already totalled £400,000 in an age when a labourer took home about seven shillings a week. His ostentatious lifestyle in the company of his mistress Mrs Fitzherbert, whom he had illegally married, aroused anger at a time when his father was gaining respect.

'Prinny', as he was called, was not politically astute. His ventures into politics were generally a pose struck in keeping with the eldest sons of previous monarchs. Politics to him were essentially personal matters. His friendship with the Whig Charles James Fox was that of a couple of drinking companions as much as anything else. Even his qualities did not meet with public approval or suit public taste. Like Charles I before him, Prince George was an art connoisseur. Just as the earlier monarch faced parsimonious hostility to his collections, the Prince Regent's flaunted tastes were conducted against a background of biting poverty and misery. In an age when reason shone its light on the very morality and need for monarchy, it was simply not acceptable, laudable as it may have been in the long run.

Engraving of the taking of Quebec by British forces, 13 September 1759.

colonies from Britain, boycotts were increased. By 1770 this pressure by the colonies had worked and most of the Townshend duties had been repealed. But a new spirit had been engendered in the colonies, and the idea that economic independence would benefit America was growing.

It was so powerful an underlying force that when Britain sought to unload quantities of surplus East India Company tea upon the colonies, anger erupted. Tea was boycotted and coffee became the drink of true patriots. 342 chests of tea were ceremoniously dumped into Boston harbour in 1774. Britain reacted sharply, closing down the port and sending troops across the Atlantic. Unoccupied lands between the rivers Ohio and Mississippi, to the west of the thirteen colonies, were given over to Quebec. To the colonies, which had been founded largely by religious refugees seeking to build Jerusalem well away from the influences of Rome, it seemed like handing the land over to popery; Quebec was now owned by England but settled by the French. A call went out for a pan-colonial congress.

When the congress met, it had no intention of making a final break with Britain. Indeed, a plan for political union, similar to the union of Scotland and England, was defeated by just one vote. But elsewhere violence was setting the pace. British soldiers attempted to seize prominent colonists and weapons at Concord, Massachusetts, in April 1775. About 100 colonists and 273 soldiers died in ensuing fights. By July it was war. Lord North, the British prime minister, attempted conciliation but it did not come about, and on 4 July 1776 the colonies declared their independence.

The army of the newly declared nation proved itself adept at surviving harsh Virginian winters and appearing fresh, if not in perfect discipline, in the spring. With its allies, France and Spain, both keen to kick an ailing trade rival, this small army defeated the British, often by a process of erosion; pitched battles were generally avoided. The British could not adapt to what often amounted to a guerilla war. American forces trapped the last British force of any size under Lord Cornwallis in Yorktown in October 1781. With his surrender it became clear to the British Parliament that the war must be ended; they acknowledged defeat in 1782.

THE SLAVE TRADE

THE SLAVE TRADE made certain sections of British society very rich, and the wealth of Bristol was largely founded upon it. British ships carried goods to Africa, slaves to America and the West Indies, and raw materials back across the Atlantic to Britain. The trade was not universally approved of and few slaves were actually imported into Britain; such as there were came into the country with their masters from the colonies. During the century the law courts occasionally freed slaves, especially escaped ones who sought sanctuary. The movement against the trade gathered momentum towards the end of the century and achieved Pitt's sanction in the 1790s when he asked William Wilberforce to lead the campaign.

Pitt's motives were probably not entirely altruistic. A ban on the slave trade would severely damage France, the old trade rival. British slavers did an enormous trade with San Domingo, the jewel of France's colonial crown and the envy of all colonial nations. The high mortality rate, due to the climate and savage conditions, coupled with frequent escapes into the mountains, meant that large numbers of slaves were needed every year. If the supply were cut off, the country's economy would collapse. In 1791, the slaves in San Domingo took power into their own hands. The revolt was inspired by the French Revolution, but it went beyond the bounds desired by Paris; under the great Toussaint l'Ouverture, the ex-slaves declared themselves independent. Despite efforts by Napoleon and the capture of Toussaint, the new nation remained independent. Under the name of Haiti, the one-time colony fell under the sway of the United States the following century.

The hard groundwork of the growing anti-slavery movement in Britain was done not by Wilberforce but by men like Olaudah Equiano, who had been a slave himself. Once free, he worked as a merchant seaman, wrote his autobiography and toured the country speaking against slavery. The abolition of the trade came early in the following century, but sadly Equiano had died beforehand.

Above right: William Pitt the Younger (1759–1806).

Below right: William Wilberforce (1759–1833).

INDIA

Art

The century began with the portrait painter Sir Godfrey Kneller, a German by birth who founded the first artistic academy. After his death in 1723, there was an interlude until the art world began to respond to influences from abroad during the reign of George II. Canaletto and Watteau, amongst others, both spent time in Britain. The Dilettante Society, formed in 1733 by veterans of the 'Grand Tour', began to send promising English artists to study abroad. Allan Ramsay went in 1736, Stubbs eight years later. Joshua Reynolds was in Italy for three years from 1749 by courtesy of his friend Keppel. William Hogarth, by contrast, was home-grown, spending no time abroad. A hard drinker, he was very much a man of the people, portraying the seamier side of London in works like 'The Harlot's Progress' (1732).

In 1768, the Royal Academy was founded by George III for the study and exhibition of art. The Academy's first president was the great portrait painter, Sir Joshua Reynolds. Thomas Gainsborough was also a foundation member; his elegant portraits are aristocratic images set against his native countryside. A later member, James Gillray, was a populist, like Hogarth; his caricatures of the royal family sold to a wide public. Joseph Wright of Derby, another portrait painter, is today best known for his studies of light and darkness and scientific experiments.

Scotland produced great artists like Allan Ramsay and Henry Raeburn. Ramsay was painter in ordinary to the King from 1767. His reputation suffered when his school produced a series of royal paintings which Ramsay had not worked on. However, recognition of his talents has restored him to the first rung of portrait painters. Raeburn was an even better painter and a member of the Royal Academy. He remained loyal to his country and stayed in Edinburgh. He was knighted by George IV.

The Hon. Mrs. Graham by Thomas Gainsborough.

GEORGE III THOUGHT that the loss of America was the first stage in the collapse of Britain's burgeoning empire and he feared other colonies would follow suit. India was a great concern. It had taken a lot of effort to secure trading rights and territory in the sub-continent, and the British did not want to lose them.

The East India Company had established a monopoly of trade with India in 1711, which continued until 1733. Exploiting the decline in power of the Indian Moghuls, the company stretched its tentacles further into the country in an effort to out-do the French. In the late 1740s, the French began a campaign to weaken British control of the east coast and captured Madras in 1746. Their attempt to secure the south of India was later prevented by the 'Heaven-born general', Robert Clive. An ex-servant of the East India Company, Clive defeated the French-backed *nawabs* (governors) on the Carnatic Coast in 1752. Four years later, however, Calcutta was captured by French-backed forces and the English inhabitants were crowded into a cellar where many died overnight – the infamous 'black hole of Calcutta'. Clive retook the town in 1757, and by 1760, the year of George III's accession, he had pushed the French out of three north-eastern provinces. Having accepted a *jagir* (income) of £3,000 per annum, he fell under a cloud of bribery accusations upon his return to England. He was only the first to do so. Another Governor-General, Warren Hastings, was prosecuted in the 1790s for seven years by Edmund Burke for supposed corruption. All Hastings' money was spent on his own defence; he was found innocent, but was ruined by the case. He was finally supported by the grant of a large pension from the East India Company.

From the 1760s, the entire relationship with India changed. The East India Company controlled large areas of the country and, by 1786, the demand was made that India come under British governance. The French Revolution and the wars against Napoleon enabled the British to destroy the French presence in the subcontinent and to prepare the way for the Raj.

Captain Cook (1728–79).

The British Empire in Australasia

Although the Falkland Islands were taken over in 1765, it was not until the last quarter of the eighteenth century that the British Empire expanded south of the equator into the Pacific Ocean. The Portuguese, Dutch and Spaniards had been in possession of the Spice Islands and the Philippines for a century and a half or more before the voyages of Captain Cook stimulated British expansion.

James Cook (1728–79) was a naval captain, navigator and explorer who had achieved fame by his work for Wolfe at Quebec, charting the St Lawrence river to the sea. At a later stage he surveyed the Newfoundland coast and was subsequently invited by the Royal Society to study the transit of Venus from the South Seas.

Between 1768 and 1779 Cook made a series of scientific voyages, visiting New Zealand and Tasmania which had been discovered by Tasman in 1642, exploring the eastern coastline of Australia and stopping at many of the islands of the Pacific. On one voyage to the Antarctic Circle in 1773, he proved that the introduction of citrus fruit into his seamen's diet was an effective means of preventing scurvy. He was murdered at the age of fifty in Hawaii.

Within ten years of Cook's death, the Australian continent was claimed as a British possession, only a week before the arrival of French ships which may have intended to make the same claim for France. The British flag was raised officially on Australian soil by Captain Phillip on 18 January 1788. For a long time, Britain's naval pre-eminence was unthreatened in the antipodes and by the time the European wars had ended in 1815, the British had established their position. However, the formation of a New Zealand Company provoked disputes between the British settlers and the Maoris who held the islands: the British Empire exerted its authority and New Zealand was annexed in 1839 by a treaty with the Maoris.

In the 1880s when European expansionism was becoming a threat, the Australasian states became uneasy about the uncertainties of annexation. A partition of spheres was inaugurated by an agreement between Britain and Germany in 1884 which divided between them that half of New Guinea, or Papua, which was not already under the formal sovereignty of the Dutch. After a brief period as a protectorate, Fiji came under the British flag in 1886. In the New Hebrides a sort of condominium was set up between the British and the French. The Sandwich Islands, subsequently known as Hawaii, went to the United States, whilst Tonga sought British protection.

THE SCOTTISH ENLIGHTENMENT

Scotland was at the forefront of the Enlightenment. The philosopher, David Hume, who wrote the first Tory History of Britain, was read throughout Europe, but he was not alone. Hume along with John Home and Alexander Carlyle formed a convivial group in Edinburgh which discussed anything from primitive humans to the creation of constitutional history. Adam Smith, who wrote the study of the economy, *The Wealth of Nations*, also had a chair at Edinburgh, before writing this book which has often been mistakenly used to justify the free market. Smith actually suggested that there was a need for the state to take control of some major institutions.

There were poets too. James Thompson wrote *Rule Britannia*, but others like Jane Elliot and Robert Burns used vernacular language. Burns was a genius who could write poetry with humour, realism and humanity. He remains one of the most celebrated poets of the three nations.

Medicine

In the early eighteenth century the mortality rates of the young were so high that parents were resigned to the death of a large proportion of their children. It is calculated that one in three infants died before the age of five. Even those who survived had a life expectancy of only thirty-five years. Typhus, cholera, dysentery, measles and influenza could all kill, though the worst scourges had already diminished: plague had vanished before the century began (possibly because the rats no longer carried it) and the effect of smallpox moderated after the mass vaccination that took place before the century was finished. As the doctors' confidence grew in their ability to cure rather than simply relieve, clusters of hospitals were founded in the provinces as well as five in London: in 1720, the Westminster; in 1724, Guy's; in 1733, St. George's; in 1740, the London; in 1745, the Middlesex. After these hospitals opened, so lunatic asylums in their old form began to close,

St. Thomas's Hospital, Southwark.

as it was deemed inappropriate and unreasonable to chain up and expose to public gaze their deranged prisoners – Bedlam, for example, closed in 1766. The new asylums tended to be gentler institutions where patients had a limited degree of liberty.

LITERATURE IN THE EIGHTEENTH CENTURY

THE EIGHTEEN-CENTURY NOVEL is generally perceived to be dominated by Jonathan Swift, Daniel Defoe and, later, Samuel Richardson, Henry Fielding and Tobias Smollett. The journey to experience was a common theme. The heroes of Fielding's *Tom Jones*, Smollett's *Humphrey Clinker* and Laurence Sterne's *Tristram Shandy* gain experience of life through a series of lusty adventures. Other novels were episodic, such as Smollett's *History of an Atom* and led to the Victorian comic serial-novels, like *The Pickwick Papers*. The story of a particular woman, such as Richardson's *Pamela* or Defoe's *Moll Flanders*, was also a popular subject – often lampooned in the popular idiom or mirrored in pornographic works like *Fanny Hill* by John Cleland.

Though these novels were written by men, there were two women novelists for every man. They created a diverse literature from a different experience, publishing well over 500 novels before the publication of works by Jane Austen early in the next century. Though often dismissed by male contemporaries, writers like Amelia Opie, Sarah Fielding, Mrs Radcliffe and Mrs Edgeworth were the mothers of the novel.

Alexander Pope was the most influential poet of the early years of the century. His work was mostly satirical, as in 'The Rape of the Lock' which lampooned the tradition of courtly love. In the second half of the century poetry began again to look at rural life, as in Thomas Gray's 'Elegy Written in a Country Churchyard' and Goldsmith's 'The Deserted Village'.

Goldsmith also wrote a comedy *She Stoops to Conquer* (1773), which is still performed, as are plays by Sheridan – *The Rivals* (1775) and *The School for Scandal* (1777).

Though little of his work is read today, the most influential literary figure of the century was undoubtedly Dr Samuel Johnson, one of whose great achievements was a dictionary which tended to stablise educated usage of the language.

9. WORKSHOPS AND WORKHOUSES

THE EARLY NINETEENTH CENTURY

WITHIN A FEW YEARS, the American Revolution acted as an inspiration to France and, in 1789, the French people began to overthrow the oppressions of the absolutist state. Britain still saw herself as the home of democracy, despite the incident with America and the fact that four-fifths of the nation were politically unrepresented. France, it was said, was repeating what the English had done in 1688 and was now using England as a model in its move, initially, towards a constitutional monarchy. But the ideas of the French Revolution exposed British democracy as a sham.

Societies sprang up all over the country, like the London and Sheffield Corresponding Societies, which maintained communications with the French revolutionaries and spread ideas of reform to the common people. Reformers like the dissenting scientist Dr Joseph Priestley and Dr Richard Price were advocating far-reaching changes to the representation of the people.

Even within Parliament, many were arguing for change. Demands for fundamental reform arose partly from a desire to see the power of the Crown and the King's ability to reward supporters diminish. The Whigs, who had been in opposition since 1783, were calling for the abolition of 'rotten boroughs' — parliamentary seats like Old Sarum, the original site of Salisbury, but now farmland — with new seats being created for unrepresented towns like Leeds and Manchester. Outside Parliament there were gentry-based pressure groups such as the Yorkshire Movement, led by Christopher Wyvill, which sought to disfranchise rotten boroughs and give the spare seats to larger counties like Yorkshire.

The Romantic Movement

THE PERIOD of the French Revolution and the other revolts and rebellions in the 1790s inspired two bursts of Romanticism in Britain. William Wordsworth witnessed revolutionary France at first hand:

> Bliss was it in that dawn to be alive,
> But to be young was very heaven.
>
> Prelude II

Wordsworth expressed in his better poems the beauty of a person's relationship with nature, dwelling on the happiness he found in rural or pastoral places like the Lakes where he made his home. Samuel Taylor Coleridge, his near neighbour and friend for many years, was more willing to force his body and mind to the limits of experience and used drugs as a means of doing so on occasion. He dabbled with the notion of creating a commune in England in the 1790s, but disillusioned with France, studied German philosophical writing. He initiated imaginative criticism which developed new concepts of organic form and dramatic psychology. During the first two decades of the century he toured extensively, giving lectures on poetry; in his later audiences sat the younger generation of Romantics: George, Lord Byron, Percy Bysshe Shelley and John Keats.

In their turn they took up the roles left by the older men. Wordsworth's poetical powers declined (yet his popularity grew when he was 'safer' and more acceptable) and he became isolated from the other 'Romantics' after arguing with Coleridge; he was later ridiculed by Byron. Coleridge was dogged by ill-health. The younger men read widely among the works of the European philosophers and poets, Goethe and Schiller; Byron and Shelley travelled extensively in Europe and Keats, with less financial means, walked his own country. Their poetry echoed the liberty they perceived in the French Revolution and the sense of freedom which Wordsworth had once felt. All died young. Keats, racked by tuberculosis, was able to escape nightingale-like and soar above the illness, but by the time Byron and Shelley brought him to the healthier climate of Rome, it was too late and he died there in 1821, the same year as Napoleon. Shelley drowned a year later in a storm which sank his boat. The intellectual courage which lay behind his atheism, and his fearless opposition to oppression are as impressive as the fine lyricism of his writing on

Lake Windermere by William Havell.

the English monarchy. Byron, who began his political career in the Lords by condemning their decision to make framebreaking a capital offence, ended his life in Greece having inspired and financed a part of their struggle against the Turks. He died of fever at Missolonghi in 1824. The Greeks treated him as a hero, the Deans of Westminster and St Paul's as an outcast. He was interred at Hucknall in Nottinghamshire, the town which had once the temerity to paint his statue purple.

Perhaps one of the most abused works of the Romantic period has been the great gothic horror novel and philosophical treatment of creation, *Frankenstein*. It was written by Mary Godwin, the daughter of Mary Wollstonecraft and William Godwin. She began the book when she was only nineteen, as part of a competition between her, Shelley and Byron, and it was published when she was twenty-one. Mary Godwin married Shelley after his wife Harriet committed suicide but Mary did so chiefly to gain custody of his children; they had lived together for some time and marriage was not something this young woman believed in. The life of the two writers was not a fully happy one: several children died in their infancy and Shelley's death dealt her a savage blow. Only one child survived, Percy. Mary published two other novels in her lifetime and wrote a lot of magazine stories, generally on historical themes. The novel *Matilda* was intensely personal and she did not publish it herself. It and many other works were published later.

TIME CHART

1789	The French Revolution
1790	*Reflections on the Revolution in France* by Edmund Burke and *Vindication of the Rights of Man* by Mary Wollstonecraft are published.
1791	*The Rights of Man* by Thomas Paine and *Vindication of the Rights of Woman* by Mary Wollstonecraft published.
1793	Britain at war with France.
1795	Speenhamland system of poor relief is introduced.
1798	Publication of *Essay on Population* by T.R. Malthus. First *Lyrical Ballads* published by Wordsworth and Coleridge.
1801	Union with Ireland.
1802	Peace of Amiens, ending war with France. Despard's Plot. Peel introduces factory legislation.
1803	War with France.
1805	Battle of Trafalgar: French and Spanish fleets are defeated by Nelson.
1806	Continental System begun.
1808–14	Peninsular War.
1811	George, Prince of Wales, is made Regent.
1812–16	Luddite risings.
1815	Battle of Waterloo: Napoleon is defeated. Corn Laws passed.
1817	Pentrich Rebellion.
1819	Peterloo massacre: 11 killed and 400 wounded by troops at reform meeting.
1820	Bonnymuir Rising and Cato Street Plot. Death of George III: accession of George IV.
1829	Catholic Emancipation whereby most Catholic civil rights are granted.
1830	Death of George IV: accession of William IV.
1830–2	Cholera epidemic.
1831	Merthyr Rising.
1832	Reform Act.
1834	Poor Law Amendment Act. Slavery abolished in the British Empire. 'Tolpuddle Martyrs' are transported.
1837	Death of William IV: accession of Victoria.
1839	Chartist Petition presented, Newport and Rebecca riots.
1842	Second Chartist Petition and Plug Riots.
1846	Corn Laws repealed. Tory Party broken.
1848	Final Chartist petition.

On three occasions, the government of William Pitt the Younger, who had been put into office by the King in 1783 at the age of twenty-four, tried to pass reform bills in Parliament, but without success.

As the French Revolution developed, reducing and then destroying the powers of the monarchy, including the monarch himself, attitudes in Britain changed. Edmund Burke, an erstwhile Whig and former advocate of reform, rallied Tories behind him when he published his *Reflections on the Revolution in France*. The extension of democracy could have only one end – anarchy. The increasing violence across the Channel gave him the example he needed and he turned his vitriolic pen on Price and the other reformers. It was a watershed in British thought.

There were, however, other reactions. Mary Wollstonecraft, who had already published work on the inadequate education of girls, went into print attacking Burke's anti-liberalism. Her pamphlet *Vindication of the Rights of Man* defended Richard Price and the principles upon which the French Revolution had been based. Thomas Paine, who had worked with the American revolutionaries, produced in 1791 a 'bestseller', *The Rights of Man*. He savaged Burke's platitudes about the British 'constitution' and challenged him to produce one. Paine was right: there is no constitution for British government, nor was there democracy in the 1790s. Paine contrasted this with the nature of French democracy and how it reached throughout the population. He recalled some of the old Leveller arguments: all people who were subject to a government should participate in the creation of that government. The present system, he declared, was not even consistent in its own terms. Many people who were theoretically eligible to vote were often deprived of the right, expecially in towns without representation but also in places where the vagaries of the borough rules on voting confined the right to small numbers. Paine's book was a success and, as it was cheaply available, was widely read amongst the working-classes in the corresponding societies.

Paine referred consistently to men, although he had, in America, proposed that women should be equal members of society; it was Mary Wollstonecraft who now extended these principles to the other half of society. In 1792,

her book *Vindication of the Rights of Woman* argued that women should no longer be excluded from political life; they had the potential to be equal partners with men. Society dictated otherwise. In marriage they lost all rights to property, in education they were fobbed off with, at most, second best, in politics they had no part. Actually, there were exceptions in the latter sphere. In cases where women, generally widows, held property, there had been cases of women voting in elections; but this was very rare. Also, of course, in Britain and Europe women had been heads of state. The potential was there, Wollstonecraft argued; it was society that was denying women their rights: they were not a weaker sex.

Wollstonecraft like Paine, Price, Priestley and the man she later married, William Godwin, became targets of the state. Britain went to war with France in 1793; the French had executed their King, promised to help European nations to overthrow their monarchies, and started to annex neighbouring states. At home, reformist ideas were ruthlessly repressed. Hired gangs of thugs, 'Church and King mobs', named after their support for George III and the Anglican Church, attacked reform meetings and on one occasion wrecked Priestley's Birmingham laboratory. The government arraigned large numbers of radical men, like Horne Tooke, on charges of treason, but these trials often collapsed as juries refused to find defendants guilty. Instead, on charges of sedition, men were imprisoned or transported. To ensure radicals were silenced, Habeas Corpus was twice suspended, which meant that people could be incarcerated without charge for unspecified periods of time. Ordinary members of society, unattached to radical causes, also suffered. Prices went up during the war and new taxes, introduced so that Pitt could finance the military efforts of France's enemies, bit hard. Windows, dogs and hair-powder were amongst the objects that were taxed, and an income-tax was introduced for the first time. Britain had become involved in a war which, apart from an eleven-month gap in 1802−3, was to last for over twenty years.

Whilst some sections of society knuckled under and radicalism disappeared for a few years, all was not quiet. The 'jolly jack tar', defender of the coasts, was certainly not feeling jolly. Below decks on a wooden ship was horrible, dirty, claustrophobic and

A French print of 1803 with imaginative schemes for the invasion of Britain.

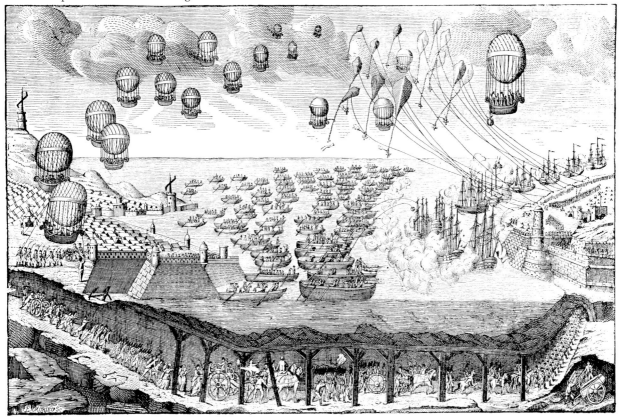

After union with Ireland in 1801 a new flag was chosen combining the crosses of St. George, St. Andrew and St. Patrick.

disease-ridden. It was violent, too; floggings were bestially severe. Pay was low and food vile: the sailors were angry. In 1797 at the naval bases of Spithead and Nore, the sailors rebelled. Although the leaders were hanged, the admiralty had to make concessions on pay and conditions before order could be restored.

In Ireland rebellion broke out. Since the 1780s there had been vocal demands for change. The Anglican Church and its adherents ruled the country, political rights were denied to dissenters and Presbyterians and Catholics were left without voting, property or religious rights. By the 1790s, the United Irishmen brought together these diverse groups and proposed radical changes. French help was sought and several attempts to coordinate a rebellion with a French landing were made. One expedition reached Bantry Bay in 1796 and failed because of the weather; storms drove the fleet, which contained the Protestant free-Irishman, Wolfe Tone, out into the bay and no landing could be made. In 1798 the Irish rose in the North and South, but this was unco-ordinated and by the time the French fleet arrived, it was all over. The Irish were savagely dealt with. In order to secure future Presbyterian support, and to divide the hitherto united religious groups, the full vigour of repression fell chiefly upon the Catholics. In the aftermath of the rebellion, an estimated 30,000 people died in prisons, on the gallows and in sectarian murders.

As the new century approached, Britain was in a state of flux. Ireland was to be absorbed into Britain, as Scotland had been in the early years of the century. The opposition had been left leaderless in the Commons, as Fox and other leading Whigs had abandoned the House in protest against the suspension of Habeas Corpus. Britain was becoming an industrial nation, but poverty was spreading and deepening. Wordsworth wrote that it was bliss to be alive, but for many, the young, the poor, the radicals, Catholics and women, it was a dark time. A romantic age and a new century were approaching, but many of the chief figures were still infants and Britain had to wait.

On 3 February 1803, the conspirator Colonel Despard was executed for 'encompassing the death of the King'. The events that led to his bizarre plot show it to have been both unnecessary and doomed. In 1802 the war with France had come to an end; similarly, the harsh repression which Pitt had displayed against even moderate reformers had also eased. The reformers were now able to preach republicanism without being accused of unpatriotic behaviour. A reform candidate of the Foxite Whigs was elected at Nottingham, openly supported by the Jacobins of the town. In plotting his conspiracy, Despard was reacting to repression which no longer existed.

His plot had been preceded by an earlier one in 1802, when a cache of arms had been discovered in Sheffield. This had resulted in the transportation of William Lee and William Rankesley for administering an illegal oath. Despard, a former colonel and friend of Lord Nelson, had far wilder intentions. His plot had entailed the seizure of the Tower of London and the Bank of England as the preliminaries to the overthrow of the government and the monarchy. Like the earlier plot, his conspiracy was exposed.

Despite the peace which had been rapidly secured by the Treaty of Amiens, reform politics were not driven underground, nor did Pitt repeat the repression of the previous decade. Reformers continued to make strides at elections. In 1807 the seats in the Westminster constituency, which had a large number of artisan voters, were won by two reformers, Sir Francis Burdett and Lord Cochrane, after a campaign using door-to-door canvassing and leafleting. Other radicals were elected in places around the country.

Martello Towers on the south coast, built to defend Britain against Napoleonic invasion. They were later adapted for defence in the Second World War.

WAR WITH FRANCE

THE WAR WITH FRANCE had a drastic effect on the country. At first Britain was chiefly involved through financing the allied powers and protecting the seas and the colonies from French naval forces. In 1804 Napoleon planned an invasion of England's south coast, precipitating the construction of Martello towers around the south and east coasts of England and the south coast of Ireland. Other coastal defence measures were taken and London was also prepared to be ringed by defence works within three days in case of an invasion.

That invasion never came. Instead Napoleon used the massive army stationed at Boulogne against Continental enemies, marching it across country at a rapid rate, defeating the Austrians at Ulm and the combined Russian and Austrian army at Austerlitz before the end of 1805. Despite Nelson's victory at Trafalgar

Napoleon Bonaparte (1769–1821).

Horatio Nelson (1758–1805).

which ruined the French and Spanish fleets, also in 1805, Pitt's hopes for a Europe united against Napoleon crashed around him as the Austrians sued for peace. Within a year he was dead and the Prussians, urged on by Britain, entered the war only to be crushingly defeated within a fortnight. Prussia was occupied and from Berlin Napoleon issued decrees establishing the Continental System which sealed off Britain, cutting all trade with the Europe which was soon, after the defeat of the Russians at Friedland in Poland, under his sway. In an attempt to further isolate the nation of 'shopkeepers', Napoleon attempted to seize Portugal; he also displaced the Spanish monarch and replaced the King with his own brother Joseph. This drew Britain into the conflict and resulted in the long Peninsular War, in which the British were led by Arthur Wellesley, who later became the Duke of Wellington. From 1812, aided by Napoleon's Russian folly and the destruction of the great invasion force, the British and their Spanish and Portugese allies pushed the enemy back towards France. In 1814 as the Continental allies forced their way into northern and eastern France, Wellington crossed the Pyrenees. Napoleon was exiled to Elba but it was only ten months before he was back, raising an army by force of personality alone. This time, defeat by the Prussians and a composite army of Netherlanders and British troops under Wellington at Waterloo, ended his spectacular career and led to his exile on St Helena, where he died in 1821.

The Evening of the Battle of Waterloo by Ernest Crofts.

The middle classes at leisure. A group playing music, sewing and writing c. 1810, by John Harden.

THE 1812 WAR WITH AMERICA

AMERICA REMAINED NEUTRAL during the Napoleonic wars, but to the British such neutrality by their former colonists was tantamount to supporting the French. French ships and English deserters could seek refuge in the United States and American competition in trade could be seen to harm Britain's war effort. Conflict between the two nations was not in the best interests of either country, yet it lasted two and a half years, concluding with the Peace of Ghent in December 1814, which resolved little and did not even put an immediate end to the fighting: the greatest battle, the battle of New Orleans, took place three weeks later on 9 January 1815. There was, however, a lesson for Britain in the war: her former colonies no longer came under British tutelage and were free to formulate their own foreign policy.

INDUSTRIAL UNREST

THE CONTINENTAL SYSTEM (the Napoleonic decrees which tried to cut British trade with Europe) had drastic consequences in Britain. Napoleon's aim of destabilising the government and forcing the formation of a sympathetic administration of Foxite Whigs failed, even when the Prince Regent took over the reins of monarchy. In 1807 the Whigs were succeeded by a Tory government; the Tories were to stay in power for more than twenty years with only the leaders changing, once because of the non-political murder of Spencer Perceval in 1812. Meanwhile, markets contracted as the European countries closed their ports, and access to cheap imports of grain was lost too. In industry, chiefly the textile sector, this forced the millowners to seek out more profitable methods of production and to cut wages.

By 1812, there were three areas where new technology undermined the jobs of the skilled workforce. In Lancashire the powered looms threatened the skilled weavers. In west Yorkshire the mechanical wool croppers trimmed the nap faster though not as accurately as the shears wielded by the skilled men; and in the east Midlands the skilled hose makers were replaced by machines producing sheets of stocking material which could be cut up and sewn to shape. This provoked

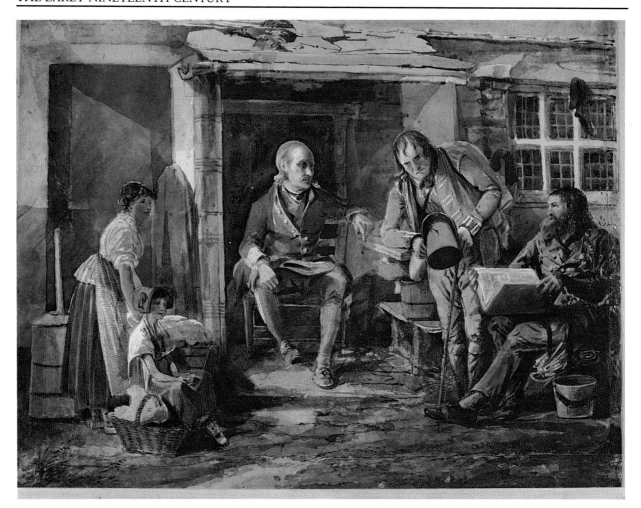

Village Group, Ambleside by John Harden. One of these is clearly an old soldier.

widescale organised attacks on the machines in these areas, lasting sporadically until 1816. The breaking of the machines by men who banded together under the supposed leadership of the mythical Nedd or General Ludd prompted the government to make it a capital offence. The young Lord Byron chose this moment to make his plea for the workers he saw shabbily treated in his native Midlands. In his maiden speech in the Upper House, he told the Lords:

When a proposal is made to emancipate or relieve, you hesitate, you deliberate for years, you temporise and tamper with the minds of men; but a death bill must be passed off hand, without a thought for the consequences.

The Luddites were spurred on by the realisation that their labour was all they had to offer and that their power was limited by their lack of capital. Some also realised that their labour and that of the working class (as they were becoming known) made an essential contribution to the wealth of the nation. Yet there was little in the way of class-consciousness and the Luddites gained only the sympathy of other workers, not material support. Their attempt to halt mechanical progress was in the end a failure, but the organisation and the leadership skills developed in the movement never left the skilled workers again.

In the agricultural sector, the landlords opened to cultivation many of the acres traditionally left waste to off-set the loss of imported corn. When the war ended and the corn flooded in at a cheap price, the landlords were forced into cutting profit margins and some went bankrupt. Agriculture still dominated Parliament and it was not long before aid came to the landowners in the form of the Corn Laws. In order to support farmers against an influx of cheap foreign corn, an Act in 1816 allowed foreign corn to be imported, duty-free, only when English corn reached the price of 80 shillings a quarter. This was later amended to include a scale of tariffs based on the English corn prices which fell in the post-war years. It went against the desires of those

who wanted a system of free trade in Europe and was seen by the unemployed as a means of keeping the price of food high to enrich the farmers.

The land was full of laid-off workers, no longer needed as the wastes fell into disuse. 100,000 soldiers and sailors returned home, no longer needed to fight the French or the Americans once the war begun in 1812 in North America came to an end in 1814. They were not needed at home either for industrial growth was slow and there was no understanding of, let alone provision for, the victims of industrial dislocation. The burden on the Poor Law increased and discontent among the workers grew too. There were to be several explosions ahead.

A GROWING REALM

IN THE WAKE of the Irish rebellion in 1798, moves were rapidly made to incorporate this other Celtic nation fully into the fold of the British Crown and government. This was the final confirmation of Pitt's belief in the weakness of Ireland. He feared that the Irish Parliament might yet have a majority of Catholics and Dissenters, therefore over-throwing the Protestant Ascendancy which the British Rule depended upon. Pitt and the British government simply planned to buy the compliance of the Dublin Parliament. The restricted franchise allowed for a Parliament which had little responsibility to an electorate. For Pitt it was merely a question of giving money, office or promise of office to the 300 members of the Dublin Parliament. It was expensive, but it was achievable. However, the Parliament rejected the proposition and Pitt had to replace the executive with a triumvirate of union supporters and it was promised that union would take place no matter how often it was rejected.

To gain further support, the Irish Parliament was suspended and behind-the-scene deals were conducted with all sectors of the Irish population. The leaders of the majority Catholic population were tempted by the promise of seats in the British Parliament which was to have thirty-two Irish peers. By January 1801 when the Irish Parliament reconvened, the British government had raised forty-eight supporters to the peerage and spent £1,260,000 on buying the support of many members of the Commons. With this support the British saw the Dublin parliament vote itself into oblivion. Instead of it there were to be a hundred Irish members in the House of Commons and the thirty-two peers. The legal system remained separate largely due to the power of the Irish bar and its successful defence against Pitt's encroachment.

George III proved to be a major problem. He refused to allow the Irish Catholics into Parliament. Pitt had promised emancipation,

The Royal Pavilion, Brighton, Sussex: George IV's 'marine pavilion'. It was begun in 1786 as a simple classical design, but was transformed by Humphry Repton and later John Nash into an Indian-style fantasy. It was not finished until 1821.

seats in Parliament and the regulation of the Catholic clergy by the British government; all these would happen as part of the temptations offered to secure Catholic acceptance of the Union. George reckoned that repealing the Test Acts which kept Catholics out of government would break his coronation oath. The King held firm and the emancipation of the Catholics had to be dropped. It was only in 1829 that most of the restrictions placed upon Catholics throughout Britain were ended.

PRESSURE FOR REFORM

THE POST-WAR YEARS were not settled ones. The Tory government of Lord Liverpool, which was formed after the assassination of Spencer Perceval in 1812 and lasted until 1827, was intent upon holding back any pressure for social or political change. The working classes were beginning to stir themselves but it was a slow process and it was the lower middle classes who formed the chief reform pressure-groups, with working-class support in the background. When the workers did become active it was generally under the leadership of the artisans. Such was the case at Spafields, London, on 2 December 1816, when a meeting to support Henry 'Orator' Hunt's attempt to petition the Prince Regent for reforms, turned into a riot. It was spearheaded by the shoemakers and other skilled workers from that area of London.

Similarly, it was a skilled worker from Sutton in Ashfield in Nottinghamshire, Jeremiah Brandreth, who in 1817 was to precipitate the Pentrich Rebellion. Spurred on by the machinations of the Home Secretary, Lord Sidmouth, artisans of south Yorkshire, Nottinghamshire and Derbyshire plotted their part in a great rebellion. They were led on by a government spy named Oliver and told that they were a part of a massive rising; in truth they and a group in the Holmefirth Valley near Huddersfield, were the sole protagonists. In the end, the group at Pentrich in Derbyshire were the only people in the Midlands ready to rise. They set off from the village on 9 June to storm the Butterley iron-works and then proceeded to Nottingham.

There they expected to link up with 100,000 men from the region. Simultaneously they expected London to fall to a similar rising. In the event, they were driven off from the ironworks and were caught by the militia at Eastwood. Brandreth and the other leaders were executed, despite a spirited defence by Denman, who, for his work, is commemorated by a public house in Brandreth's town of Sutton in Ashfield.

The government had succeeded in provoking a rebellion and used it as an excuse to fend off calls for change. Nevertheless, mass

Right: The 'Peterloo Massacre', 16 August 1819.

meetings of well organised and disciplined people continued to meet. In 1819 one of these meetings gathered at St Peter's Field, Manchester to hear Henry 'Orator' Hunt speak on reform. The crowd was attacked by the militia on orders from the magistrates.

There was no police force to carry out the removal of the demonstrators and so the magistrates had to use the armed forces to break up the meeting. There was no excuse for the brutality which resulted in the deaths of eleven men and women and 421 injuries from sword cuts and hooves. Nor was there any

excuse for the Prince Regent's praise for the magistrates; even Lord Liverpool was more circumspect in his reaction. The name Peterloo, ridiculing both the 'bravery' of the troopers and the supposed fruits of the fight for Britain's freedom, was given to the affair.

The government enacted the Six Acts which curbed the ownership of weapons, drilling of demonstrators, the organisation of meetings and the publication of 'seditious' pamphlets. As a result, protest was driven underground and into violence. In 1820 there were two events which revealed this tendency. In

London in February, Arthur Thistlewood led a gang of men into a trap laid by the government. His men planned to attack the Cabinet whilst it dined out. The plotters, based at Cato Street, had the sympathy and perhaps support of the artisans of Westminster, but they were deceived: the very dinner was a sham and when the attack was launched the diners turned out to be soldiers well prepared for the plotters. A strike in Glasgow during early April was concluded with an armed rising similar to the Pentrich one. The Scottish workers set out for the South convinced that they were a part of a wider rebellion. They were confronted at Bonnymuir and defeated in a fight.

The following decade was quiet partly due to the government's suppression of public debate, and Liverpool's government carried on in power, succeeded briefly by George Canning. However, neither of the following two prime ministers, Goderich then Wellington, was successful in stemming the demand for reform, as pressure within the House of Commons was growing and the Tory party could not restrain it for much longer. The pressure came from the wealthier middle classes who demanded the say in power that their contribution to the economy and the government coffers deserved. They were in the driving-seat and the working classes were behind them.

However, it was to be the agricultural workers of the southern counties who opened the decade of reform. Wages in the rural sector were still low and the corn laws still kept food prices high. The depression in agriculture kept many men and women unemployed and with this pool of labour the employers knew they could always dispose of troublesome workers and hire others. In 1830, workers took matters into their own hands and attacked the threshing machines which they saw as a symbol of their unemployment. They destroyed the machines and burned hay-ricks in the South-east. Although their risings, led by the shadowy figure of Captain Swing, were put down speedily, little was done to end the causes of the problem.

Four years later, a union of men was organised in secret as the Friendly Society of Agricultural Labourers at Tolpuddle in Dorset by George Loveless. It was affiliated to the General and National Consolidated Trade Union formed by the Welsh utopian Socialist Robert Owen and, whilst not illegal in itself, the members had sworn illegal oaths. It was on charges of administering these oaths that Loveless and five others were arrested and transported. Almost immediately the men became heroes of their class and the injustice of their case was taken up by middle-class agitators whose protests secured the early return of the men.

Pressure for political reform continued. By 1831 it was no longer a question of whether there was to be reform, but which party would shape it. The main target was the rotten boroughs and their corruption. From these places, seats were to be taken away and given to the rising towns like Leeds and Manchester with their huge and growing populations. After the 1830 election occasioned by the death of George IV, it befell the Whigs under Lord Grey to implement changes in the electoral system with the Reform Bill of 1832.

The Tolpuddle 'martyrs'.

Behind the in-house machinations, large popular demonstrations were held around the country and the fear of rebellion gripped MPs. These mass meetings of the working class were not always peaceful – Nottingham Castle and the Bishop's Palace in Bristol, seats of anti-reform peers, were both attacked by rioters – and there was always the implication that if reform did not come, then more violence would ensue.

Reform did come, but the right to vote was still hedged about with restrictions in all three mainland countries. New boroughs were created, but some small towns still held on to a seat, leaving the great towns still under-represented in the Commons. The electorate in England, Wales and Scotland was increased by numbers drawn from the middle classes in the towns. A government survey estimated that less than one in fifty men from the working class would have a vote: even this was an overestimate. As for women, the Reform Act expressly excluded them by stating that electors were male, whereas before it had not been unknown for women with property to be allowed by the sheriffs to have a vote. The Reform Act became known as the great

Above: 'The Political Drama' – a contemporary cartoon about the 1832 Reform Act. The cartoonist suggests that William IV is more concerned about the effects of partial reform than politicians like Wellington.

Below: New Lanark, Robert Owen's attempt to create a community with decent housing and working conditions.

231

betrayal, as the working-class men and women who had backed the pressure for reform throughout the United Kingdom, realised that they had been left out.

THE POOR LAW

ALMOST STRAIGHTAWAY the new-found power of the middle class was felt and the government began to examine the problem of the Poor Law. The dreadful economic readjustments in the post-war period had resulted in a great increase in the demand on the Poor Law. This strain on the pockets was felt by the middle classes to be unbearable and a Royal Commission reported on the need to tidy up the Poor Law and the collection of adjustments made to it since 1601. Philosophic pressures were brought to bear. At one end of the scale, the Reverend Thomas Malthus had created somewhat of a scare in 1798 that the population was growing and with it the numbers of the poor. He concluded that, without serious checks like plague and famine to keep numbers low, unrestrained population growth would ruin the nation's resources. Utilitarians led by Jeremy Bentham and James Mill believed that everything, in particular government bodies, should be judged by its usefulness and efficiency. To them the Poor Law was a mish-mash in need of change. Simplicity and efficiency coupled with low costs would save the nation money. Such a principle was used in the prison system where new prisons were built as panopticons, like that at Strangeways in Manchester. A central core for wardens was placed in the middle of a set of radial wings, thereby enabling a small number to observe the whole place from the middle of the prison. Some of these prisons still form the core of twentieth-century establishments. Further reductions in prison costs were also made by working the prisoners; they generated power on treadmills or produced goods to be sold outside.

Such principles of efficiency were to be applied to the Poor Law. The people on the Royal Commission who created the legislation – the Poor Law Amendment Act of 1834 – were concerned to cut the numbers

Over London by Rail by Gustave Doré.

of poor receiving relief. Therefore they adopted the principle of making fewer eligible for help. They intended to stop out-relief, the money given to the poor in their own homes, and to insist that relief could be given only in the workhouse. The workhouses were to become grim and forbidding, entailing the separation of children from parents and husbands from wives (this would stop the poor from breeding and therefore becoming the burden Malthus had calculated). Entrants would have to be without possessions: craftsmen would have to sell their tools and thus their method of escape from poverty. Inside, food was cheap but supposedly planned on the lines of a strict scientific diet. Inmates worked, often picking oakum from old rope to make mats.

Some workhouses were reportedly run by sadists, but these were weeded out and, in any case, it was not the individuals in charge who made the whole system evil (some wardens actually attempted to educate and cultivate their inmates). Rather it was founded on wrongheaded principles. There was no understanding of the reasons behind unemployment, which was seen as temporary and often as a sign of laziness. Nor did the system cater well for the old and infirm — they too, at the end of their working lives, were pushed to the grim unions as the parish workhouses were known.

Workhouses barely coped with the reality of the system in the agricultural South, where the designers of the Amendment Act drew up their ideas: in the north of England and industrial Wales, they were utterly incapable of working. These new Bastilles, as they were termed, were attacked by Rebecca Rioters in Wales and riots in the North greeted their appearance at the end of the 1830s when a downswing in the economy resulted in their widespread introduction. Despite this, the Poor Law Amendment Act (Scotland) extended the provisions of the English system into Scotland in 1845. Out-relief was ended and parishes were banded together into unions as they had been in England since the 1780s, with the same results and the same disregard for the poor. The effect was perhaps most passionately expressed by Dickens when he put these words, possibly heard by him whilst working as a journalist in London, into the mouth of Betty Higden in *Our Mutual Friend*:

Pitlessie Fair by Sir David Wilkie. The early nineteenth century was a golden age of Scottish painting. Wilkie was the foremost genre painter.

...Kill me sooner than take me there. Throw this pretty child under the cart-horse's feet and loaded wagon, sooner than take him there. Come to find us all a-dying, and set light to us all where we lie, and let us blaze away with the house into a heap of cinders, sooner than move a corpse of us there.

RAILWAY BOOM

THE IDEA of running a loaded wagon on wooden or metal rails was not new. Mines had employed railways for years before the

eighteenth century. Horses were able to pull heavy wagons more easily if the carts ran on rails, and some enterprising people had even hauled wagons up inclines by using stationary steam engines to draw them. Steam engines that were capable of self-locomotion were known to work – Richard Trevithick had built one early in the century – but up until the 1820s they were still fairly inefficient. One of the earliest operational prototypes was George and Robert Stephenson's 'Loco-motion' which worked on the first commercial line, the Stockton and Darlington, opened in 1826. The real impetus for progress came when the Stephensons

developed a better, more heat-efficient boiler using a number of tubes passing through the water in the boiler, carrying the hot gases from the firebox. This heated the water much faster and produced a reliable source of power. The first engine to carry this was 'The Rocket' which they entered in the Liverpool competition. The competition was to find an engine and engineer to build a commercial railway. In 1829 the Rainhill Trials set the competing engines a series of tasks to perform, carrying various loads set distances with limited amounts of fuel. The Stephensons' Rocket was the winner and the railway contract went to the two Geordie engineers.

Above: The Rocket

The Liverpool line caught the public imagination, leading figures from government presided over its opening and the affair was marred only by the first passenger fatality as George Huskisson, a former President of the Board of Trade, stepped into the way of a passing engine.

Throughout the 1830s lines were built across Britain and helped, due to low costs, to promote the economic boom of the decade. In the following years, as England, Wales and Scotland were linked into a growing network, the railways themselves became the economic miracle. People joined in an investment mania unseen since the South Sea Bubble. This had two main drawbacks: first, like any other bubble, it burst, leaving people broke and lines unbuilt; second, it resulted in the creation of large numbers of small lines which were never profitable. It also meant that many places had several stations, each built by different companies. George Hudson built himself an Empire of Railways centred upon York, to where he dragged all the local lines. He was, however, corrupt and paid dividends out of

Below: The London and Greenwich Railway.

capital invested to maintain his boom. The collapse came in the late forties as the economy swung down again. The government, trying to keep a *laissez-faire* attitude, was forced to step in to regulate the process of line building, partly as a result of Hudson's behaviour. The railway-building spelled the end for canals. Once their monopoly of several routes declined, their problems – limited routes, relative slowness – hampered continuous progress. Some were bought out and deliberately run down by profitable railway companies, but most were simply unable to compete with the cheap, convenient and fashionable way to travel.

Britain was changed by the railways. It was easier to keep a synchronised time throughout the nation for a start. The postal system, helped in 1840 by the Prime Minister Robert Peel's introduction of a one-price stamp system marked by adhesive stamps – the first being the Penny Black – grew beyond all bounds. Large numbers of newspapers, freed from the crippling duties applied to stop seditious papers in the second decade of the century, came into being. It was easier to deliver them nationally using the trains and the debt they owed to railways is marked still in names like *The Daily Express*.

William IV (1765–1837)

VICTORIA REGINA

THE EXCESSES of the Prince Regent, later George IV, were not matched by his brother William, who succeeded him in 1830. William IV had spent much of his life 'messing about in boats'. He served in the Navy and was a friend of Nelson. As George III became incapable of maintaining his mental faculties, William had returned to England to play a closer part in the family. With George IV childless, it befell the royal princes to father an heir. On the face of it, William looked admirable in this respect. His partnership with the actress Mrs Jordan boasted nine children. Under pressure, William set Jordan aside and married Princess Adelaide of Saxe-Meiningen. Despite her role as intended breeding mare, the Princess rose above the standards set by the male members of the royalty and proved intelligent and thoughtful. She also loved William's children born to Mrs Jordan, but

sadly for her the Princess's own two daughters died in infancy.

In 1830 William ascended the throne with some sensitivity. As it was a time of great economic distress, he tried to side-step a coronation on the grounds of its wasteful expense. The monarchists prevented this care from being fully realised, but William recognised that there were social evils to be dealt with and did not hold back the demands for reform. He died in 1837 with no sons and was succeeded by a young woman, daughter of his brother, the Duke of Kent.

Queen Victoria took the throne at the age of eighteen. Although very young, she was serious and capable of running the Privy Council from the start. At first she trusted and depended upon the Whig party of Lord Melbourne. This enabled her to force the issue in 1839 when Peel and the Tories almost formed a government on Melbourne's

Above: Lord Melbourne (1779–1848).

Opposite: Queen Victoria as a young woman. A watercolour sketch by A.E. Chalon.

Below: Prince Albert (1819–61).

resignation. Victoria refused to see her ladies-in-waiting changed, as was customary, to Tory women and refused to let her erstwhile servants go. In the end Peel admitted defeat and Melbourne returned to power for a further year. This was to be one of the last occasions when a British monarch was able to enforce her will about the choice of government.

In 1840 Victoria married Prince Albert of Saxe-Coburg-Gotha. The couple had nine children many of whom were married off throughout Europe, further uniting the monarchies of the Continent in an exclusive but not united club. Victoria was, more than many monarchs, to become a symbol of her nation, but she was to undergo personal tragedies and there would be a loss of public faith in the monarchy before this proved to be true.

In 1841, the Whigs under Melbourne fell from power. This time Peel was more subtle in his approach to Victoria and won the Queen's favour. However, the problem of the Corn Laws was insoluble. Many in the Tory party wanted to abolish the laws and there was a powerful pressure group in the country – the Anti-Corn Law League – dedicated to their extirpation. By 1846 in the face of a dreadful famine in Ireland, Peel too realised that the laws must go and he forced through their repeal in the face of opposition from most of his party. The Tories were split and Peel's career came to an end. The split was great enough to ensure that it was over twenty years before a wholly Tory government was formed again.

CHARTISM

THE 1830S AND 40S were not peaceful times in Britain. Wales had seen violent rioting in Merthyr in May 1831. This was tied in with the agitation for the Reform Bill and opposition to truck shops – ones owned by mill or pit owners and charging high prices for goods purchased with tokens handed out as wages, ensuring that the workers bought goods exclusively from their employers. Real violence extended from the many demonstrations throughout Wales. Under a banner proclaiming 'Reform for Ever' and the Red Flag, the rioters attacked debtors' courts,

Sir Robert Peel (1788–1850).

MPs, equal constituency size and annual parliaments. Women's suffrage was to have been a seventh point but several of the leaders of the movement thought that it would hamper the chances of the rest of the petition. Some Chartist groups kept up the demand for the women's vote and most of the leaders expected it to follow, once the other points had been accepted. There were two strands to Chartism. Moral force was represented by leaders such as William Lovett who believed in the constitutional method of persuading the ruling classes to expand democracy. Physical Force Chartists believed in using violence to achieve ends, and the great leader in the North, Feargus O'Connor, editor of the paper, *The Northern Star*, advocated this until 1847. In Wales the Physical Force Chartist, John Frost, led the risings in Newport before the Commons' rejection of the Charter, and the 1,208,000-signature petition backing it, in June 1839 by 235 to 48.

Disturbances greeted this news in England, causing troops to be sent into the North; Wales again saw conflict as the militia battled against the armed workers of Newport who rose expecting a national rebellion in November 1839. Twenty-four people were killed in the fighting and the ringleaders were transported. Whilst in England there was now a lull during which men and women organised local Chartist societies, dedicated to educating and politicising the working classes, Wales was steeped in yet more violence. In the north of the country men, disguised as women led by a 'woman' Rebecca on horseback, began to attack the symbols of economic exploitation, such as the toll houses on roads and workhouses. The toll houses had been established after the government allowed private companies to maintain roads. In poor areas there were many toll gates to ensure a return on investment and to the Rebecca rioters and the society they represented, this was intolerable. They treated the gates as they would treat those who broke the rules of the community – with a rough ride (in England this was called a Charivari or Skimmington ride). This social justice, roughing up the culprits of bastardy and fornication, was extended to the gates that offended the farming community. The term, Rebecca, was taken from the biblical line 'And they blessed Rebecca, and said unto her, Thou art sister; be

returned distrained goods to their owners and finally, under the leadership of Lewsyn yr Heliwr (Lewis the Hunter), they took on the militia. Within days the south of Wales was in revolt and it took two pitched battles before the English government restored order. Melbourne, at that time Home Secretary, and Lord Grey covered up the true nature of the events in Wales, claiming it was just a riot and dealt with it in that manner. Lewsyn's confederate, Dic Penderyn, was hanged and Lewsyn transported. The great unrest in Wales was channelled during the decade into the Chartist Movement and into the Rebecca riots at the end of the decade.

This second series of troubles developed from the Chartist programme launched in London in 1838. The disappointment and sense of betrayal felt by the working-class supporters of the Reform movement was immense. By 1835 the General Working Mens' Association of London had begun to develop a charter of rights. In 1838 this matured as The Charter, a six-point set of demands for the working class: manhood suffrage, secret ballots, no property qualifications for prospective MPs, salaries for

Chartist procession at Blackfriars Bridge, London, 1848.

thou mother of thousands of millions, and let thy seed possess the gates of those that hate them' (Genesis, chapter 24, verse 60). Rather more than gates were at stake here. As they marched and fought under banners demanding justice and food, the Rebecca men were also influenced by Chartism and their aims spread beyond the destruction of toll booths and workhouse riots. In the end they were met with violence, but the English were not fully effective in putting down the risings and court cases were rarely successful. Eventually, changes in the economic climate and the growing demand for an educated Wales took away the fire.

The violence exhibited by the Chartist groups angered their middle-class supporters and after the first petition they tended to drift into other reform movements, many joining the Anti-Corn-Law League. By 1842 Britain was back in economic slump and the Chartist societies presented their petition again with well over 3,000,000 signatures. Again the Commons threw it out and northern England witnessed many protest riots as the plugs of steam-engine boilers were removed, bringing mills to a standstill. After this failure, the Chartist movement branched out into trying

to build up rural communities of its supporters on plots of land bought by a co-operative and rented out cheaply to followers. This was never a success as the land cost could not be recovered from the low rental income. Meanwhile, the men and women of the movement built up their societies, some joint, some largely single-sex groups – about a fifth of the clubs around the country were women's groups, formed out of working-class women and small traders like Mrs Sweet and Mrs Smith of Nottingham, adept at organising trade boycotts of opponents and fund-raising events. There were also popular women lecturers like Caroline Williams who toured the provinces drumming up support. All of this was channelled into the third presentation of the Charter in 1848, after O'Connor had become Nottingham's M.P. This time there were riots and looting in Glasgow as the petition was again rejected after only 1,975,496 of the 5,700,000 signatures were declared genuine. Chartism broke up after this failure into small, largely unconnected groups. Some of these kept going for years and members of the societies continued their political education and activity into the second half of the century.

10. GREAT EXPECTATIONS

THE LATE NINETEENTH CENTURY

THE GREAT EXHIBITION

IT SEEMED as if all might be possible, and the Great Exhibition of 1851 expressed the confidence of the age. Prince Albert had the original idea of setting up a grand fair showing the produce, art and technological achievements of the world in a purpose-built exhibition centre. However, the chief aim of the exhibition in the Crystal Palace built in Hyde Park was to show the achievements of Britain and her empire. Albert was not wholly popular and the idea had many detractors; nevertheless, Joseph Paxton designed a vast conservatory-like structure for the occasion and in May 1851 Victoria opened the exhibition.

It was a huge success with its exhibition hall full of exotic and beautiful crafts and arts from the fifth of the world under Britain's dominion. There were the latest machines on display, from textile machinery to the standardised screws of the Nasmyth and Whitworth company of Manchester. There was also a harbinger of things yet undreamed of. One of the exhibits from Germany was a massive breach-loading cannon from the Krupps factory. The British people who flocked to the exhibition, the middle classes on the 'five shilling days' and the working classes on chartered trains on 'one shilling days', could feel proud. Britain produced over half the pig-iron in the world, her streets were gas-lit, the population which, including Scotland, had stood at 10,500,000 at the turn of the century was now over 21,000,000 and most of the workers were in industrial work, not agriculture. Britain's overseas trade was of a value greater than that of the nearest rivals, Germany and France, added together. There seemed to be nothing that the people of Britain could not aspire to. Yet the exhibition was an icing. The glories of British workers were praised in the halls of the exhibition, but the working conditions had not materially improved.

THE BEGINNING OF STATE SCHOOLS

THE REFORMERS IN PARLIAMENT had managed by 1845 to exclude women and young children from working on the coal face in coal-mines, but they had not improved the wages of the male miners, who now had the burden of a whole family to support. Factory hours remained long; not all places had seen a reduction to the ten-hour day legislated in 1847. Children still worked and not every employer was as keen to educate the workforce as the utopian socialist, Robert Owen, had been in his factories at New Lanark, although the working classes did continue to seek evening-class teaching as they had done in the Chartist period.

Schooling was not actually compulsory until 1880, but the government of 1830 had begun to finance schools immediately, giving money to the Church of England to establish National Schools and to the dissenting sects to create British Schools. In both cases the

Opposite: The opening of the Great Exhibition by Queen Victoria, 1 May 1851.

TIME CHART

1851	The Great Exhibition. Harriet Taylor publishes *The Enfranchisement of Women*.
1854–6	Crimean War.
1857	Indian Mutiny.
1857–8	Second Opium War opens China to European trade.
1859	Charles Darwin publishes *Origin of the Species*
1861	Death of Prince Albert.
1867	Second Reform Bill.
1868	First Trades Union Congress. Disraeli's first Conservative government.
1868–74	Gladstone's first Liberal government.
1869	Opening of the Suez Canal.
1870	Education Act allows all children to attend elementary schools. Dickens dies.
1872	Scottish Education Act reorganises schools.
1873–80s	Great Depression.
1876	Victoria becomes Empress of India. Massacre of Christians in Turkish Bulgaria leads to anti-Turkish campaign in Britain.
1878	Congress of Berlin reaches agreement on Turkey. Britain gains the island of Cyprus.
1879	Zulu War: British defeat at Isandhlwana, victory at Ulundi.
1880–1	First Anglo-Boer War.
1882	Britain occupies Egypt.
1885	Death of Gordon at Khartoum. Burma is annexed.
1886	First Irish Home Rule Bill introduced by Gladstone's government.
1888	Matchgirl's strike.
1889	Docker's strike.
1890–1903	Booth's study of London poverty published.
1893	Second Irish Home Rule Bill defeated in Lords.
1896	Sudan conquered.
1899	Rowntree's survey begun.
1899–1902	Second Anglo-Boer War.

Isambard Kingdom Brunel (1806–59), the great engineer whose suspension bridges and steamships came to symbolise the industrial achievement of Victorian Britain.

The National and British Schools were largely free of government interference for some time, despite the fact that in 1850 they were costing the state some £200,000 a year and educating only about thirteen per cent of the nation's children. Not until 1870 did all children aquire the right to elementary education, partly to ensure that the larger voting population was capable of making an educated judgement at the ballot. The newly created School Board oversaw access to these schools although attendance was not compulsory until ten years later. After 1880 the limited aims of the three 'Rs' (reading, writing and arithmetic) were extended to a much broader curriculum. The teaching profession was increasingly educated in training colleges and by 1895 there were 53,000 teachers.

Three-fifths of these professionals were women. Nevertheless the education of women lagged far behind that of men. Women were taught subjects that fitted them only for the home. The principles of the Chartist Women who had taught politics were generally swamped by the sex-role modelling of the Victorian system which was to prove remarkably resilient. Even the women teachers were paid less than their fewer male counter-parts. But there were outstanding exceptions; in 1854 the college founded for

government put up half the cost of founding and running a school and the local church or chapel the rest. Literacy had traditionally been high in Britain compared with other countries and the Sunday School movement, established in the 1780s, shares some of the credit for this; by the time of the exhibition there were about 2,500,000 youngsters learning the basics there along with Christian teaching.

women by Charles Kingsley and F.D. Maurice became the Queen's College for Women. One of its pupils was Frances Mary Buss who established the North London Collegiate School for Ladies. In Cheltenham the principal of the Ladies College founded a residential college for women and an associated Hall, St Hilda's at Oxford. It was not until 1871 that a college for women, later Newnham, was inaugurated at Cambridge and a second followed in 1872 – Girton. Oxford later saw the establishment of Lady Margaret Hall and Somerville. London University accepted women in the late 1870s.

In Scotland schoolteachers' status was boosted by an act in 1861 which gave them higher pay, and the system as a whole became a national one in 1872 when the Scottish Education Board was created. In the localities, as in England, the mass of local governing bodies was superseded by School Boards, at least as far as the Presbyterian schools were concerned. The Episcopalian and Catholic schools could still remain outside the system.

The Welsh education system was revealed to be in a dreadful state in the middle of the nineteenth century when the Blue Books, resulting from an inquiry, were published by the government. There was a mixture of old grammar schools in the towns and country schools, taught by retired soldiers with no real experience of education, and a smattering of modern schools in the industrial areas of the South. The English system of British and National Schools was inadequate in Wales, for the dissenting groups who formed the majority in many areas lacked the resources to meet half the cost of a school. The Baptists and others were unwilling to send their children to National Schools where they would receive Anglican teaching and so schooling was informal in such areas. Whilst the Blue Books highlighted the problems, the Anglocentricity within them was overbearing. The Welsh language was stigmatised as a barrier to culture and learning. This 'Treachery of the Blue Books' further asserted that the dissenter women of Wales had loose morals thereby compounding the 'immoral effects' of the language. Yet remedy came from within and not from the overbearing Anglicans behind the reports of 1844. Hugh Owen, a political mover in Westminster who advised Disraeli on the second Reform Bill, pressured the

Lord John Russell (1792–1878).

dissenters into making efforts to use the money offered and establish schools. The Welsh language was upheld as a cultural medium by Lady Llanover who acted as a benefactor to Welsh poetry and music, supporting the Eisteddfodau, poetic and artistic gatherings. These had been established by followers of Iolo Morganwg, the revolutionary Painite at the beginning of the century who had linked the ideals of the French Revolution with a Welsh cultural rebirth. Wales was to progress into the new age on its own terms, at least culturally, despite the crusade of the English.

TOWARDS PARLIAMENTARY REFORM

THE REPEAL OF THE CORN LAWS in 1846 had largely been forced upon the Prime Minister, Peel, when the Irish Famine pressed the need to find cheap food quickly. It had resulted in a split in the Tory Party which the Whigs tried to exploit. The succeeding government was led by Lord John Russell, the architect of the Reform Bill. This government was a coalition of the Whigs and their radical allies and is seen rather as a Liberal

Life at the Seaside (Ramsgate Sands) by William Powell Frith — Victorians relaxing on holiday in 1851.

government instead of the older Whig Party; nevertheless the Whig members were holding the majority of government posts. Until the 1847 election, it was a minority government made possible only by the split in the Tory Party, which had created two implacably opposed camps unable to unite in the face of the Liberals. In the Commons the leader of the Tory Party was considered to be Benjamin Disraeli, yet there was a large anti-Jewish faction in the party which shrank from accepting Disraeli's leadership and the official leader was the Earl of Derby. The Peelite Tories proved impossible for the hard-working Disraeli and Lord Derby to win back, and one in particular drifted to the Liberal Party: William Ewart Gladstone. In the 1850s he devised the Liberal balanced budget,

forging in time a Liberal Party which lasted through into the twentieth century.

Russell proved a difficult man to work under and, increasingly, sections of the party refused to serve under him, whilst he refused to serve under anyone else. When his government failed to hang on to power in 1852, it was succeeded briefly by the Earl of Derby but as he could not gain a firm majority, the Earl of Aberdeen, a Peelite Tory, formed an administration out of the Peelites and the Liberals. This in turn was succeeded by Lord Palmerston's Liberal government in 1855 after the Commons supported Lord Russell's demand for an inquiry into the conduct of the Crimean War which appeared to have been fought badly and at great cost in manpower and money.

Lord Palmerston (1784–1865).

Palmerston succeeded in holding together a party, which still had many disparate elements within it, by maintaining a liberal policy at home, enquiring into the working conditions in factories to keep the support of the radicals and yet continuing an aggressive imperialist policy abroad to prevent uniting the Tories against the Liberals. This, coupled with Gladstone's sound budgeting policy, forged a party which would have long experience of government. On the opposite benches Disraeli and Derby worked hard attempting to win back Peelites and began to build an effective opposition party by the dawn of the 1860s, although the Conservative government of 1858 lasted only a few months. Palmerston's government had fallen over the alleged complicity in the Orsini Plot to assassinate the French Emperor Napoleon III when it was found to have been planned in London.

Palmerston returned in 1859 and continued an aggressive policy towards China, forcing the country to accept more foreign trade and causing the Imperial Summer Palace to be burned down after twenty English people and other foreigners had been killed. Meanwhile, at home, Gladstone continued to try and lessen the burden of income tax, which Peel had introduced in 1842, by increasing some direct taxes. Palmerston died in office in 1865,

the last of the leading Whigs of the nineteenth century except for his successor Lord John Russell. In 1866, Russell's government fell after failing to pass a Reform Bill, whereupon the Conservative Party of Lord Derby took office and committed itself to a new Reform Bill, which was eventually passed in 1867. Soon after, Derby resigned as Prime Minister and was succeeded by Disraeli. The Second Reform Act increased the number of working-class voters and doubled the total electorate by reducing the voting qualifications, but it did not relate constituency populations to the number of seats and working-class voters were rare: it was 1874 before the first working-class MPs, Thomas Burt and Alex MacDonald, sat in the House. Despite an organised campaign, women were still excluded and, out of a population of about 30,000,000, only just over 2,000,000 could vote in what was until 1872 an open ballot. When Disraeli took his party to the country and subjected it to an election hoping to capitalise on his role as a reformer, the new electorate rejected it. William Gladstone and his Liberal Party became the first Reform government.

THE CRIMEA

As the once-great Ottoman Empire declined, the other nations of Europe hung greedily around looking for spoils. When a dispute grew over the maintenance of the Christian sites in the Holy Land, these nations reached the brink of war. France had responsibility for looking after the sites, but neglected it. The Sultan of Turkey, out of necessity, gave the rights to the Russian Orthodox Church. France under its ambitious Emperor, Napoleon III, attempted to reassert its right. The Sultan came to a sensible compromise, only to see the Russians press their claims. The Turks rejected the Russian right to guard all Christian holy sites and, in 1853, Russia invaded the area of the empire which is now Rumania. Although Russia withdrew a year later on the intercession of Austria, war-mongering on the part of France and Lord Palmerston in Britain ensured a conflict. The French and British landed a force in the Crimea to destroy the naval base at Sebastopol.

Despite the bravery of the British and French soldiers, the lack of imagination of their commanders, the determination of the Russians and the awful winter ensured a humiliating war. The major battle of Balaclava (1854), in which the heavy brigade cavalry battered back the Russian attack, is remembered for the disastrous charge of the Light Brigade when too many men who could not question why, were killed because of the incompetence of their supposed betters and leaders. They attacked the wrong guns in the wrong positions and were slaughtered by gunfire. The action is commemorated by, what is sadly, Tennyson's most famous poem. Brave men remembered for a terrible blunder; a great poet remembered for doggerel.

FLORENCE NIGHTINGALE

SEBASTOPOL, the Russian naval port on the Black Sea, was eventually captured, but the war dragged on until 1856 and many soldiers died in the dreadful trenches and in the hospitals. It was the latter which attracted the condemnation of the people at home. Florence Nightingale undertook the task of instilling a professionalism into the nursing of the sick at Scutari Hospital from 1854 onwards. The treatment of the sick and injured was wretched and Nightingale, in the face of opposition from time-serving doctors and inefficient nurses, battled successfully to change it. This fight for better conditions she continued back in England, striving not only for hospital improvements but for the great cause of the age: equal status for women whom she saw as wasted in the Victorian society of the mid-century. Within a few years Elizabeth Garrett was struggling against hostility and ignorance to gain a doctor's qualification. She achieved it in 1865 by a combination of professional experience in England, Scotland and abroad only to be barred from a position because of her sex. She formed her own surgery in Upper Berkeley Street and it became a haven for the women of the area and beyond, who were unable to afford or unwilling to accept male doctors.

THE STATUS OF WOMEN

THE CAMPAIGNS outside Parliament for the Reform Bill and to elect John Stuart Mill, the philosopher son of the Utilitarian James Mill, were marked, like those of the Chartist movement, by the support of womens' societies. Mill had promised to campaign

The charge of the six hundred, Balaclava.

The Governess by Richard Redgrave.

actively for the women's vote to be included in the bill. He was influenced in his aims by the fact that he lived with an active feminist, Harriet Taylor, who had written articles and the pamphlet *The Enfranchisement of Women* at the tail-end of the Chartist period, arguing for an improvement in the status of women. Her daughter, Helen Taylor-Mill, carried on the campaign as did Mill, who incorporated the work of Harriet Taylor in his own book *The Subjection of Women*. The issue of the vote was only one of the topics engaging feminists and their male supporters: in fact, the whole status of women was in question. Men had sought to exclude them from the vote; equally, they had been kept out of underground mine-work through well-intentioned middle-class reformism, though they had not been included in the decision process. Women who were married had few rights over property, which all went to their husbands on marriage and in divorce. Moreover, Victorian children were

deemed to have only one parent, or two bound up in one legal personage: the father. In a divorce the father usually gained custody whatever the circumstances, and women were not allowed to sue for divorce on equal terms with men.

There was a great deal of confusion over the nature of woman. There was essentially a view that women did not work, that they existed to beautify the home and complement the bread-winner. This view of course took no account of the fact that over half the women in the country worked and had always worked. Nor did it allow for the fact that women often had little choice, not only in the working class, where most families could not survive without the income of two working adults, but also in the middle classes where there was always a significant number of women who were unmarried and not part of a family. Poverty was common amongst middle-class women trapped in the uncertainty of governess's posts

or in sweated labour as seamstresses – the only manual labour considered suited to the 'gentle' classes. To women concerned with these matters, the vote was only one issue and attempts were made to organise the women in such trades and later in the unskilled and skilled labour groups as well. By 1896 there were 142,000 women in trade unions, most concentrated in the textile industries. Much of the responsibility for this was due to Emma Patterson's Women's Trade Unions League which struggled hard both to encourage women to join unions and to get unions to accept them.

The groups of women's committees which had supported Mill in 1865 went on to organise pressure for changes to the franchise in 1866, with prominent societies in Edinburgh and Manchester appearing a year later. Throughout the following decade, the women's groups built up support in the Liberal Party, both in and out of Parliament. The Liberal governments after 1868, led by W.E. Gladstone, contained many supporters of women's suffrage and were greeted with hope, but despite the backing of over half the party by 1884, the leading Liberals were not in favour. Indeed, in 1884 over half the House of Commons had pledged its support to suffrage, yet the Liberal government so controlled time for business that no time was found for the debates, though desired by many, including Disraeli and a significant part of the opposition front bench. Largely because of this failure, Lydia Becker and Millicent Garrett-Fawcett, sister of Dr Elizabeth Garrett, strove to keep the ailing movement from political affiliation during the late 1880s. This split the movement for some years. Becker died in 1890 to be succeeded in the leadership by Mrs Fawcett, who managed to oversee the re-unification of the disparate groups in 1895 at the time of the general election, after which a policy was adopted of encouraging those who supported women's suffrage regardless of party.

In the next two years, seventeen major societies became the National Union of Women's Suffrage Societies. The executive comprised chiefly middle- and upper-class women and provided general directions for the movement, ensuring that its chief aim was to gain the vote for women on broadly the same principles as those that extended it to

Women's fashions of 1868.

men, who formed an electorate of around five million after extensions to the franchise in 1884. The regional groups often went their own way, with a large input from the dissenting churches, continuing the long tradition of radical politics. In the Northern England Society for Womens' Suffrage, Eva Gore Booth, the poet, and Esther Roper worked in the 1890s to bring the unionised women of the textile industries into the campaign on the basis that only electoral equality could lead to fair labour regulations. The society as a whole was heavily geared to a patient campaign built upon the tried and trusted methods of fund-raising at functions and the quiet persuasion of the Members of Parliament in an attempt to gain a majority of supporters, despite Gladstone's opposition to the extension of the franchise. It was a policy which soon after the end of the century was questioned by a number of women activists.

The arguments of the feminists had several strands: justice was one; their payment of taxes over which they had no control because of their exclusion from Parliament was another. They also appealed to history, showing that in the past women had proved themselves eminently capable of holding government or administrative office. Naturally Elizabeth I featured prominently in this catalogue, but the

Calcutta in the late nineteenth century.

present Queen proved more problematic. Victoria, whilst happy to support the education of women, was less concerned for the claims for political equality. She suggested that Josephine Butler who, by campaigning against the Contagious Diseases Acts, defended the rights of prostitutes in an age when fallen women were considered as redeemable Magdalenes or vile women who lured men into pleasures of the flesh, should be horse-whipped.

THE WIDOW OF WINDSOR

VICTORIA'S own life went through several changes in the latter half of the century. Her beloved Prince Albert died in 1861 only four years after Victoria succeeded in making him her Prince Consort. Victoria shut herself away, overwhelmed by grief. Albert had not been a popular man and the Queen's sadness and retreat from public life won little sympathy. The Widow of Windsor's popularity declined sharply and the whiff of republicanism could be detected as the people saw less and less return for their taxes, which paid for royal expenditure — the Civil List.

THE INDIAN MUTINY

NEVERTHELESS British progress to even greater heights continued; so did confidence in the empire and the nation's seemingly unique role in the affairs of the world. The empire stretched from Canada to the antipodes, embracing the farmers of the great plains of Canada and the industrialists of the colony in South Africa founded by Cecil Rhodes. The centre of this empire was undoubtedly the sub-continent of India.

India had been incorporated into the British Empire piecemeal as the East India Company steadily increased its powers. The company dealt with the parts of India outside Calcutta, Bombay and Madras as friends or enemies as the need arose, invading those which proved troublesome. In Britain people believed that by such methods the British way of life and Christianity was spread throughout the world. In 1857 a religious issue caused a mutiny in the Bengal army. Cartridges were issued which were greased with cow fat or pig fat, a practice which was offensive to the beliefs of, in the first case, Hindus, and in the second, Muslims. The mutineers marched to Delhi and engaged the support of a descendant of the Mogul

Benjamin Disraeli (1804–81)

Disraeli was the son of a literary man and grandson of a stockbroker who had migrated to England from Italy in 1748. Though a Jew, he had been baptised into the Church at the age of twelve, a fact of subsequent significance for he could not have otherwise entered Parliament until 1858 when professing Jews were first admitted.

He established his reputation as a young novelist before he entered Parliament for Maidstone, Kent, in 1837. Two years later he married a widow, thirteen years older than himself, who brought with her an income of £4,000 a year, possibly of no small interest to Disraeli whose finances, unlike those of the rich Gladstone, were always perilous. His was, however, a most happy marriage and his wife was later to say: 'Dizzy married me for my money, but if he had the chance again, he would marry me for love'.

In 1843 he became leader of the 'Young England' movement. When Peel abandoned the Corn Laws in 1846, Disraeli, as self-appointed advocate of Toryism against the 'Conservative' cabinet, was followed as a champion of Protection, a cause which he was to drop within a few years as Protection was no longer valid in the climate of prosperity. But by the late sixties, his success was ensured when he managed to carry the Reform Bill in 1867, giving the vote to householders. In his own words, this 'dished the Whigs'. When Lord Derby resigned the premiership in 1868, Disraeli succeeded, though only for the remaining ten months until Gladstone's first Liberal administration. However, Disraeli's second administration lasted from 1874–80. In this period he was noted for his vigorous foreign policy. He purchased shares in the Suez Canal for £4,000,000. He empowered Queen Victoria to

assume the title of Empress of India (1876). He attended the Congress of Berlin in 1878 to settle the vexed question of Russian, Bulgarian and Turkish power. This was a (temporary) political triumph, but colonial failures in Afghanistan and South Africa contributed subsequently to his electoral defeat.

By now he had become Earl of Beaconsfield, accepting the peerage that the Queen had offered him. His relationship with Victoria had always been to his advantage. His wit, charm, flattery and humanity had restored her zest for life, and, after his death, she told Granville that Disraeli had been 'one of the kindest, truest and best friends and wisest counsellors she ever had'.

Emperors. It was a protest about the harsh attitudes of the East India Company which developed into a vicious war. The mutineers massacred the British inhabitants of Cawnpore and when the British regained the initiative, they indulged in almost unparalleled brutality, hanging suspects summarily or deliberately executing them in a manner which destroyed their bodies (the suspects were tied to the barrel of a loaded cannon which was then fired); this affected their

afterlife according to Hindu faith. On the other hand, the attitude of the company was deemed unacceptable even to the jingoistic Palmerston who had rejected as squeamish the calls for a halt to the brutality. Henceforth India was to be ruled by a viceroy in the field and given a secretary of state in the British government. The Jewel in the Crown, as India was known, later provided the British Monarch with the imperial title and Victoria became Empress of India in 1876.

THE BRITISH IN AFRICA

IN OTHER PARTS of the globe, British people forged their rough passages through areas uncharted by the white races. The Scot, David Livingstone, fought against slavery in Bechuanaland in his work for the London Missionary Society and went on to explore the Zambezi River, naming the magnificent falls he found there after his Queen. He advanced further in the late 1860s to search for the source of the Nile. After five years of silence from Livingstone the world community demanded news and the *New York Herald* sent Welsh-born Henry Morton Stanley to find him. In 1871 the two met at Ujiji on the eastern shore of Lake Tanganyika. Livingstone refused to return and within two years died from illness. His body was transported back to London where he was buried in Westminster Abbey.

Sir Richard Burton also explored the 'dark continent' with John Hanning Speke in the 1850s. Burton is one of the people who brought cultural benefits to the nation from the colonial possessions, which were too often treated only as sources of raw materials and profit. Burton, in love with oriental civilisation, translated the magnificent *Arabian Nights* into English, enriching the culture of Britain.

In the 1880s Britain became embroiled in Egyptian affairs when Britain and France persuaded the Sultan of Turkey, Egypt's overlord, to replace his Khedive (viceroy) with a man more sympathetic to the European powers; after all, they could argue that the economy of Egypt was controlled by the nations which had built the Suez Canal. This of course did not take into consideration the desires of the Egyptians, and two risings, that of Arabi Pasha in the north of the country and Mohammed Ahmed in the Sudan, attracted much support. The northern rising was put down after Alexandria was bombarded and General Garnet Wolsey defeated the nationalist forces. In the South, the British suggested a quiet withdrawal in the face of the rising led by Ahmed who declared himself the Muslim

Above left: David Livingstone (1813–73).

Below left: General Gordon's Last Stand by George W. Joy.

Omnibus Life in London by William Maw Egley. This was painted in 1859, three years after the formation of the London General Omnibus Company. Omnibuses were a popular means of public transport in Victorian times and Egley's painting shows how effectively conductors could cram the vehicle with both 'inside' and 'outside' passengers.

Messiah — the Mahdi. Unfortunately, the man in charge was General Gordon to whom withdrawal was virtually an anathema. Instead, he hoped to inflict defeat upon the Mahdi. For ten months he was trapped in Khartoum by the Mahdi's forces which stormed the town two days before a relief force arrived to find Gordon and loyal supporters dead. At home he became a hero, defending the empire to the death. In truth he failed either to understand the purpose of his role in Sudan, or he simply disobeyed orders. It was some thirteen years before British forces under Lord Kitchener recaptured the territory won by the nationalists after the battle of Omdurman in 1898.

Charles Darwin (1809–82)

Darwin was born in Shrewsbury, the grandson of Josiah Wedgwood and Erasmus Darwin, the physician and poet. He studied medicine at Edinburgh, then went up to Christ's College, Cambridge, with the intention of entering the Church. His interest in natural history, however, took precedence and it was here that he applied himself seriously to zoology and geology with the encouragement of the botanist, John Henslow. It was the latter who secured for him the position of naturalist on HMS Beagle, which was to sail on a scientific survey in South American waters (1831–6). This expedition was crucial to the young scientist, furnishing him with the detailed knowledge of flora, fauna and geology that he would use for his later theories.

In 1839 Darwin married his cousin, Emma Wedgwood, and from 1842 lived at Downe, Kent, surrounded by his birds, his conservatories and his garden. Within a few years he had published studies on the zoological and geological aspects of his voyage and had won recognition as one of the foremost of contemporary scientists. Private means enabled him to apply himself concentratedly to his work and perpetual poor health did not prevent its continuation.

The gestation of his theories was prolonged, beginning with a few notes in 1842, developing into a mass of detail and culminating in the publication in 1859 of *The Origin of Species by Means of Natural Selection*. The work provoked turbulent controversy and Darwin had to sustain violent attacks on his book but, out of the corpus of scientists who shared his views on evolution, he was to prove the first to be granted wide expert credence for his theory. The noisy response did not interfere with Darwin's productivity and he followed this most famous book with numerous other supplemental treatises, notably *The Descent of Man and Selection in Relation to Sex* (1871) which derived the human race from a hairy relative of the orang-utan, chimpanzee and gorilla.

By the time of Darwin's death, his work had bequeathed a legacy with a rather different dimension in the form of 'social Darwinism'. In the 1880s and 1890s the notion of 'the survival of the fittest' was applied somewhat less to individuals than to nations. Contemporary opinion began to express a widespread feeling that certain 'races' had acquired a superiority over others, an idea that was linked to imperialism. Thus the language of race became a common currency.

IRELAND

THE BRITISH ROLE in Ireland also thrust itself into the political arena in the last quarter of the century. Gladstone made a decision in favour of some measure of home rule for the country and a re-established Parliament in Dublin. He had been urged on by Charles Stuart Parnell who had entered the House of Commons in 1875. In 1877 Parnell had become leader of the home rule party and he headed the Irish contingent in disrupting the business of the Commons by exploiting the inability of the House to interrupt a speaker on his feet. His supporters read passages from the Bible and lost no opportunity to confront the House with the state of Ireland and its exploitation by absentee landlords, over which the Irish people had no control. In Ireland itself, there was a massive campaign to withhold rents – it was called 'boycotting' after Captain Boycott, a man who so angered

William Gladstone (1809–98)

Gladstone was Prime Minister for four Liberal administrations: 1868–74, 1880–5, 1886 and 1892–4.

He was the fourth son of a businessman who had made a fortune as a trader and planter, owning large estates in the West Indies. Gladstone entered Parliament as a Tory, was rapidly singled out by Peel for promotion (he was President of the Board of Trade by the age of 34), but resigned after the repeal of the Corn Laws. As Chancellor of the Exchequer he reduced income-tax and other tariffs and led the newly formed Liberal Party to victory over Disraeli, who was to be his enduring political adversary. Indeed, from 1865 to 1880, British politics consisted of Disraeli versus Gladstone. As a result Gladstone's family, especially his wife, Catherine, was so antagonistic towards Disraeli that a bitter rift developed between the two men, building on the personal differences of parties, outlook and temperament. It was exacerbated by Queen Victoria's evident antipathy towards Gladstone and her appreciation of Disraeli.

In Gladstone's first ministry, his immediate task was to disestablish the Irish Church. He also enacted a Land Act to protect Irish tenants and introduced the secret ballot. His second ministry saw the Reform Act of 1884 and his third and fourth administrations attempted to carry through a Home Rule Bill for Ireland.

As scholar, theologian (this did not prevent him defending the right of atheists to sit in

Parliament), popular orator and statesman, the breadth of his abilities and activities was unrivalled. In age, he was referred to by his followers as the Grand Old Man, though his detractors claimed that G.O.M. stood for God's Only Mistake, or, when the letters were reversed, for 'Murderer of Gordon', a reference to General Gordon's death in 1885 at Khartoum, for which Gladstone was blamed.

his own community that he was alienated from it. Boycotting was backed by the rick-burning of the Moonlighters (the term derived from their nocturnal activities). In 1881 Parnell was arrested for suspected involvement in the rioting, but released after the violence increased. When Lord Frederick Cavendish, Chief Secretary for Ireland and the under-secretary, Thomas Burke, were murdered in Phoenix Park, Dublin, in 1882, revulsion in the government put a brake on the moves towards Home Rule. There was a greater concentration on general reform and the third Reform Bill was passed, again broadening the franchise. The immediate beneficiaries seemed to be the Conservative Party which, under Lord Salisbury, came into power with a minority government in the

reformed elections.

In new elections in 1886, the Irish increased their numbers in Parliament, holding the balance of power and putting Gladstone back in office after Lord Salisbury's minority government of the previous year had fallen. Gladstone embarked on his first Home Rule Bill. He proposed a single-chamber assembly for Dublin. Even though Britain would control foreign affairs, defence and trade, this was more than certain factions could agree to. About a hundred Liberals seceded from the party under the leadership of Joseph Chamberlain. Gladstone took the issue to the country and lost to the Conservatives, who allied with and then absorbed many of the Liberal Unionists within a number of years. The Conservative government under Lord

Lord Salisbury (1830–1903)

The third Marquis of Salisbury, the leader of the Conservatives after Disraeli, was Prime Minister for four administrations (1885–6, 1886–92 and, twice, 1895–1902), longer than anyone else in the second half of the nineteenth century. Although he was universally respected as a steadying force in Europe, Conservative MPs were initially cautious about supporting his leadership. His intellectual distinction was not in question but Disraeli, admittedly an opponent within the Tory party, had called him 'a master of gibes and flouts and jeers' and stated that he was 'not a man who measures his phrases'. Later, 'a salisbury' became the synonym for an outrageous indiscretion.

The rupture with Disraeli had occurred over Lord Salisbury's opposition to his Reform Bill. Salisbury feared the effects of household suffrage and resigned from the Cabinet in 1867.

Some twenty years later Lord Salisbury led the opposition to the Irish Home Rule Bill. Abroad, he was responsible for the administration of Indian affairs, though remembered most for his handling of African concerns, with the Boer War (1899–1902) in his last premiership. His policy of eschewing major foreign alliances was summed up, in his phrase, as 'splendid isolation'.

The last Prime Minister to wear a beard, he was noted for his simple, austere manner of living despite his magnificent family home of Hatfield in Hertfordshire. His nephew, Arthur Balfour, succeeded him as Prime Minister.

Salisbury ruled Ireland with an iron hand, evicting tenants and holding juryless trials. Parnell made political capital of the situation. His standing rose even higher after he was cleared of a false accusation: it was claimed in *The Times* that he had been involved in the murder of Cavendish and Burke in 1882 — and the evidence was shown to be a deliberate forgery. But his affair with Kitty O'Shea scandalised the Irish people and his support split, just as the Liberals had done. Gladstone returned to office in 1892, at the age of eighty-three. He pushed his last Bill for Home Rule through the Commons but failed to get it through the Lords in 1893.

The Murder of Lord Frederick Cavendish

The following extract from the diary of Lucy Cavendish records her learning of the death of her husband. The aunt and uncle to whom she refers are William Gladstone and his wife.

. . . the door opened and Lou came in. No thought of fear struck me at first; I knew she wished for a talk, and I only thought that on her way home from the Admiralty she had looked in so as to find me alone. But as soon as I saw her face, the terror seized me, and I knew something must have happened to my darling. She had the dreadful telegram in her hand — but it said 'dangerously wounded,' and I clung to the hope he wd get over it. She could not tell me, but I felt that she did not say a word of hope.

Then Meriel came in, and then the whole anguish fell upon me. All my blessed joy of many years wrecked in the darkness. In the midst of the black storm a confused feeling came over me that it wd kill Uncle W. who had sent him out in such hope — as indeed a 'son of his right hand.' But then Uncle W. himself came in with Atie. Pussy — I saw his face, pale, sorrow-stricken, but like a prophet's in its look of faith and strength. He came up and almost took me in his arms, and his first words were 'Father, forgive them, for they know not what they do.' Then he said to me, 'Be assured it will not be in vain,' and across all my agony there fell a bright ray of hope, and I saw in a vision Ireland at peace, and my darling's life-blood accepted as a sacrifice for Christ's sake, to help to bring this to pass.

At Bowood, Wiltshire, the styles of two different centuries exist side by side: the nineteenth-century Italianate parterre overlooks the eighteenth-century landscape designed by 'Capability' Brown.

INTERNATIONAL COMPETITION

THE 1880s brought a check to the optimism of the British: Egypt had given the nation a hero, but there had been a major defeat. Moreover, the economy destroyed its great expectations. Britain could not hope to remain the top nation for ever. The United States had expanded during the century in size and wealth. By the 1880s the frontier had all but gone and the whole landmass was united as one nation south of Canada. The vast prairies were opened up to white settlers as the American Indians were moved into often sterile reservations. With huge amounts of British, particularly Scottish, investment, the American railroad system expanded throughout the country uniting the agricultural South and Mid-West with the eastern seaports and thereby Europe. Refrigerated ships were able to bring the carcasses of the cattle trailed and then later railroaded from the South to Britain.

Germany, too, was a major competitor with

Britain after its final unification at the start of the 1870s. Investment in the iron and steel industry allowed for the development of completely new plants which took advantage of the latest production techniques: in Britain these were delayed because of reluctance to rebuild the furnaces to incorporate the innovations. By the end of the century Germany, with her drive to industrialise rapidly and build a fleet to rival the Royal Navy, was a major threat to Britain's place in the world.

The colonies, too, were able to inflict damage on the home industries. Meat and wool were being imported into Britain from Australia and New Zealand. The refrigerated ships plied the seaways via the Suez canal, their steam-powered engines ensuring a constant supply of imported cheap beef and mutton. In the 1880s this competition drove the British farmer to distraction. It was difficult to compete with the cheap meat and grain from America and the colonies, despite great

Queen Victoria (1819–1901)

It was apparent that Queen Victoria, William IV's niece, would become his successor to the throne, only after his legitimate children died in infancy. She had a difficult childhood, for when it was clear what her destiny would be, her mother, the widowed Duchess of Kent, kept her under constant supervision: her daughter was not even allowed to sleep alone.

Victoria was crowned Queen in 1837. She was to reign for 64 years, longer than any other monarch. In the beginning she was greatly sustained by her Prime Minister, Lord Melbourne, a witty, charming and worldly Whig, and between the pair the affectionate feelings of father and daughter flowered. The importance of her personal relationship with all her ministers was to prove a characteristic of her reign, not infrequently tempting her to overlook the demands of constitutional propriety as she favoured one minister above another, or approved or condemned an action.

On 10 February 1840 Victoria married Prince Albert of Saxe-Coburg-Gotha in the Chapel Royal, St. James's Palace. They were to be the paradigm of the devoted husband and wife, making their family nest in their two most personal and informal homes, Osborne House on the Isle of Wight and the tartan-furnished Balmoral in Aberdeenshire, which Victoria preferred to the stricter environment of Buckingham Palace or Windsor. She bore nine children but she found the continual pregnancies 'more like a rabbit or a guinea-pig than anything else'. Her labours were difficult and it was with relief that she received the new-fangled administration of chloroform for her later births.

Marriage emphasised the contraditions in her character, for she was both submissively feminine as well as dominant, traits which developed in response to her role as wife and mother on the one hand, and, on the other, her position as the heart of the Empire. This position was precious to her and her domestic life did not deflect her from her responsibilities as Queen of England. However, her desire to be fully involved and informed about the policies of her governments led to friction with some ministers, notably Lord Palmerston whose foreign policy she abhorred and whose indifference to her wishes she resented. Some years later she was to find William Gladstone not only tiresome but almost as offensive.

1861 began with her mother's death. It ended with her husband's. Victoria was widowed at forty-two. Her grief was desperate and prolonged, her need for seclusion paramount. Public opinion began to turn against her, and on 1 April 1864 *The Times* published an article rebuking the Queen for her failure to participate in the nation's life. Her nervous breakdown remained unremitting and it was not until 1865 that she began gradually to come to terms with her widowhood. Two very different men helped to restore her. One was the sympathetic Disraeli, leader of the Conservatives. The other was her loyal but independent-minded servant, John Brown, who had been one of the royal ghillies in the Highlands. At her doctor's suggestion, he was brought to Windsor. The move inspired public gossip but Victoria was unconcerned.

After 1874 and the fall of Gladstone's ministry, Victoria found in Disraeli a Prime Minister who charmed, entertained and relaxed her. To him she was 'the Faery', though he admitted in private that he found her exhausting. When he made her Empress of India, he was fulfilling her own ambition. Public opinion was less enthusiastic but on 1 May 1876 she was proclaimed Empress with great pomp in Delhi. After John Brown's death in 1883, Victoria took on an Indian as her personal servant.

Colonial failures led to Disraeli's resignation, and the Queen was compelled to face the irritant of the returning Gladstone. She talked of abdication, but was forced to concede. Gladstone's ministry was marked by disagreements with his sovereign. She deplored his foreign policy, she blamed him for the death of General Gordon at Khartoum, she was impatient with his mission to 'pacify Ireland'. Indeed she feared his programme for Home Rule would threaten the Empire with disintegration. She rejoiced in the Bill's rejection which she had tried to secure.

In 1887 she celebrated her Diamond Jubilee though age and exhaustion compelled her to receive guests in her wheel-chair. By now the years of her unpopularity were long over. She had become an institution and enhanced the reputation of the monarchy. In the New Year of 1901 she died and her coffin was laid beside her husband who had died forty years before. Victoria's reign had seen the high point of the British Empire and the country was richer than at any previous era.

Above: Membership card of the International Working Men's Association. It has been signed by Karl Marx.

improvements to farming techniques which equalled the innovations of the previous century. Steam power was applied in the farms; drainage ditches, essential to the opening up of new lands, were dug by steam-powered bores. The fields were being ploughed with two huge steam-engines (often belonging to a company dedicated to the hiring out of such machines) pulling an anti-balance, double-headed plough back and forth across the fields. Threshing-machines were harnessed to steam-engines which either toured farms under their own power or were dragged around by horses. New fertilizers were spread on the land; they were produced by the growing chemicals industry, which was also in competition with German companies. The costs of such investment, preceding the depression caused by the price decline induced by the cheap imports, meant bankruptcy for some farmers and a drastic fall in profits for others. Workers were threatened with unemployment and the free-trade policy of the Liberals and some of the Conservatives looked in tatters as the goods poured in.

Below: The new Houses of Parliament, designed by Sir Charles Barry with Gothic detail by A.W.N. Pugin, were finished in 1860.

The summer smoking-room at Cardiff Castle, richly ornamented with murals, astrological symbols and medieval scenes, a brilliant example of the romantic attitude of the Victorians to history.

TRADE UNIONISM

IN THIS SHATTERING of confidence, the vulnerable worker began to cast about for some greater protection than was offered by the state. As trade became ever more international with major or growing businesses like the toy industry being dominated by foreign producers, the vagaries of the market were increased by factors well out of the control of governments.

The working classes, led by the skilled sector, began to turn to unions in increasing numbers to protect them. There was as yet no attempt to repeat Robert Owen's creation of an all-embracing union on the model of the General National Consolidated Trade Union which had sought to include all labour under its banners; but from 1868 onwards, there was a call for a national umbrella organisation over individual unions. In that year at Manchester, thirty-four union delegates representing 118,000 members met at a Trades Union Congress. In 1871, Gladstone tidied up the trade union laws, allowing them to hold corporate property and to bargain collectively for wages and conditions. Disraeli further ensured that the picketing of companies with disputes could occur peacefully. The successful match-girls' strike of 1888 proved that, with good leadership, even the most exploited could organise and reject their exploitation. In this case the young women employed by Bryant and May, led by the Marxist socialist Annie Besant, took action for better pay and conditions.

A year later a major strike of dockworkers met with success and secured the docker's

Above: Queen Victoria's huge family, many of whom were to marry into other royal families of Europe. This group portrait was painted in 1897 to celebrate her Diamond Jubilee.

Opposite: Charles Dickens (1812–70)

tanner – six pence an hour. Following this, union membership grew from 750,000 to 1,576,000 by 1892 and on to 2,022,000 by the end of the century. The Liberals at first were able to exploit this to their advantage by appearing as the party of the working man. The first Labour MPs sat as a result of this alliance between the Liberals and the trade unions. Yet there was discontent about this situation in the 1880s. In the following decade many workers found their unions fighting in courts against the very men they were expected to support at the polls, as even liberal employers challenged the growing unions.

For the last thirteen years of the century every TUC conference saw this issue debated hotly. Eventually, in 1899, there was an agreement to establish a special conference to increase the number of Labour MPs in the Commons. This created the Labour Representation Committee which, within six years, became an independent Labour Party.

CHARLES DICKENS

THE CENTURY SAW many great novels, often dealing with the social issues of the times. Perhaps the greatest of these were by Charles Dickens, a journalist, novelist, social commentator and a brilliant performer of the climactic episodes of his own novels. Born in 1812 to a family with an impecunious father who provided a model for Mr Micawber in *David Copperfield*, Charles Dickens grew up in penury from the age of ten. Forced to earn his own income as a blacking factory-boy at the age of eleven, he saw the horrors of the exploitation of children at first hand. After this he attended a school run by a sadist who later became, in part, the character of Wackford Squeers in *Nicholas Nickleby*. He then progressed through a couple of solicitors' offices where he grew to hate solicitors and the law, which inspired the Jarndyce versus

Ophelia by John Everett Millais (1829–96). Millais was a founder member of the Pre-Raphaelite Brotherhood in 1848. The group, which took their approach from the Italian masters prior to Raphael, were distinctive for their choice of subject which was often religious, elaborately detailed, and executed in brilliant colour.

Jarndyce case in *Bleak House* (as well as Pip's experiences in *Great Expectations*). Dickens went on to work for several newsheets and papers, gaining by observation knowledge of life he had not experienced.

He used these experiences in the serialised novels which appeared in various papers from the 1830s onwards, including his own *Household Words*. From then on Dickens was enormously productive, gradually destroying his health. He seemed to have a fear of poverty unrelated to the increasing wealth which the novels brought him. Through his work he opened the eyes of mid-century Victorians to the horrors that lay hidden below the surface of British success. Undoubtedly his writings spurred on the creation of the many charities for the relief of the needy which existed in the middle of the century. He was not beyond direct action either; with Angela Burdett-Coutts he established safe houses for London prostitutes who wished to escape the streets.

WOMEN NOVELISTS

DICKENS had not been the only writer to examine critically the state of the nation during the middle years of the century. Mrs Gaskell had done no less in her novels, and in *North and South* she revealed a sympathy with the industrial worker which Dickens sometimes found difficult to do. George Eliot (the pen name of Mary Ann Evans) also concerned herself with issues of class and, more particularly, explored the social and acceptable roles given to men and women, depicting the frequently boring nature of the expected female role, a subject which the three Brontë sisters had examined in their work too. All these novelists together with another writer, Mrs Oliphant, created female characters who challenged the passionless and inert role thrust upon women – characters like Emily Brontë's impassioned Catherine in *Wuthering Heights* or Mrs Oliphant's determined and shrewd heroine in *Miss Marjoriebanks*.

Daisy, one of the first three textile prints designed by Morris.

William Morris (1834–96)

The goals of socialism were cherished not only by the working classes. Other people found the idea of an equitable distribution of the national wealth an attractive idea. William Morris, the artist, craftsman and philosopher, turned in the 1880s to political activity. He was a man of genius, founding with Edward Burne-Jones and others from the Pre-Raphaelite Brotherhood a company dedicated to the production of beautiful textiles, wallpapers and furnishings to combat the world of tawdry mass-production. The workshops of the company, in which talented men and women worked, seemed to evoke a world that had long disappeared, a world of the skilled craft worker; yet as Morris was aware, the distribution of income in the favour of the owners of capital goods and the means of production, resulted in the fact that the work of the company was not affordable to the 'craft worker', but only to the well-off.

In the 1880s much of Morris's energy went into the Social Democratic Federation to which he gave a socialist direction. In 1884, when the federation split, he led a faction which formed the Revolutionary Socialist League. As each person had to dedicate his abilities to socialism, Morris donated his artistic and poetic talent, writing prose and poetry for the cause. The poem, *A Dream of John Ball*, linked the nineteenth-century workers with the peasants of the fourteenth century in the struggle against the ruling classes. Morris was not alone in placing his art at the service of the 'people'. Walter Crane produced some of the greatest images of the Victorian period, celebrating the glory of toil in a romantic manner, which gave it a dignity beyond that usually accorded to the working women and men of the country.

STUDIES OF POVERTY

Neither Dickens's nor Gaskell's illustrations nor even Henry Mayhew's graphic accounts of London life communicated the scale of the problem facing Britain from within. In the 1850s Mayhew had shown the depths to which sections of society had sunk, supplementing the picture of the north of the country revealed by Friedrich Engels's study of the working class in the 1840s. The ignorance about the poverty in Britain was likened by Mayhew to the lack of knowledge

of a most unusual African tribe, and it was not until the 1880s that poverty was fully revealed. Many believed it to concern a submerged tenth of the people, and thought the problem often self-induced and at variance with the true state of the country, even if Henry George had shown in *Progress and Poverty* that both aspects of society were linked. Moreover, a tenth was surely a proportion which charity could cope with, even if the Charity Organisation Society showed almost total confusion. William Booth continued Mayhew's earlier assertion by comparing the destitution with Africa in *In Darkest England* and *The Way Out*. He suggested agricultural re-training – the sending of the unemployed back into the countryside – and emigration. Still no statistical support was available to reveal the extent of the problem.

In 1886 and 1887 Charles Booth, a Liverpool merchant, began studies of Tower Hamlet and Hackney. Over the next ten years the work was published as *Life and Labour of the People in London*. It showed that there were actually thirty per cent of the population in a state of poverty. The main causes were old age and the attendant inability to work and, amongst the able-bodied, casual work and earnings. Not everybody believed that Booth's statistics were founded on a sound basis or that they were true of places outside London. At the very end of the century Seebohm Rowntree of the Quaker chocolate manufacturer family began work in York with a clearer notion of poverty than Booth had begun with. He defined primary poverty as a state in which people could not afford the basics of food and rent, and secondary poverty to mean that these could be afforded but no saving could be made against future unemployment. 28% of the 46,754 people Rowntree surveyed lived in families in either primary or secondary poverty. All of this formed a sobering backdrop to Victoria Regina Imperatrix's Diamond Jubilee in 1897, and one which Lord Salisbury's third government, formed once again of Conservatives and Liberal Unionists, had to address with housing legislation. It was a start on a road which led into widespread welfare legislation. More than just the century was set to end.

The pomp of Empire – Indian durbar in 1903.

269

11. THE
DELUGE

THE EARLY TWENTIETH CENTURY

WARS IN SOUTH AFRICA

WHILST SEEBOHM ROWNTREE continued to publish his results, there was more startling evidence of the poor state of the nation's people. A third of the soldiers volunteering for the war in South Africa were proven to be unfit for military service due to the poor state of their health. The question of the state of the poor began to develop imperial overtones. It seemed as if the greatest empire on earth could not depend for its defence on its own people. The wars in South Africa were embarrassing for further reasons. In the first place, the British defence of the Dutch Boers against the Zulus of King Cetawayo in 1879 had not been a total success: the Zulu forces had proved superior at Isandhlwana before they were defeated at Ulundi in their attempt to fend off the incursions of the whites. A year later the British forces were humiliated in their attempts to defeat the nationalism of the Boers in the Transvaal, following which Paul Kruger had established an authoritarian regime.

The British then attempted to support an uprising in 1895 of the latecomers to the Transvaal, people searching for the gold around Johannesburg and called 'Uitlanders' by the settlers. This was an attempt to destabilise the Transvaal to enable Cecil Rhodes to build his railway from the Cape to Cairo, as well as a desire to settle old scores. Only a small rising took place when an adventurer, Dr Leander Jameson, launched an

The Defence of Rorke's Drift by Lady Butler (detail). This action, which took place the day after the battle of Isandhlwana, halted the Zulu advance.

TIME CHART

1901	Queen Victoria dies; accession of Edward VII.
1902	Boer War ends. Balfour's Education Act. Anglo-Japanese alliance formed to gain naval security in the Indian Ocean and Pacific.
1903	Women's Social and Political Union formed.
1906	Liberal Government begins welfare reforms.
1908	Asquith's Liberal government introduces its Old Age Pension plans.
1909	Lloyd George's budget rejected by the Lords.
1910	Edward VII dies: George V becomes King.
1911	Parliament Act establishes five-yearly elections.
1912–14	Third Home Rule Act (for Ireland).
1914–18	The First World War.
1916	Battle of the Somme.
1917	Battle of Passchendaele.
1918	11 November, end of the War. Lloyd George coalition government elected.
1919	Peace in Europe secured by the Treaty of Versailles.
1922	Conservatives break up coalition government.
1924	First Labour government.
1925	Britain goes back on the gold standard.
1926	General Strike.
1929	Wall Street Crash precipitates Depression. Second Labour Government, led by Ramsay MacDonald.
1931	Financial crisis and run on the pound. Britain abandons gold standard. Ramsay MacDonald resigns and returns to head coalition National government.
1936	Death of King George V. Abdication of King Edward VIII. George VI becomes King.
1938	Munich Crisis.
1939	The British guarantee to defend Poland.
1939–45	The Second World War. British Empire declares war on 3 September 1939.
1940	Churchill succeeds Neville Chamberlain as prime minister. Battle of Britain.
1941	British cities blitzed by the *Luftwaffe*. Soviet Union and the United States enter the war.
1942	Singapore lost. Montgomery victorious at El Alamein.
1944	D-day invasion of Europe.
1945	8 May, war ends in Europe. 15 August, war ends in Far East.

A Boer trench.

attack on the Transvaal at the end of the year. The defeat of Jameson's raid left Kruger more powerful. Rhodes's reputation was damaged by his links with the raid and he resigned as governor of the Cape Colony. However, British ambitions in the region were not satisfied and in 1899 Britain went to war with the Free State and the Transvaal. It was a poorly handled war: the Cape Province was invaded, the major cities of Ladysmith, Kimberley and Mafeking came under siege and the army was defeated by the end of the year.

In the new century the garrisons of Ladysmith and Kimberley were quickly relieved but Colonel Baden-Powell, who was under siege in Mafeking, had to wait until mid-May. His rescue proved an occasion of rejoicing despite the paucity of much to celebrate. The war dragged on for two years,

Edward VII (1841–1910).

the Boers inventing commandos, small effective guerilla groups. Lord Kitchener's response was to herd large numbers of the Boer civilian population into wired prison camps, where they were starved of decent food supplies and medical attention. A fifth of the settlers in these 'concentration camps' died. Twenty thousand people were the victims of a deadly portentous experiment. In Britain there was outrage. "When is a war not a war," asked Sir Henry Campbell-Bannerman who had succeeded Lord Rosebery as the Liberal leader: "when it is carried on by methods of barbarism in South Africa."

In the midst of these body-shocks, the old Queen died on 22 January 1901, having outlived the glorious years of her reign and seen the dark days of the future loom. She had outlasted all the other monarchs of the British

nations, witnessed the population of her home-nation double since her accession, watched her empire grow to cover a fifth of the world landmass, and yet also seen it challenged and defeated by the anger of those it trod upon and the jealousy of others who saw it as an asset to be emulated. Her fifty-nine year old son Edward VII refused to be crowned until the war in the Cape was over. His pressure and the new government of Arthur Balfour's Conservatives and Liberal Unionists brought the shoddy and unsuccessful war to an end in 1902. The government of Britain recognised the independence of the South African states and provided for £300,000 compensation for the destruction and depredations caused by the army of Lord Kitchener.

WELFARE REFORMS

THE PHYSICAL DETERIORATION REPORT of 1904 which examined the recruits for the Boer War linked poor diet to the condition of the

The Edwardian Era

Nearly 30 per cent of the population lived in relative poverty, but for the middle and upper classes life in Edward VII's reign could be easy and affluent.

Above: A Tennis Party at Hendon, by H.G. Stormont.

Left: Hestercombe House, Somerset, a magnificent example of a country house garden created by the architect Sir Edwin Lutyens and the garden designer Gertrude Jekyll.

potential soldiers. Suggestions were made that some attempts to provide children with at least one full balanced meal during the day could be made within the school system. Schools could also provide physical examinations now that school attendance was compulsory. The Liberal government of 1906 led by Campbell-Bannerman attempted to take up the challenge and enacted the free school meals bill. They also added to the Education Bill the Physical Examinations Bill, which had been introduced by Labour members of the Lib-Lab alliance. It was a period of great welfare reform and the

foundation for the modern welfare state. It is usually credited entirely to the reforming Liberal government, though it was the Labour members who impelled the government of Bannerman and then Asquith, who took over the party on Bannerman's death, to take measures like the Workmen's Compensation Act and the Trade Disputes Bill.

There was to be one great battle for perhaps the most basic of requirements — pensions for those too old to work. Many commentators before and including Booth and Rowntree singled out old age as one of the great causes of

poverty. Pensions had been suggested in the last decade of the previous century, but there had been little action. The qualifications for the pension (whether the recipient should have contributed to it during his or her working life or not) was a major area of dispute. Booth was against contributions, but successive government reports backed some form of contribution to offset the costs. The bill of 1908, a scheme which was drawn up by Asquith before he became Prime Minister – though it was seen through by the 'Welsh Wizard', Lloyd George – tried to meet this challenge. Only people over seventy got a pension, on condition that they had not been in prison within the previous two years nor in receipt of twenty-eight pounds a year. The rate was five shillings (25p) a week for a single person and seven shillings and sixpence (37.5p) for a couple. No contribution was due. Some members of the House of Lords thought it would reduce self-reliance and wanted the enrolments of new pensioners to stop in 1915. Restrictions in England meant that only about 44 per cent of those over seventy took up their pensions. In Scotland, 55 per cent collected. In Ireland, where there were no records for many parishes, many turned up claiming to have been born in the year of the 'great wind' which was coincidentally 1838 – that is, seventy years earlier, and the take-up rate was 98 per cent.

Insurance for the most vulnerable workers was brought in too. Lloyd George and the ex-Conservative, Winston Churchill, introduced insurance for shipbuilders and others in answer to socialist calls for complete insurance schemes and to accommodate the Royal Commission report of 1909, which had criticised the Poor Law and wanted to overhaul the system thoroughly. The minority report, written largely by Beatrice, wife of Sidney Webb, the Fabian or philanthropic Socialists, had wanted complete insurance for all the workforce, administered by the government and charities through a Public Assistance board and a Ministry of Labour. Churchill met this some way by creating a system of Labour Exchanges which were designed to ease the problems of unemployment by providing a method of matching the needs of local industries with the availability of the local unemployed.

The accompanying National Insurance Bill

Above: Herbert Asquith (1852–1928).

Below: Keir Hardie (1856–1915), the first socialist to be elected to parliament in 1892. He founded the Independent Labour Party in 1893 and led the Labour Party in the House of Commons.

progressed through the House of Commons. It was a limited, compulsory arrangement for those industries that suffered from the vagaries of trade cycles. It was a contributory scheme in which the employer paid 4d (2.8p) per week, the employee 3d (2.1p) and the government 2d (1.4p). No-one in seasonal work or condemned to casual work and no women at all were eligible for the scheme. Though limited in its provisions, it took the fire from the socialist parties – it went only a little way down the path that the Labour Party wanted and yet they could hardly be seen to oppose the bill. Not so with the Lords: they objected and held the bill up. It was part of a struggle with the Commons. The Lords contained a majority of Conservative supporters and was used by the party at times, after Lord Salisbury suggested that the Upper House possessed an instinct for the good of the nation, to block Liberal bills when it was powerless to stop Liberal legislation in the Commons. The Insurance Bill went well beyond the limits that the Conservatives were prepared to accept; so did the 1909 Budget and they rejected both, prompting a constitutional struggle which saw

the Liberal Government put itself before the electorate twice in 1910. On both occasions it was victorious, although its majority fell. This and the threat of creating a large number of new peers to force the bills through the Lords, put enough pressure on the Upper House to ensure its compliance.

EUROPEAN ALLIANCES

LLOYD GEORGE'S BUDGET of 1909 increased various taxes – tobacco and spirit duties as well as death duties and Public House licences. Income tax went up by 2d (1.4p) in the pound and a super-tax was imposed on high incomes. It raised government income by 12 per cent. Much of the burden fell upon the wealthier classes and this was what the Lords had baulked at. The added income was to pay not only for the welfare reforms but also for the construction of new battleships – the massive iron ships known as Dreadnoughts. There was an arms race in progress between the German nation and the British Empire. Britain had set

H.M.S. Dreadnought, 1907.

a model for others to follow and the Germans wanted a 'place in the sun' with sources of cheap raw materials to feed growing industries. To protect the empire that Kaiser Wilhelm II was amassing, he demanded a fleet comparable to that of his English cousin, Edward VII. The British did not want such competition and objected to the number of ships Germany was building; the Kaiser replied that he had a lot of catching up to do. There was a growing state of tension in Europe and the world that the Europeans dominated.

The European nations were divided into two camps. The Triple Alliance or Central Powers consisted of Germany, the Austro-Hungarian Empire of Franz Josef and Italy. The Triple Entente involved Britain, France and Russia. Each alliance committed its members to mutual defence. This presaged a great catastrophe. The Agadir Crisis in 1911 had revealed the potential for all the states to be dragged to war over a conflict between two of the opposed nations. Germany had attempted to seize parts of France's African possessions and the alliances stood by the antagonists. Luckily a negotiated peace ended the problem.

The Wars in the Balkans in 1912 and 1913 showed that the great empires had other internal difficulties – nationalism. The Balkan state of Serbia expanded into the neighbouring areas, encouraging the Serbian peoples of the Austrian Empire. With the Russian Tsar, Nicholas II, supporting the Serbs of whom he claimed to be 'father', the situation promised only trouble for the future, as a conflict between Austria and Russia could not fail to embroil the other nations of Europe because of the inevitable involvement of their allies.

THE SUFFRAGETTES

WITHIN BRITAIN the struggle to achieve equality for women intensified. Although women had managed to gain a higher social status – property rights in marriage had been granted, women were allowed to sit on school boards and on local councils – they were still excluded from the vote in general elections and from seats in

Mrs. Pankhurst on a suffragette march.

Parliament. The National Union of Women's Suffrage Societies (the NUWSS) continued its campaign of lobbying the members of Parliament and on five occasions there had been successful first votes on the issue in the Commons, but each had been talked out later or refused extra time to proceed. The Liberals who had seemed the best hope were not keen; Campbell-Bannerman urged patience and Asquith was out of sympathy. In 1903 Emmeline Pankhurst led a break-away group in Manchester which became the Womens Social and Political Union. This group was at first mainly associated with the working classes, growing in a region where the unionisation of women textile workers had met with success. The WSPU was also linked to the independent Labour Party and Mrs Pankhurst's husband was a member of this group, which eschewed connections with the Liberals.

In 1907 when a massive rally at Hyde Park, held in atrocious weather conditions, was dismissed as unimportant by Asquith, the WSPU began an escalating campaign of disruption. Political candidates who opposed the suffrage movement were heckled and public meetings disrupted. In the years following, windows were broken, letter-boxes fire-bombed and the houses of prominent men attacked. The campaign brought the vote issue to the forefront of public attention and kept it there. After 1907 the WSPU broke its connections with the Labour Party and

ignored a constitution drawn up by Theresa Grieg-Billington. This prompted a split in the movement and the founding of a socialist organisation, the Women's Freedom League, with its own journal *The Vote*. In 1909 at the Bermondsey by-election acid was thrown by the WSPU women at a meeting and violence stepped up in response to the Home Secretary's, Herbert Gladstone's, harsh treatment of the women arrested for suffrage actions. Women in prison had begun to go on hunger strikes, forcing the government to release them as they became ill. In response Gladstone had ordered force-feeding. Tubes were forced down a woman's nostrils, through the throat and into the stomach. The restrained woman was then 'fed' a liquid diet which was poured down the tube. Many women withstood this horror, women of all social classes, although those from the working class were treated much worse. Lady Constance Lytton disguised herself as a working-class woman, Jane Wharton. As Lytton she was treated gently because of her heart condition. As Wharton there was no tenderness, only brutality which probably contributed to an early death. The Liberals, attacked within Parliament by the Labour member George Lansbury and elsewhere by men of their own party, introduced the 'Cat and Mouse' Act, releasing women from prison when they were ill, only to rearrest them as they recovered.

The WSPU concentrated on becoming a tight-knit, almost militaristic group, strongly led from the centre by Emmeline Pankhurst and her daughter Christabel. Its numbers fell, whilst the NUWSS grew in size as it broke links with the militant campaign, stressing the peaceful methods of its suffragists as opposed to the violence of the suffragettes. Its campaign of education through its paper, *Common Cause* contrasting with the vote-centred aims of the WSPU's *Votes for Women* attracted the sympathy of many women. The support within and without Parliament grew. Although the actions of the WSPU turned some people against the movement, it kept it clearly in the public eye allowing the work of the NUWSS to build on firm foundations support for an unignorable issue. In 1913, Emily Davison died in her attempt to draw attention to the cause by trying to halt the King's horse in the Derby. The event was

filmed and seen in the Kinemas and Electric Theatres on the exciting medium of celluloid. She became a national martyr, and was buried in the tradition of the great reformers like the Levellers of the seventeenth century, surrounded by many supporters. Asquith had already acknowledged the importance of the women's case for he had put the vote issue before Parliament in the Reform Bill of 1912.

THE OLD LIE

THE DANGEROUS SITUATION in Europe gave the world of 1914 an air of gloom. The confidence of the last century had given way to some uncertainty. The sinking of the *Titanic* on her maiden voyage on 14 April 1912 had in some way emphasised this decline in spirits. The ship, built in Belfast by Harland and Wolff for the White Star Line, was supposed to be unsinkable. It was not and the company knew this but to the public the unique system of electric doors and watertight compartments that would limit the effects of a leak, meant that the ship was invulnerable. She struck an iceberg in the Atlantic and sank after two hours and forty minutes taking over a thousand men, women and children with her.

In June 1914 at Sarajevo the heir to the Austrian Empire was murdered by a member of the Black Hand, a Serbian-based nationalist movement. Germany was inevitably drawn into supporting Austria's bellicose demands of Serbia. Russia supported Serbia as the father supports the child. France, as ally, was therefore drawn to support Russia. Germany, to ensure its own survival against a two-pronged attack, had to operate the Schlieffen Plan. This involved an attack on northern France via Belgium, which Britain was committed to defend. The British expeditionary force went to France following Britain's declaration of war. The declaration was greeted with great joy. Volunteers rushed to join up before the war was over. They believed that it would end by Christmas. Instead, the war turned into an entrenched static slogging match. The Schlieffen Plan collapsed as forces were taken from the German's main attack to fend off the temporarily successful Russians. The Germans failed in their aim of capturing Paris, and the three armies, the French, the British and the

H.M.S. Dunraven V.C. in action against the submarine that sank her, 8 August 1917 by Charles Pears.

The War at Sea

At sea the British defeated the German navy at a battle in the South Atlantic but faced appalling casualties in a war against German submarines preying on the merchant navy. In December 1914 the German fleet bombarded Scarborough, Whitby and Hartlepool without interruption, and the submarines in the North Sea kept the Royal Navy in the North at Scapa Flow. It was not until May 1916 that the British Fleet under Jellicoe came into conflict with the main German Navy at the Battle of Jutland; although the British lost more ships, the German surface fleet did not enter the North Sea again. Even their submarine campaign had been restricted in 1915 after a German U-boat had sunk the passenger ship *Lusitania*; the outcry in America had nearly brought the United States into the war. By January 1917, however, the British naval blockade was starving Germany of supplies and the decision was made to torpedo all vessels in the Atlantic, Allied or neutral.

German, dug two lines of trenches stretching from the English Channel to the Swiss border. On the Eastern Front the Russians soon suffered a major defeat and in the winter their war with Germany slowed to a deathly pace.

In 1915 there was an attempt to strike at the 'soft underbelly of Europe' by attacking the Dardanelles, cutting the Turkish Empire off from their Austrian allies and then driving northwards. Regrettably, the attempt to secure the beach-heads at Gallipoli, which fell to the Australian and New Zealand forces as well as to the British and French, could not be sustained. Other attacks on the Turkish Empire met with more success in Palestine, organised with Arab help by T.E. Lawrence, following a successful defence of the Suez Canal.

On the Western Front the conditions in winter were appalling: the trenches built by

Above: Col. T.E. Lawrence (1888–1935).

Above right: Gallipoli. A Faugh-a-Ballagh (Royal Irish Fusilier) teases a Turkish sniper by holding his helmet above the trench on his rifle.

Below right: The battle of Albert (Somme). A wiring party of the Royal Warwickshire Regiment going up the trenches, Beaumont Hamel, July 1916.

the British and French filled with water, and disease and lice were rife. The monotony was relieved by bombardment. Gas was used in 1915; mustard gases drifted across the no-man's land between the trench lines, blinding and tearing the insides of lungs. In 1915 several attempts were made to break the stalemate, but the offensives failed in the mud of no-mans land. The following year the Germans launched an attack on Verdun, seen as the gateway to Paris. The French commanders asked the British to relieve the pressure by attacking the Germans on a broad front based on the river Somme. The British soldiers were raised by Kitchener's recruiting drive, fronted by posters showing his pointing finger and the message 'You are the man I want' ('which had the power to send my

Troops of the Canadian Mounted Rifles with tanks making a practice attack, Bonny, June 1918.

generation to hang dead on the barbed wire of the Somme . . .' according to H.V. Morton in *I saw Two Englands*). In the summer on the Somme, British soldiers, weighed down by 60lb of kit, could advance only at a slow march in their attack on German defences which were scarcely damaged by the massive bombardment that preceded it. British casualties were colossal: 60,000 soldiers died on the first day of the five-month battle.

In 1917 the Russian soldiers, angered by ill-treatment and the constant defeats, were at the forefront of the revolution of February which ended the reign of the Tsar. The provisional government which replaced Nicholas II wished to continue the commitment to the Triple Entente but was itself overthrown by the Bolshevik revolution in November. British and French soldiers also mutinied but the high commands of both retained their nerve and there was no mass support in the country for revolution; in any case, news of the mutinies did not reach the public domain. The French and British were bailed out from the threat imposed by the enlarged German army when the United States entered the war. The Germans must have realised that the United States would not remain neutral after the resumption of their unrestricted submarine campaign against all Atlantic shipping in February 1917. The American President, Woodrow Wilson, was reluctant to commit his country to war even when news of sunken ships began to arrive; but if America did not remain neutral, Germany intended to take the war to her by proposing to Mexico that she reconquer American territory. Britain

A German Attack on a Wet Morning, April 1918 by Harold Sandys Williamson.

intercepted and deciphered a telegram from the German minister, Alfred Zimmermann, which contained this proposal, and handed it to Wilson. On 6 April 1917 America declared war.

The German offensive of 1918, Operation Michael, failed because of the arrival of the Americans in Europe and this spelt the end for the German war effort. There were drastic food shortages in the country and the government of the Kaiser fell in the autumn. On 11 November 1918 at eleven o'clock the war ended. Britain had lost 750,000 of her young men; officers and other ranks who should have contributed to the wealth and

knowledge of the nation had died in the trenches of 'the war to end all wars'.

The war poets, Wilfred Owen and Siegfried Sassoon amongst others, proved that there could be a survival of the spirit amongst the horrors of war. They rejected the appeals that had inspired the people to enter the ranks or had permitted the introduction of conscription in 1916. It was Owen who wrote of the senselessness of the notion that 'Dulce et decorum est . . .' to die for one's country when faced with the horror of the gas attack.

Women too committed themselves to paper, expressing the horror that they felt at the losses on the Continent. Many served as

A Busy Scene in a Shell Factory of Messrs. Vickers, 1915, by J. Matania.

welfare measures. The Women's Freedom League led by Sylvia Pankhurst, artist and daughter of Emmeline, was pacifist in intent, campaigned for the end of the war and worked on relief projects in the East End of London. At the end of the war the Representation of the People Act gave the vote to all men aged over twenty-one but only to women over thirty and younger graduates. It was often asserted that the work of women in the war was the major reason for their being awarded the vote on this limited scale, yet the impetus for the vote was unstoppable before the war began and the war probably held it up.

'A FIT COUNTRY FOR HEROES TO LIVE IN.'

A T THE START of the war, it was increasingly obvious that the Liberal Party was in great difficulty. The needs of war did not fit easily with their attempts at internationalism and the conscription imposed on the men of Britain at the end of 1915 was more than many could bear. Lloyd George had long protested that the war had to be fought vigorously with scant regard to peacetime values. In 1916 he ousted the Prime Minister, Asquith, and formed a government with the support of Conservatives and Unionists. Indeed, towards the end of the war the Cabinet was chiefly Liberal whilst the Conservatives provided the majority of the support in the Commons.

volunteer nurses at the front giving their skills and their lives to the desperate struggle to relieve some of the horror. Other women were employed in jobs such as driving buses and trams, or working in the dangerous conditions of the munitions factories and in the fields of Britain.

The WSPU threw itself behind the war effort with a ferocity which Mrs Pankhurst inspired. The NUWSS, whilst on the face of it supporting the war, did not hitch itself to the militaristic bandwagon. Individual groups within the organisation were pacifist and instead of taking part in the troop-raising actions of the WSPU, concentrated instead on

David Lloyd George and his wife.

David Lloyd George (1863–1945)

Lloyd George, the Welsh Liberal Prime Minister, was born in Manchester though moved at the age of two to Wales when his schoolmaster father died. His uncle, Richard Lloyd, took over the paternal role and, recognising the latent brilliance in his nephew, gave him every support. Through his own self-sacrifice he enabled the young but shrewd and ambitious boy to educate himself sufficiently to become a solicitor.

In 1890 Lloyd George's political career began when he was elected as an advanced Liberal for Carnarvon Boroughs. His eloquence, grit and scathing speeches made an immediate impact on the House of Commons, but for some years he was considered merely as a vivid orator whose talents were confined to the platform. To these critics it was a surprise when he was appointed President of the Board of Trade in 1905. He held the post for three years during which he disproved those who had dismissed him as a mercurial and radical firebrand. His talent for negotiation and his ability to promote schemes achieved settlements which won him a solid reputation.

From 1908–15 he was Chancellor of the Exchequer. However his Budget of 1909 ('for raising money to wage implacable warfare against poverty and squalidness') which introduced a land-tax and a super-tax on the incomes of the very rich was thrown out by the Lords, causing a constitutional crisis and the subsequent Parliament Act of 1911 which limited the Lord's veto to two years.

Until the outbreak of the First World War, Lloyd George had been considered a pacifist, as he had been a passionate opponent of the Boer War in South Africa. Now, by contrast, with equal zeal he threw himself behind the moral justification for the 1914 War, when little 'five-foot five' nations like Belgium were invaded by Germany. In 1915 he was appointed Minister of Munitions, in 1916 became War Secretary and in the same year superseded the increasingly feeble Asquith as the Coalition Prime Minister, when all Party barriers were thrown down. Lloyd George's main support came from his former opponents – all the great posts went to Unionists (Conservatives) – and he had no front rank Liberal in a government which included Labour members and businessmen until he gave office to Churchill half-a-year after its formation.

The position he held over the government was virtually impregnable whilst he devoted himself to the War. Bonar Law, the future Conservative Prime Minister, said of him in 1920: 'He thought of nothing and aimed at nothing and hoped for nothing except the successful end of the war ... [His was] not merely the courage of dogged determination, but was accompanied by a brilliant hopefulness which was an example and inspiration to everyone who worked with him'. He was called 'the man who won the war' and was one of the three at the peace negotiations.

Although Lloyd George won the election in December 1918 in triumph, his Liberal party base had dwindled and in the years that followed, he failed to achieve his goal to establish a Centre party. The Coalition continued for four more years until its collapse in October 1922, but it was weakened and prey to increasing tensions between Lloyd George and his Conservative colleagues. The latter in particular opposed his negotiations with the Sinn Feiners in 1921 and his concession of the Irish Free State in 1922. By now Lloyd George's political reputation had become tarnished and his philandering and financial carelessness inspired a lack of trust. Though he retained his seat until the year of his death, he was in effect a political outcast.

Asquith's Liberal and some Unionist MPs sat as an opposition party in the difficult position of not wanting to appear traitorous by failing to support the war.

At the end of the war, Lloyd George capitalised on his role as the man who had won it and the election was fought between his Coalition, the Liberals of Asquith and the Labour Party. The electorate had trebled in size. Asquith lost his seat, the Coalition won and the Labour Party gained forty seats at the expense of the Liberals. On the crest of the post-war boom, it appeared as if there was little need to worry and the land which Lloyd George promised to the heroes might come about with little trouble. However, there was soon widespread unemployment as the soldiers returned and disruption in the labour market as the munitions works closed and other industries re-tooled. Moreover, the British economy was exhausted and dependent upon loans from the United States, whilst many overseas customers had begun to set up their own industries to replace British ones separated from them by war. In particular, India established its own cotton manufacturing industries, thus damaging the textile trade in Britain. Strikes for higher wages to cope with inflation and riots backed by British

Communists, inspired by the Bolshevik revolution, broke out in Glasgow. Troops had to be sent to the Red Clyde and tanks appeared on the streets of Britain. Not all the army was happy at taking on this role. The Soldiers' Sailors' Airmens' Union was a socialist union with 10,000 members by 1919 and it strongly opposed the use of troops on the streets of the country. In May the headquarters were raided and the nation told that it had escaped from disorder. Yet the SSAU was a pressure group, not a revolutionary force. Its aims were to secure better conditions for the servicemen awaiting demobilisation and a quicker return home for those still abroad.

THE IRISH FREE STATE

IN 1921 THE GOVERNMENT survived major strikes and ended the civil war in Ireland with the agreement for the self-government of all but the six counties in the North, which remained under direct British rule. This latter was a major, if flawed achievement. Liberal plans for Home Rule had been shelved when war broke out in 1914. In 1916 the Irish nationalist movement, Sinn Fein (We

Dublin: the Easter Uprising, 1916.

Ourselves), who had rejected the constitutional means represented by the Nationalist MPs in Westminster, seized the Post Office in Dublin on Easter Sunday. The revolt lasted until the following Friday and it ended in bloodshed and reprisals. In 1920 the six counties of Ulster, which had Protestant majorities, became Northern Ireland, whilst the southern counties and three northern Catholic ones came under the government of a limited 'parliament' in Dublin. To many this was unacceptable and a terrorist war broke out, ending only when Lloyd George's government allowed greater power to Dublin and acknowledged the country as the Irish Free State. It was thus still a British dominion, until full independence was granted in 1949.

DECLINE OF THE LIBERAL PARTY

EDUCATION BUDGET CUTS and foreign investment scandals led to Lloyd George's downfall and Bonar Law formed a Conservative administration in 1922. The general election at the end of 1923 saw the first Labour government take office. Labour had built up support as the Liberal Party declined, but in 1924 it still depended on the Liberals to stay in office. As a result, Ramsay MacDonald's Labour government had to water down many of its welfare proposals because of Liberal pressure. It was a short-lived government: the Liberals left Ramsay MacDonald stranded when the Tory press published a forged letter purportedly from the Soviet Union suggesting that the Labour Party was in the pocket of the Bolsheviks. The Conservatives returned to power in November 1924 under Stanley Baldwin, who had succeded Bonar Law in 1922. Baldwin was perhaps the most influential inter-war Prime Minister, though by 1923 he had only limited government experience as President of the Board of Trade in the Coalition government from 1921 and the office of Chancellor of the Exchequer under Bonar Law.

James Ramsay MacDonald (1866–1937)

Ramsay MacDonald, the first British Labour Prime Minister, was born in Lossiemouth, Scotland. Educated at a board school, he was poor but clever and stayed on as a pupil-teacher rather than earn his living as a fisherman.

He came subsequently to London where he became a member of the Fabian Society and of the Independent Labour Party in 1893. His ambitions were only beginning to lift him from poverty and obscurity when he married. With the support of his redoubtable wife (who was regrettably to die early, in 1911) Ramsay MacDonald gained in confidence and his career began to flower. He became secretary of the Independent Labour Party in 1900 and an MP in 1906.

However, at the outbreak of the First World War, he resigned the chairmanship of his party, to which he had succeeded, denouncing the government for having blundered into conflict. His opposition to the war (which lacked conviction to sincere pacifists) made him an outcast for many years, and it was fortuitous that he found a constituency to return him to

left: Ramsay MacDonald and his daughter.

One and a half years later, the miners went on strike as the recently restored coal-mine owners, who had lost control of the pits under the war-time administration, tried to offset falling sales by lowering wages. The miners were joined by the distributive trades, and many other industries and workers went on strike. The General Strike lasted a week. Although it failed and only the miners stood by their cause into the winter, enduring great hardship and hunger, the government had experienced a scare and had mobilised the middle classes into driving trains and supporting the army-driven food convoys into the cities. To counter the striker's newspapers, Baldwin appointed Winston Churchill, now back in the Conservative camp, to edit *The British Gazette*.

Baldwin's Conservative government lasted through the next three years as the nation was swept by a consumer boom similar to that in America.

It was a time of excitement with new dance crazes and jazz music coming over from the

WOLSELEY

Comfort and Visibility

Four doors and six spacious windows at the sides, one at the back, and a clear, unobstructed view ahead for everybody in the car—this six-light Wolseley fabric saloon combines arm-chair comfort and protection with the airiness and freedom of view which makes many motorists still cling to the open tourer . . . Tastefully upholstered and finished in matching duotones. The engine is the Wolseley "Silent Six" and gives the top-gear perform-ance for which it is famous. Also in full measure, the elegance, reliability and easy control which are special points in all Wolseleys. A car for comfort and long, satisfying service. A choice of four colours—blue, lake, beige and black . . . . . unequalled value at £375.

You can purchase out of income for a small initial outlay.

WOLSELEY MOTORS (1927) LTD., WARD END, BIRMINGHAM

Wolseley Six-cylinder Six-Light Fabric Saloon — £375
Extras—Wire wheels £10; Triplex Glass £15, Specially Painted wheels £1

Motorcars established themselves as a major industry in the 1920s.

---

the Commons. Subsequently, however, others of the socialist Left were to remember his anti-war stance as the sign of unflinching opinion in the face of abuse, and he was elected Leader of the Labour Party in 1922. His Utopian idealism and internationalism won him an increasingly enthusiastic response from the country and the first Labour government was elected in January 1924. Ramsay MacDonald was its Prime Minister until it fell in November of the same year. With his rugged handsomeness, elegant dress, his private means (his wife had benefited from settlements) and his ability to mix with the elite, he was remarkable in the broadness of his appeal not only to the hard Left of Clydeside but also to the aristocrats of the London Establishment.

In the election at the end of 1924 he lost office, but was returned again to form a second Labour government in 1929. It was a disastrous period and he responded to the financial collapse of 1931 by forming a predominantly Conservative 'National' government, from which most of his Labour colleagues were excluded. It lasted until 1935, whilst Ramsay MacDonald, though its official head, became weakened and increasingly isolated.

United States. Women, with the vote over the age of thirty (and after 1928 over the age of twenty-one as with men), were perceived to have greater freedom. Young flappers, women in beautiful clothes, dancing into the late hours, epitomised the middle-class bright young things. Those with disposable incomes in the later 'twenties bought cars and opened up the country roads of Britain. The Highlands of Scotland and the West of England echoed to the motor horns of the young and moneyed evoked in Evelyn Waugh's books, *Vile Bodies* and *Decline and Fall*.

When the great stock-market crash occurred in October 1929, Britain was dragged into the pit. The loans, used to bail her out of the post-war depression, had tied her to the international money markets, based chiefly on Wall Street in New York. The Labour government of 1929 was faced by economic problems which no government proved able to handle alone.

287

STRANGE TUB-FELLOWS

Dr. Goebbels. "The British Empire is one long story of oppression, bloodshed and tyranny!"
Marxist Orator. "Comrade, you take the very words out of my mouth!"

THE GREAT DEPRESSION

THE DEPRESSION of the 1930s caused enormous distress to the people of Britain. Some ten per cent of the workforce had remained unemployed during the twenties, even when the economy had improved. The old staple industries had not recovered and as the depression followed, other industries, even the modern technological ones, were in trouble. The unskilled labour-force suffered worst and there was widespread unemployment. Some areas, like the north-east of England and the south of Wales, joined the industrial areas of Scotland in seeing mass unemployment and the hunger marches of the people who suffered most. In the valleys of Wales the coal-mining areas fared a little better than the rest of Wales and some of the industries managed to survive, but slate-quarrying had already suffered from competition. Many families upped and moved across the border to England looking for work there that was already scarce enough.

In 1931 the Labour government, faced with having to balance its budget by cutting unemployment pay, tore itself apart and nine members resigned. Ramsay MacDonald reluctantly came to the conclusion that a government of national salvation on the model of that in France, was necessary. The National Government became a coalition of Labour and Conservatives with some of Lloyd George's Liberals. Other Liberals under Sir John Simon, and most Labour members remained aloof, with the Scot James Maxton becoming a leading figure in the Independent Labour Party. This organisation attracted great support in the Welsh valleys where the Labour Party had more of a crusading zeal, personified by Aneurin Bevan and Jennie Lee. The National Government, which from 1935 was led by Baldwin, won an election victory in late 1935, leaving Labour in opposition with 154 and the Conservatives dominating the coalition. It had little to offer to the unemployed and the marchers. The welfare system administered by the Public Assistance Board was still inadequate and the means-testing which governed the issue of the dole was reminiscent of the now-abolished Poor Law requirements and penalised those people who had saved money whilst in work.

Above: George VI (1895–1952).

Opposite: In the depression of the 1930s many people began to look at new political ideas. The confrontation between fascism and marxism led to violent scenes on the streets of British and European cities.

ROYAL ABDICATION

IN 1936 THE NATION was temporarily distracted from the depression by the death of George V. He was succeeded by Edward VIII. The young uncrowned King was a popular man. He had toured the most depressed areas of the country and agreed with the unemployed that something must be done. Naturally he had no responsibility for making improvements, but he was trusted and his sympathy welcomed.

Edward did not particularly favour the princesses of Europe who were paraded before him as heir. Instead, he fell in love with Wallace Simpson, a married woman, once divorced. By the time of the death of his father, Edward and Mrs Simpson were having an affair and a constitutional crisis loomed.

There were suggestions that a morganatic marriage could be arranged if Mrs Simpson were divorced from her husband. This would mean that Wallace would not be a queen and their children would have no claim to the

Stanley Baldwin (1867–1947) and his wife.

the monarchy at that time. The abdication crisis had not served its reputation well: once again whispers of republicanism had been heard and the wealth of the monarchy amongst the poverty of the times was commented on.

All but overshadowed in the last month of 1936 was the most notable of the hunger marches. Jarrow in the North-east had unemployment running at 67.8%. The ship-building industry was destroyed there and there was nothing to replace it. Ellen Wilkinson M.P. organised the march, which left for London in October. Two hundred of the unemployed set out and were fed and looked after in the towns along their route.

Their march made newspaper headlines, but had little effect otherwise. It was a symbol of the hopelessness of the unemployed in areas where the staple industries were in decline and showed up the inactivity of government.

The period gave rise to some excellent literature like Walter Greenwood's *Love on the Dole*, but not all the 1930s were concerned with the depression. There was also a growth in the wages of those who were employed and an improvement in the housing conditions of many. The suburbia of George Orwell's *Coming up for Air*, also revealed an aspect of the period – the lower-middle-class frustrations with the limitations of life. However, these limitations for some – a house with indoor toilets and sunrise gates – also represented the hopes and dreams of many others.

THE RISE OF FASCISM

THERE WERE NO SIMPLE ANSWERS to the problems of the 1930s but John Maynard Keynes suggested government spending in certain industries could stimulate the economy by creating purchasing-power in the employed sector which would spur on other industries as demand grew. Others took up more drastic solutions. Some drifted into the British Union of Fascists led by the ex-Labour MP, Sir Oswald Mosley. These black-shirted thugs unfortunately tapped a vein of bigotry which refused to accept that the growth of

throne. This was impossible, Stanley Baldwin asserted in the Commons, as the concept of a morganatic marriage was not acknowledged in British law. Whilst the affair became a great news matter in the American press, the British papers remained mute. In October Mrs Simpson filed for divorce and Edward made public his intention to marry her. To the Establishment, to the family and to many others, this was not acceptable. A twice-divorced woman was not considered suitable to hold the title of queen. Baldwin, whose position as leader of the National Government had looked doubtful, had boosted his standing by convincing the King of this fact. In November the King, still uncrowned, announced his abdication to the nation on the wireless. He married Wallace in June 1937 and they became Duke and Duchess of Windsor.

In May his brother George, Duke of York, became the second stammering younger brother to be thrust to the throne (Charles I was the first). George was a different man from his brother, quieter and seemingly more serious. He and his beautiful wife, Elizabeth Bowes-Lyon, and their daughters Elizabeth and Margaret, injected the stability needed in

Opposite: The Arrival of the Jarrow Marchers in London by Thomas Dugdale.

Adolf Hitler (1889–1945).

Nations, and Germany was defying the terms of the Versailles Treaty that had been imposed on her at the end of the Great War. This ultimately led to territorial demands in the east of Europe once Germany had annexed Austria, her ally in the Great War. Hitler wanted to reunite all Germans, those living in Czechoslovakia and Poland in particular.

In a desperate attempt to fend off the possibility of war, Neville Chamberlain, the British Prime Minister since 1937, and Daladier of France, flew to Munich in September 1938 and accepted the supposed compromise drawn up by Mussolini, which actually represented what Hitler had intended to gain from the meeting. To avert war Britain and France gave Hitler part of Czechoslovakia. He went on to take all of it within six months of Chamberlain's return from Munich, when he had waved the piece of paper representing 'peace with honour – peace in our time'. Meanwhile, even before the Munich Crisis, the British had dug air-raid shelters and had been issued with gas masks. When Hitler attacked Poland on 1 September 1939, Britain demanded his withdrawal; but Hitler did not believe that the politicians who had granted him Czechoslovakia intended war. Yet, as Chamberlain announced that Britain was at war and the air raids sounded, the British did not doubt it.

Some of the British people had already fought against Fascism. In 1936 many had joined the International Brigade fighting to save the democratically elected socialist government of Spain. The Fascists there, under General Franco, invaded the country and in a brutal three-year civil war took over the nation. Many Europeans and Americans gave their lives for the cause of socialism and democracy in a war against the Fascist forces of Spain, Germany and Italy. The tragic war left us many great works of art and literature, among them Picasso's *Guernica* and Hemingway's *For Whom the Bell Tolls*. From the British writers who supported the Spanish government we have W.H. Auden's *Spain 1937*. Auden served as a not-very-good ambulance driver during the war but the poem was perhaps the greatest political poem of the 1930s. Just as Auden in 1937 recognised that the struggle in Spain was a battle of historical significance, many in Britain in 1939 believed that there was an historic struggle to come.

British society was due to the multiplicity of different racial input. The chief but not the only target was the Jewish community of the country, especially that in the East End of London, where there were running battles between the Fascists and those people, gentiles and Jews, who refused to accept the racism of the Blackshirts.

Mosley and the movement he led were emulating the National Socialists of Germany and the Fascists of Italy whose leaders – Hitler who had come to power in 1933 and Mussolini who had led Italy since 1923 – seemed to represent the modern world's dynamism. The simplicity of the Nazi solution to the economic problems – to rearm, employ people in government projects and build up an army – appealed to the right-wing of British political life and to the easily-led lay people. At the same time these very movements caused great problems for the British government and the government of France. Italy was building an empire by invading Abyssinia in defiance of the League of

A column of Jews guarded by German soldiers is marched through the streets of Warsaw during the winter of 1940. The number of Jews who were to die at the hands of the Nazis in the greatest attempt at racial extermination the world has known totalled 6,000,000.

WORLD WAR TWO

THE MOMENT OF TRUTH did not come straightaway. The war began with a long period of inactivity for the British people. Poland was carved up by Germany and Soviet Russia. Russia then attacked Finland whilst the British stood by. The British Expeditionary Force (BEF) went to France from where the air force dropped leaflets on the Germans. In April 1940 the war intensified as Germany invaded Norway and Denmark. The British force sent there was withdrawn when Hitler attacked northern France, Holland, Luxembourg and Belgium on 10 May 1940. Chamberlain was thrown out by a concerted attack launched in the Commons from both the government and opposition benches. He was succeeded on 13 May by Winston Churchill who brought Labour men,

Clement Attlee and Ernest Bevin, into a coalition Cabinet.

The BEF and the French army were swiftly overcome by the speed of Hitler's *Blitzkrieg* and by 19 May the retreat had begun. 338,000 men from the BEF and the French army were taken off the beaches of Dunkirk by a flotilla of Navy ships and pleasure boats crewed by all sorts of British civilians. It was a partial success as a retreat, but as an intervention in a major European war it was a disaster.

Hitler hoped to invade Britain and his air force, the Luftwaffe, began raids on aerodromes. The RAF fighter squadrons suffered badly in August and September, losing many valuable pilots and machines. The British were backed in numbers by Poles and Czechs as well as by volunteer Canadians and Americans. Fortunately the Germans changed their attack strategy to raids on London to break morale. This gave the RAF time to

recover and they and the Navy defeated the invasion plans by wrecking the air cover and the attempts to create an invasion flotilla. The Battle of Britain, after the cancellation of the invasion, became a series of bombing raids on the great cities of Britain and their interception by the fighters of the RAF. Coventry, Bristol and London still bear the scars.

The war spread across the world with Japan attacking British colonies in the Far East from late 1941, whilst the Italians sought to take over colonies and dependencies in Africa. It was in Africa in 1942 that the tide made a slow turn in Britain's favour when Field Marshal Montgomery defeated the Afrika Korps of Rommel at El Alamein on 23 October. Before that, however, the Axis powers, Germany, Italy and Japan, had made three great mistakes. Germany had to rescue Italian forces trying to conquer Greece in spring 1941, which delayed the attack on Russia. Secondly, the invasion of

Russia began in June and the Germans soon became bogged down in a fierce winter. Finally, on 7 December Japan, starved of raw materials by an American embargo aimed at hindering Japan's imperialist war against China, attacked Pearl Harbor naval base and the economic might of America was brought into the war.

American forces aided the destruction of the Axis forces in North Africa by capturing the French colonies of Morocco and Algeria. Churchill and President Roosevelt met at Casablanca and decided to accept nothing short of Germany's complete surrender. The plan was to help Russia by opening a second front, and, even though it was too early to attack northern Europe, it was decided to strike at the soft underbelly of Europe once North Africa was under control. To this end, in July 1943, Allied forces landed in Sicily. Mussolini was overthrown once the Allies entered Italy in September; but German

Pearl Harbor: USS Oklahoma capsized alongside USS Maryland.

Above: First Sortie by Jeremy Whitehouse. This painting depicts Pilot Officer Cyril Babbage of 602 Squadron in his Spitfire encountering a German Messerschmitt over Hampshire, 18 August 1940.

Right: Pilots running for their aircraft, 25 July 1940.

The Battle of Britain

'Never in the field of human conflict was so much owed by so many to so few.' Churchill's words are an eloquent tribute to the pilots of Fighter Command who, during the months July to October 1940, resisted the attempts by Hitler's *Luftwaffe* (air force) to destroy British air defences as a prelude to a seaborne invasion of Britain. The Germans began by attacking Channel shipping and ports, hoping to engage and destroy British aircraft over sea; they then attacked airfields and radar installations before eventually starting the bombing campaign of London that became known as the 'blitz'. The Royal Air Force lost 915 planes during the battle, but the Germans suffered 1733 losses and their invasion plans were thwarted.

Sir Winston Churchill (1874–1965)

The political tradition into which Winston Churchill was born made it inevitable that he would follow in the footsteps of his father, Lord Randolph Churchill, whose career had, however, been disappointing and who had died when only forty-five. Churchill was born at Blenheim Palace in Oxfordshire where his father was the Tory representative for Woodstock. After an education at Harrow and Sandhurst, Churchill was gazetted to the 4th Hussars in 1895, the year of his father's death. The risky exploits of his early army career were followed by his equally dramatic experiences as a newspaper correspondent during the Boer War when he was captured in an ambush, escaping with a £25 price on his head.

In 1900 Churchill entered the Commons as the Conservative MP for Oldham. Soon the intractable bent of his character became apparent and by 1904 he was a declared opponent of Balfour's Unionist government, as a consequence of which he broke with his party and joined the Liberals in 1906. He became Colonial Under-Secretary, then President of the Board of Trade (1908–10), Home Secretary in 1910, and the following year First Lord of the Admiralty. Meanwhile, in 1908 he had married Clementine Ogilvy Hozier who was to give him comfort and stability throughout a marriage that lasted nearly sixty years.

Churchill's record in the First World War sealed his fame but also his censure, for he was made a scapegoat (though was later exonerated) for the disastrous Dardanelles expedition, an epic of military mismanagement in which there were very heavy casualties among the forces sent to Gallipoli. He resigned his position as First Lord of the Admiralty. Though his reputation had been badly damaged, he returned to office and became Minister of Munitions for Lloyd-George in 1917, producing thousands of tanks at his own initiative; Secretary of State for War and Air (1919–21); and from 1924 (when he was returned for Epping as a Constitutionalist supporter of the Conservatives) until 1929, he was Chancellor of the Exchequer. In 1925 it was Churchill who resolved to return to the gold standard at the pre-war parity. The valuation of both coal and steel increased too greatly in consequence and so did the unemployment of the men who produced these commodities.

During the 1930s he diverged from the Tory mainstream because of his uncompromising views on Indian self-government. For years he was in the political wilderness, spending his spare time in middle age on the crafts of bricklaying and painting. Isolated and unpopular, he was consumed with prophetic anger at the ineffectualness of the National government in the face of the belligerent European dictators. To Churchill, Munich was 'a total and unmitigated defeat'; and his views found an echo in popular feeling.

In May 1940 Neville Chamberlain lost power as eighty Conservatives rebelled against the leadership; when he resigned, Churchill formed a Coalition government. He saw the period as his destiny, one for which all his previous life had been mere preparation. His war leadership was the most inspiring the British had ever experienced and was to bring him international veneration. He worked with incessant urgency, nursing the delicate alliance with the Soviet Union which had entered the war in June 1941, whilst maintaining close contact with President Roosevelt, committing his forces to the Mediterranean and, as an even higher priority, to the Middle East, broadcasting continually to Britain and Europe, fighting too his own periodic bouts of depression – his 'black dog' – at such dreadful losses as the surrender to the Japanese of Singapore and 80,000 British and Empire troops in February 1942. Churchill called this watershed in the downfall of the Empire 'the worst capitulation in British history'.

But when the July 1945 election came, the statesman who had won the war was rejected. Churchill became the leader for the opposition. Again he was to utter prophetic warnings about the tyrannical regime behind the Iron Curtain (a term that he coined) and encouraged as a buffer the potential for European and Atlantic unity, the germ from which NATO developed. In 1951 Churchill became Prime Minister once again at the age of seventy-seven, beginning a period of prolonged Tory rule that was to last until 1964. Even when a mere back-bencher after 1955, he was honoured for the sustained and superhuman nature of his achievements.

Opposite: Winston Churchill at his desk wearing his 'siren suit'.

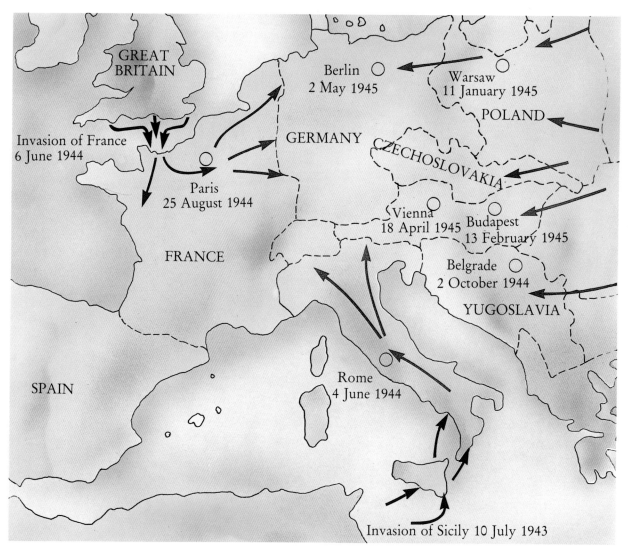

The invasion of Europe by Allied forces, 1943–5, with the dates on which capitals were liberated.

troops invaded the country too, reinstated Mussolini and continued Italy's commitment.

On 6 June of the following year, France was invaded by the Allies under Dwight D. Eisenhower in the massive Operation Overlord. During the next eleven months, British and American troops aided by French regular units and the Resistance drove the Germans back to the Rhine.

In the East, the Russians began to push the Germans out of their country and, at the beginning of 1945, the Allies closed in on Hitler's Third Reich. In May, as the Russians swept in from eastern Europe and the British and Americans crossed the Rhine, Hitler committed suicide and the war in Europe ended. The horrors of the German nation under Hitler's Nazi regime were revealed when soldiers, civilians and reporters like

Richard Dimbleby saw the concentration camps — Auschwitz, Dachau, Belsen — which were used to herd people together. Here, Jews, gypsies, Slavs and anyone else the Germans considered inferior, were imprisoned and murdered in their millions.

The Asian arena saw several more months of military action. American forces were relentlessly fighting across the Pacific from island to island; the British, who had seen 'the worst capitulation in British history' when 80,000 troops surrendered at the fall of Singapore in February 1942, had contained the Japanese in Burma. Japanese defeat was inevitable, but casualties in this eastern war were high on both sides; the final assault would be even bloodier and the American President, Harry Truman, decided to put a quick end to it by exploding two atomic

Above: General Montgomery and Winston Churchill on the Normandy seashore, 12 June 1944.

Right: A mushroom cloud rises to 20,000 ft. over Nagasaki after the explosion of the second atomic bomb, 9 August 1945.

bombs in Japan: on Hiroshima on 4 August and on Nagasaki on 9 August 1945. Hundreds of thousands of people died instantly and many more over the following years. These forced the Japanese to surrender.

Churchill wished his government to continue in office throughout the period following the war, but many of the opposition were keen to hold an election. The Labour leader, Clement Attlee, offered a compromise but Churchill, aggrieved by this, resigned, banking on a victory at the polls. He even went so far as to claim that the socialists would act like the gestapo – the Nazi secret police. The voters rejected pre-war Conservatism. They did not want Churchill, whose peacetime record had included the despatch of troops to break up miners' strikes in Wales while a Liberal Home Secretary.

THE LATE
TWENTIETH
CENTURY

12. FROM THE
CRADLE
TO THE
GRAVE

During the war years, plans were drawn up to rebuild Britain, but there were those in Parliament, the forces and the nation at large who saw physical reconstruction as only one of the jobs facing the new Britain. It had been a people's war that had come every day to British cities and homes, and a feeling spread in the country that it would be a people's peace for which the old order would have to be re-written. Reconstruction was to be a comprehensive re-evaluation of the needs of the individual and society.

William Beveridge, the Liberal economist who had studied the problems of unemployment earlier in the century, proposed wide-ranging social welfare reforms. The aim of these reforms was to remove the threat of poverty caused by unemployment and ill health. After the war the nationalisation of the health services was intended to support such welfare reforms, caring for the British citizen from the cradle to the grave.

St. Paul's, rising above the remains of burnt-out buildings in the City of London.

TIME CHART

1945	Labour wins general election.
1945–9	Large-scale nationalisation and the creation of the Welfare State.
1947	Severe winter. Nationalisation of coal and other industries. Power transferred to independent India, Pakistan and Burma.
1949	NATO is founded.
1950	Labour win general election with reduced majority.
1951	Festival of Britain. Conservatives win election.
1952	Death of King George VI. Queen Elizabeth II ascends the throne.
1956	Suez Crisis.
1959	Macmillan wins election.
1963	Profumo scandal. French veto British application to join the European Common Market. Macmillan resigns through ill-health.
1964	Labour wins general election.
1968	Homosexuality partially decriminalised.
1970	Conservative government under Edward Heath is returned.
1973	The United Kingdom joins the European Community.
1974	National miners' strikes: consequent three-day weeks and power cuts. Two general elections and Labour government returned both times by narrow margin.
1975	Referendum in favour of British membership of Common Market.
1976	Britain in recession: seeks help from International Monetary Fund.
1979	Mrs Thatcher becomes first woman prime minister. Independence given to Zimbabwe (Rhodesia). Scottish and Welsh devolution plans rejected.
1982	Falklands War.
1983	Mrs Thatcher's Conservative government returned with landslide majority. Continuing privatisation of nationalised industries.
1984	Miners' strike defeated.
1985	Anglo-Irish Agreement.
1987	Conservatives win third successive election under Mrs Thatcher's leadership.
1990	Mrs Thatcher forced to resign. John Major is voted to replace her as prime minister.
1991	Channel Tunnel links Britain and France. Britain, as member of United Nations allied forces, embarks on war to liberate Kuwait from the invading forces of Iraq.

A 'SOCIAL DEMOCRACY'

WHEN THE NEW SESSION opened in Parliament and the overjoyed, recently elected Labour members stood on the seats, singing 'The Red Flag', it seemed as if a fresh era was beginning. The rejection of Churchill was quite dramatic and it was largely due to the soldiers' vote that the Labour Party came to power with 393 seats and a majority of 146 over other parties. It should not have been surprising: regiments in Cairo had held their own elections which had returned a 'parliament' consisting overwhelmingly of Labour and Liberal representatives. In the actual British elections, where factors like the party funds and machinery had an effect on the outcome of the election, the Liberals gained only twelve seats.

In some ways the programme of reforms that the Labour Party promised was based on the work of the Liberal, Sir William Beveridge. Beveridge had, like Rowntree, studied the causes of unemployment and between 1909 and 1915 had administered the Labour Exchanges. His Report in 1942 suggested flat-rate contributions for a series of insurance proposals to cater for illness, unemployment and old age. Parliament had debated it and altered it and shelved it. It was only the Labour Party which felt able to take on the suggestions. Labour also came into power committed to taking the major industries and services into national ownership. The next few years saw the Bank of England, the railway companies, the mining industries, electricity industry, gas industry and civil aviation taken into 'the public sector'.

The economy was in difficulties because of the restructuring necessitated by the end of the war. The Americans withdrew the support offered during the war and when Maynard Keynes negotiated a loan, the U.S.A. wanted a proportion of the money spent on importing their products, which did nothing to allow the purchasing power of the British people to stimulate home industries. Moreover, the new nationalised industries did not get off to a good start. The winter of 1947 was extremely severe. There were coal shortages and power cuts; paper shortages stopped weekly magazines and cut down the size of

The Avengers with Patrick McNee and Diana Rigg – one of the most successful drama series on television in the 1960s.

Broadcasting

Following the First World War, many people began to buy radio sets, excited by the potential for communicating through the air waves. Radio manufacturers contemplated the establishment of a service providing regular broadcasts to people with receivers. The British Broadcasting Company was born and the first manager was John Reith who dedicated the company to the principle of providing educational as well as entertaining programmes. The company held a monopoly of wireless broadcasting; in 1925 this was examined and from 1926 regulated by the government when the company became a corporation still led by Reith. Driven by a conviction of his educational mission, he was to stamp his imprint upon the organisation.

In the 1920s, John Logie Baird had carried out a series of personal experiments on the transmission of pictures by radio waves. The technique was developed and improved, and from 1936 the BBC began to broadcast pictures from Alexandra Palace to the few owners of the new television monitors. But, whilst the radio voice of the BBC played an important role in transmitting propaganda and information to

Britain and occupied Europe during the Second World War, television broadcasts were suspended between 1939 and 1946.

In the 1950s the BBC's monopoly was removed when regional independent stations were permitted by Act of Parliament (the Independent Television Authority was created in 1954). The new companies were not funded by the sale of receiving licences like the BBC, but by the sale of airspace to advertisers. Commercial breaks appeared in programmes, though, unlike the system in the United States, they were not inserted directly into programmes. In the 1960s a third channel was granted and BBC2 began to broadcast at almost the same time as colour transmissions appeared. Although television had infiltrated most people's homes by the 1990s (97% of the population possessed a television set), only one more channel – Channel 4 – had been added to the mainstream broadcasting network. In addition, satellite television offered an alternative to the existing network. But whilst it increased the number of channels, it did not substantially alter the type of television programmes.

"Oh, Johnny!—that's our last egg for the month. On my lovely polished floor too!"

"Sorry, Mum! I can't get another egg but I'll soon make the floor bright again with a rub of 'Mansion' "

MANSION
ANTISEPTIC
WAX
POLISH
FOR FLOORS, FURNITURE AND LINO
Use sparingly—still in short supply

Chiswick Products Ltd., London, W.4   MP/SR

Shortages and rationing continued after the war, and this fact of life was reflected in the advertisements of the time.

newspapers. Unemployment soared despite all attempts to prevent a slump like the one which followed the Great War.

These difficulties saw Emanuel Shinwell discredited as Minister of Fuel and Power and replaced by Hugh Gaitskill. It was the Chancellor of the Exchequer, Sir Stafford Cripps, who did most to get the country out of the depression. As the economy improved he removed many of the wartime austerity measures still in place. He even upheld the legislation against strikes in certain industries until 1950. At the same time he imposed heavier direct taxes and death duties, shifting the burden of tax from the working classes to the middle classes and the landed gentry.

By 1950 many of the latter could not afford to maintain their estates. The National Trust, an organisation founded at the end of the nineteenth century to preserve Britain's heritage, acquired some of these properties, restored them and opened them to the public.

The notable feature of the post-war Labour government was the creation of the Welfare State. This consolidated the achievements of the Liberal government earlier in the century and attempted to end the mish-mash of legislation enacted after the First World War by successive administrations. The reorganised welfare system aimed to look after the British citizen from the cradle to the grave. The 1945 Family Allowance Act provided money for the support of families with more than one child, to help with the costs of parenthood and to facilitate a growth in the birth-rate. A National Assistance Act in 1948 provided means-tested benefits for the people not eligible for other insurance benefits. It was established that everyone had a right to an income set at a certain level. The old Poor Law finally disappeared and those workhouses that were still standing became hospitals or old peoples' homes (a well-intentioned but scarcely welcome initiative to those who still saw them as grim Bastilles).

Those in work were protected further against injuries in the workplace by a contributory scheme. Compensation was decided by a tribunal and there were no limits set to the amounts due to the injured party. The most embracing of all was the National Insurance Act 1946 which established extensive benefits running from maternity benefit to increased old-age pensions, unemployment pay and sickness pay. The icing on the cake was the National Health Act of 1949 engineered by Aneurin Bevan. This nationalised the hospitals and made doctors employees of the state. The costs were high if measured in money terms, but the benefits were immeasurable: the health of the nation improved and illness was no longer accompanied by the threat of a huge financial burden.

Labour did not retain power for long. The austerity measures were unpopular and the redistributed income resulted in a new middle class of people who worked in new industries and wanted better standards for themselves. Instead of continuing with the socialism which had brought them thus far, they turned to the Tory party which promised to 'set the people free' from the rationing of food stuffs and the nationalised road transport system. Although more people voted for the Labour Party in the 1950 election than in 1945, a million more people voted for the Conservatives. The

304

Housing was a desperate problem after the war. Homes had been destroyed by the bombing campaigns and the problem was aggravated by the returning servicemen. Prefabricated houses – 'prefabs' – were erected as a temporary measure; they made good homes and some survived for many years.

Liberals were crushed between the two giant parties. Although Labour held power there could be no major initiatives and the economy was still problematic. Churchill attacked the Labour party for mismanagement and certain parts of the leadership of the party quarrelled. In October 1951 Attlee called an election to try and increase the working majority, but the gamble failed and Churchill came to power with a majority of twenty; the Liberals again lost seats. The Conservatives presided over an improving economy and entranced the people with a massive house-building scheme initiated by Harold Macmillan, who achieved this largely by cutting the cost of each house by 10 per cent.

THE END OF THE EMPIRE

IT WAS CLEAR to many that the Second World War, like the Great War, had ended an era. There was clearly no role for the British Empire in the new world. The major component, the Indian sub-continent, had been agitating for independence for many years. The Indian National Congress led by Mahatma Gandhi had long waged a non-aggression campaign of civil disobedience against British Rule, but there was a significant problem with the large Muslim community who did not wish to see itself as part of a nation dominated by Hindus. The Congress was largely Hindu, yet Gandhi did not consider this an obstacle if India remained united. The Mahatma's pacifism and tolerance could not prevent the violent collision between the two communities, leading to the partition of the sub-continent into India and two sections of Pakistan. When Lord Louis Mountbatten was sent to the colony as Viceroy in 1947, it was to oversee independence. Britain surrendered Burma and Egypt, too, in the years after the war. Its part in the establishment of Israel also lost Britain the sympathy of the Arab nations with whom it had once been allied. The original intention of the British had been to establish a Jewish and a Palestinian homeland in the region, but in 1948 when Britain withdrew from Palestine, only an Israeli state emerged, founded in part by the surviving victims of the European 'holocaust'.

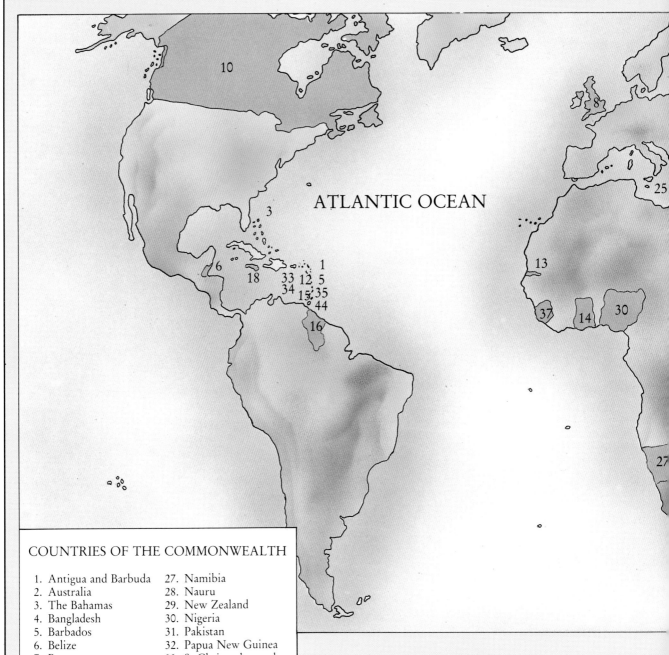

ATLANTIC OCEAN

COUNTRIES OF THE COMMONWEALTH

1. Antigua and Barbuda	27. Namibia
2. Australia	28. Nauru
3. The Bahamas	29. New Zealand
4. Bangladesh	30. Nigeria
5. Barbados	31. Pakistan
6. Belize	32. Papua New Guinea
7. Botswana	33. St Christopher and
8. Britain	Nevis
9. Brunei	34. St Lucia
10. Canada	35. St Vincent and the
11. Cyprus	Grenadines
12. Dominica	36. Seychelles
13. The Gambia	37. Sierra Leone
14. Ghana	38. Singapore
15. Grenada	39. Solomon Islands
16. Guyana	40. Sri Lanka
17. India	41. Swaziland
18. Jamaica	42. Tanzania
19. Kenya	43. Tonga
20. Kiribati	44. Trinidad and Tobago
21. Lesotho	45. Tuvalu
22. Malawi	46. Uganda
23. Malaysia	47. Vanuatu
24. Maldives	48. Western Samoa
25. Malta	49. Zambia
26. Mauritius	50. Zimbabwe

The Commonwealth

The Commonwealth succeeded the British Commonwealth (the term was discarded in 1951) which in its turn had developed out of the British Empire. It is a voluntary association that links fifty independent and sovereign states. It represents a quarter of the world's population — over a billion people of differing cultures, races and economic status. It ranges from India with its population of 800 million to Tuvalu in the Western Pacific with only 8,000 people.

The process whereby the Empire matured into the Commonwealth had its roots in the nineteenth century. Canada was made the first Dominion in 1867, a term which implied an

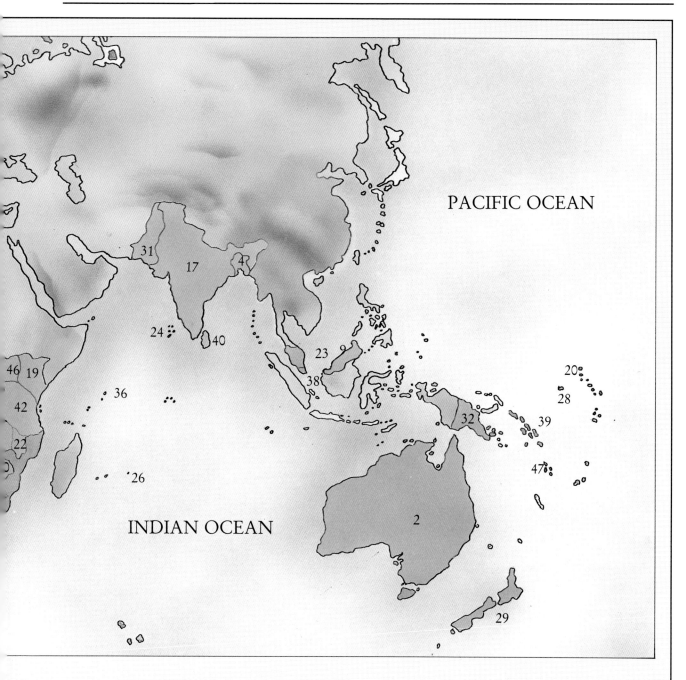

PACIFIC OCEAN

INDIAN OCEAN

equal rather than subservient status with Britain. Australia became a Dominion in 1900 when its states united into the Commonwealth of Australia. The process accelerated when these countries, together with the Dominions of New Zealand and South Africa, were given full legal independence in the Statute of Westminster of 1931. India's decision to remain within the Commonwealth after its independence in 1947 was a significant development, pointing the way to the multi-racial Commonwealth of today. Its example was followed by Ceylon (now Sri Lanka) in 1948 and Malaya (now Malaysia) in 1957. Other colonies in Asia and Africa followed accordingly.

To a minor extent the membership of the

Commonwealth fluctuates. Commonwealth opposition to all forms of racism forced the withdrawal of South Africa in 1961 because of its apartheid policy. Pakistan also withdrew in 1972 as a protest against the recognition of Bangladesh (formerly East Pakistan) by some member countries. In 1989 it rejoined, however. Fiji's membership lapsed in 1987 when it declared itself a republic.

Britain's monarch, now Elizabeth II, is head of the Commonwealth and symbol of the association. All members subscribe to the recognition of both this and a set of common ideals: these include liberty for the individual and opposition to colonial domination and to racial oppression.

The 'winds of change' blew through the British dependencies and the West Indian and African colonies freed themselves during the 1950s and 1960s from the shackles of empire. Most remained within a network of nations under the Commonwealth presided over by the British monarch, but the Empire which had once stained the world map a reddish-pink ceased to exist, except, perhaps, in the clubs of London and the clubhouses of the expatriates in the one-time colonies.

A NEW AGE

THE LABOUR GOVERNMENT planned to commemorate the Great Exhibition of 1851 with a second exhibition a century later, emphasising the new Britain, a show-case for the modern world of culture, science, art and technology. The idea, like the original, was not popular with the press who attacked Labour for wasting money in a time of austerity. Yet again such critics were wrong and 8,500,000 people flocked to the exhibition. The work of designers, furniture-makers, scientists and poets from the whole of the United Kingdom was on display to the world, but also, as the brilliant poet Dylan Thomas wrote:

the 'British Character' that stubborn, stupid, seabound, lyrical, paradoxical farrago of uppishness, derring-do, and midsummer moonshine all fluting, snug and copper-bottomed.

London's South Bank was aflame with the festival; something of recovery was seen there, and in that it was a success.

The symbol of the new age, Elizabeth II, came to the throne following the death of her father George VI in 1952. Her coronation, broadcast live and shown on television in many homes and to many people, crowded lap to lap, bottom to knee, in living rooms around the country, had the air of a fantasy. Even her name seemed to offer historic promise: the new Elizabethans looked to a golden age. It seemed to happen, too. The economy, strengthened by the booming world markets recovered and went to new heights. A consumer explosion hit the country and this buoyancy was sustained by the Conservative government. At the end of the decade Harold Macmillan, the Conservative Prime Minister,

Suez 1956. British parachute troops move into airport buildings at El Gamil Airfield, Port Said, after their airborne assault on 5 November 1956. The man on the left can be seen still getting out of his parachute.

declared that Britain had 'never had it so good'. For many it was true. The young people – the teenagers – came into their own and developed a separate culture, quite different from that of their parents. The fusion of American country music and Black Afro-American music – Rock and Roll – came in from the States on record and on film, inspiring home-grown talent like Tommy Steele and Cliff Richard who, whilst pale imitations of the real thing, built up huge followings. The 'Teddy Boys', named from their Edwardian style of dress, filled the Palais de Dance halls throughout the land.

The 1950s were not, however, a peaceful decade. The cold war which had developed between the western powers and the Russian-backed communist regimes of eastern Europe and the Chinese nation after the success of the Communist Party there, showed no sign of a thaw. The Berlin Blockade of 1949 had seen the North Atlantic Treaty Organisation flying food supplies to beleaguered Berlin, which was divided into two parts representing the sectors controlled on the one hand by Britain, France and the USA and on the other by the Russians. British forces were also involved in the United Nations army in the Korean War (1950–3), where the Chinese-backed Communists of the North attempted to unify the whole country.

In 1956 Britain was humiliated in the Middle East when the President of Egypt, Colonel Nasser, nationalised the Suez Canal to raise money for the construction of a new Aswan Dam. With the connivance of Britain and France, Israel attacked Egypt. The plan was for the two European nations to send a peace-keeping force to hold back the two sides. The peace-keeping force's territory would surround the Suez Canal which Britain wanted to control to ensure the oil supplies that Nasser was seen to be threatening. The unexpectedly tough fight put up by the Egyptian army ruined this plan. In any case, the British were forced to desist when it was reported by Harold Macmillan, Chancellor of the Exchequer, that the pound sterling was in trouble and that the USA was putting powerful pressure on Britain, preventing her withdrawal of money from the International Monetary Fund until the invasion was reversed. The British and French peace-keeping force which had begun to arrive in the region, was pulled out and United Nations

Maurice Harold Macmillan (1894–1986).

troops replaced it. The canal remained blocked by sunken ships. Britain was discredited around the world, censured by the United Nations and even mistrusted by the French, who felt that Britain's ending of the action had been precipitate.

Suez ended the prime-ministerial career of Anthony Eden, the man who had succeeded Churchill in 1955. Into the position stepped Harold Macmillan who oversaw petrol rationing and an increase in charges for school meals and NHS services. There was a constant threat of inflation in the spend, spend, spend, atmosphere of the late fifties and early sixties, yet it was largely contained, even though the economy did not remain stable. An upswing in 1958 enabled the Conservatives to cut income tax on the eve of the 1959 election, which resulted in another Conservative victory. Yet beneath all of this there was industrial discontent with many strikes and a rejection of wage restraint by the TUC. The policy of trying to regulate the economy by putting a brake on investment when there seemed to be too much activity, and reversing this in a period of slow-down – the policy of 'stop-go' economics – put a dampener on investment programmes and as the 1960s dawned, unemployment began to rise.

309

There was a growing concern in the country about the proliferation of nuclear weapons. Both Russia and America developed the powerful hydrogen bomb in the early 1950s and Britain had a significant nuclear armoury. The full horror of the damage caused by the weapons which had been exploded on Hiroshima and Nagasaki was now being revealed to the world, which realised that the effects lasted long after the explosion. The Campaign for Nuclear Disarmament, which demanded a complete rejection of nuclear weapons, attracted a great deal of support in the Labour Party even though a decade earlier it had been the Labour government that had been instrumental in devising Britain's nuclear weapons policy. In 1959 Labour Party members put forward a disarmament motion at the Party conference. The most evident of all attempts to bring the issue to the fore were the annual marches to Aldermarston, the atomic weapons research establishment, led by the veteran philosopher, Bertrand Russell, and by the MP, Michael Foot.

THE 1960s

FOR MANY OF THE YOUNG these issues passed unnoticed. There was still money in their pockets and retail industries aimed to extract it. The popular music industry grew rapidly in the 'fifties and waves of musical crazes swept Britain in the 1960s. The most successful group, and the one whose music has been the most enduring, was the Beatles, whose Liverpool origins were soon exploited by other musical Liverpudlians. As with the American star, Elvis Presley, the Beatles went into films, producing movies which were immediately successful and then lingered on as cult classics. Much of the music of the period ventured into social and political issues, again influenced in some ways by American singers like Bob Dylan and Joni Mitchell. John Lennon of the Beatles became an active peace campaigner in a period in which many young people became politicised by their opposition to the war in Vietnam, where the Americans fought at the request of the South to protect

Britain accepted many immigrants from Commonwealth countries during the boom years of the 1950s and early 1960s.

A scene from the Beatles' film *Help*.

them against Communist invasion by North Vietnam.

The Conservative Party's monopoly of power came to an end as their unity dissolved. By 1962 the support for the party in the country was shown to be declining. By-elections were giving unfavourable results and Macmillan wanted a change of ministers. Younger pro-European men were brought into the Cabinet after seven ministers resigned under pressure. Although many reforms were promised, unemployment rose and the popularity of the government fell further. In the following year it was revealed that the War Minister, John Profumo, had been involved in an affair with a society prostitute who had also liaised with a known Russian agent. Once this became public in 1963, Profumo resigned after first denying the affair. Although the subsequent report revealed that there had been no security leak, the Conversative government was reeling. The Labour Party, now under the leadership of Harold Wilson, was able to attack the government effectively and was confirmed in its claim that the

government was disunited after Macmillan was taken ill at the Party Conference in 1963. An argument developed over the succession which opened wide gaps in the party. When Macmillan resigned through ill-health, Lord Home, who renounced his peerage and became Sir Alec Douglas-Home, took over the reins of government. It was a short prime-ministerial appointment, as in the election the following year Labour won.

There was only a small majority for the first government of Harold Wilson, yet quite a lot of progressive legislation was achieved. The 1965 Race Relations Act made discrimination illegal and was extended in 1968 to cover housing. There had been a great influx of immigrants from the Commonwealth countries in the 1950s, encouraged by the booming economy and the superior welfare system in the country. There was a backlash by some of the British who perceived that the recent immigrants were taking their homes and jobs. This resentment seemed to be given official backing by the maverick Conservative politican Enoch Powell who suggested that if

some curbs on immigration were not introduced, then there could be 'rivers of blood' in Britain. This offended the Conservatives, and Powell left the party. Sadly, the racial tensions of the 1960s did not go away and saw more virulent expression in the following decades.

The 1960s became known as the permissive decade. There were several features of this which gave rise to the idea that moral norms were changing. The use of the X certificate in the cinema from 1951 enabled films featuring sex and violence to be shown to a limited audience. Censorship of the theatre, hitherto in the hands of the Lord Chancellor, also ended, leaving the way clear for plays featuring nudity like *Hair* or *Oh Calcutta!*. D.H. Lawrence's banned novel, *Lady Chatterley's Lover*, was successfully defended in court in 1960, became acceptable literature and opened the way for the publication of hitherto suppressed work. There was also a franker discussion of sex and sexuality, which opened up previously unmentionable subjects. There were, of course, drawbacks: the publication of pornography increased and became seen as acceptable within limits, which were, however, sometimes exceeded in underground networks which harked back to Victorian child prostitution.

The Liberal MP, David Steel, introduced and successfully steered a bill which made abortion more accessible to women. This did much to end the tragic scandal of the back-street abortionists, resorted to by women who were desperate, for a variety of reasons, to terminate their pregnancies. Whilst decisions on abortions remained in the hands of the doctors, women as individuals now had the right to chose whether or not to remain pregnant.

The question of homosexuality also came to the fore. The history of the gay community in Britain is a long one. Though homosexuality is often seen as a vice or even an illness, there is no doubt that homosexuality is a long-standing phenomenon of human sexuality and individual homosexuals have contributed greatly to the nation's history. However, the legislation of 1968 withheld full legislative status from both this section of the community and from lesbians whose role in Britain's past and present is still often hidden.

Underlying all these social changes were deep economic problems which the Wilson Government had to come to terms with. These slowed down the implementation of a greater range of reforms. In the field of education, the 'sixties were a mixed decade. Higher education was expanded and a number of new universities were opened. Some like York were entirely new creations; others like Loughborough were derived from older institutions. Access to these institutions and the older universities was expanded and numbers in higher education doubled. This trend was continued in the 1970s with the development of polytechnics, which offered the degrees of the universities but were not initially geared to concomitant research.

In the field of secondary education, the tripartite system of grammar schools, technical schools and secondary moderns initiated by the 1944 Education Act was very slowly being overtaken by the comprehensive system. The comprehensives were all-embracing schools with a range of children in one institution. At the end of the 1960s the right-wing Black Papers criticised the standards of literacy and teaching of the state schools at the end of a period of experiment. In Scotland, where the comprehensive system was far more prevalent than in England and Wales, schools had met with more success by the 1970s. In England by 1980 only 80 per cent of the pupils in secondary schools attended comprehensives.

THE EUROPEAN COMMUNITY

THE EUROPEAN NATIONS considered ways of strengthening their economic ties in the face of the COMECON nations under Russia's wing. The NATO alliance provided military strength but in 1957, as the result of ties between the Benelux countries and Germany and France, Italy hosted the signing of a treaty uniting Belgium, Netherlands, Luxembourg, Germany, France and Italy in a common market, The European Community. Britain considered joining the Community, but there were fears of a loss of sovereignty. Instead, Britain assisted in the creation of a

Right: This poster publicises an evening devoted to the arts and their censorship organised by the National Council for Civil Liberties.

"**The Arts & Censorship**"

The National Council for Civil Liberties and   The Defence of Literature and The Arts Society

Composing, writing, directing, performing: Larry Adler   John Antrobus John Arden Dame Peggy Ashcro
Samuel Beckett Edward Bond John Bowen Georgia Brown A Gala Evening concerning Depravity and Corruption Kevin Brownlow Cornelius Cardew Carl Davis
Ronald Duncan Frankie Dymon Jnr. Tom Eastwood Andrew Faulds Fenella Fielding Richard Findlater William Gaskill Peter Gill The Grateful Dead
Sheila Hancock Stuart Hood Joseph Horovitz Ann Jellicoe Philip Jenkinson Paul Jones Bettina Jonic Christopher Logue Jonathan Lynn Charles Marowitz
Roger McGough & Scaffold George Melly Derek Mendel Adrian Mitchell Warren Mitchell George Mully Richard Neville Donald Ogden Stewart John Peel
Geoffrey Reeves William Rushton Maxwell Shaw Johnny Speight   Fritz Spiegl Crea Tarrant John Tilbury Rita Tushingham
Billie Whitelaw Nicol Williamson **Royal Festival Hall** Charles Wood Etc. Etc. Etc.
General Manager. John Denison C.B.E.

8pm. Monday, 9th December, 1968   Designed by Alan Aldridge Ink Studio

The south front of Blickling Hall, Norfolk; the house was largely reconstructed between 1619 and 1625.

The National Trust and the National Trust for Scotland

The National Trust was formally established at the end of the nineteenth century. Two men and one woman are credited with its foundation: Octavia Hill, Robert Hunter and Hardwicke Rawnsley, though Hugh Lupus Grosvenor, Duke of Westminster, is acknowledged as an honorary founder. The Trust came into existence as the indirect offspring of an existing conservation movement. Octavia Hill, the most active of the group and an experienced campaigner for social and housing reform, was a prime mover in the Commons Preservation Society which she joined in 1875. It was this Society's help that Hardwicke Rawnsley sought in 1893 when he was exercised with the problem of saving an area of the Lake District that was due for sale. Octavia Hill accordingly proposed the idea of a public trust to the Duke of Westminster. As a result, in 1895 The National Trust for Places of Historic Interest or Natural Beauty was formally registered, its constitution drawn up by Robert Hunter who had been solicitor to the Commons Preservation Society.

The Trust's first acquisition cost £10 in 1896: it was the Clergy House at Alfriston in Sussex, a fourteenth-century building of key antiquarian importance, sited in a delightful village (see page 119). It was a small property, and it was not until 1904 that the Trust took over its first grand property, Barrington Court in Somerset. This was a magnificent mid-sixteenth-century house with spiral chimneys and finialled gables, though part of its interior was gutted and the staircase with its oak panelling and balustrading had been removed.

The Rose Garden at Mottisfont Abbey, Hampshire.

By 1913 the Trust's acquisitions had reached fifty-nine and it continued to increase the number of properties in its care until the slump and the Second World War slowed its activities. Nonetheless, public opinion began to offer vocal support to the cause of the preservation of the countryside and its beauties. As the Trust grew, the properties it acquired in the next decade became more varied, ranging from part of Hadrian's Wall in the North, to Beatrix Potter's Lakeland hill farms with their Herdwick sheep, to grand gardens.

Meanwhile, the National Trust for Scotland had come into existence in 1931, instituted by prominent Scotsmen who were concerned at the destruction of their country's heritage of landscape and architecture. Though separate from the English organisation, it shared its aims to promote the care of fine buildings, historic places and beautiful countryside. Crathes Castle in Grampian (see page 139), the Royal Palace of Falkland, and the magnificent pass of Glencoe are amongst its gems, and its preservation work at Culloden battlefield is an outstanding achievement.

The first National Trust garden was at Hidcote Manor in Gloucestershire, the brilliant and influential creation of an American called Lawrence Johnston. Other famous gardens include Bodnant in Wales, Mount Stewart in Northern Ireland and, the most popular of all to judge by attendance figures, Sissinghurst Castle in Kent, created by Vita Sackville-West and her husband Harold Nicolson. At the present time, more than a hundred gardens are owned by the Trust, and the planting and care for three-quarters of these was for many years the responsibility of the horticulturalist, Graham Stuart Thomas, former Gardens Adviser to the National Trust. The Rose Garden at Mottisfont Abbey in Hampshire is one of his most glorious creations.

Since the Second World War, the Trust's membership has grown explosively, reaching one and a half million by 1988. This has the advantage that it has become a thriving commercial business, exceeding by far the vision of its founder members. Inevitably, however, the concomitant scrutiny of its subscribing members has exposed it to criticism as well as gratitude and its agenda and decisions have become the subject of public debate.

The European Community

THE COUNCIL OF MINISTERS

– consists of a minister from each member state, ministers changing according to the subject under consideration. The Council is the body ultimately responsible for adopting new measures. The European Council is a meeting of the political leaders of the member states.

THE COMMISSION

– consists of 17 commissioners appointed by member states, each with his own portfolio of responsibilities. The Commission proposes policies and legislation to the Council of Ministers and European Parliament.

THE EUROPEAN PARLIAMENT

– consists of deputies elected directly by member states. They scrutinise and report on Commission proposals, but have no powers to enact legislation.

THE ECONOMIC AND SOCIAL COMMITTEE

– consists of individuals proposed by member states – employers, trade unions, professions etc. It is an advisory body to the Council and Commission.

THE COURT OF JUSTICE

– consists of eleven judges and is the ultimate arbiter in matters of community law.

The EC was originally established by the Treaty of Rome in January 1958. The founding members were Belgium, France, Germany, Italy, Luxembourg and the Netherlands. Great Britain, Denmark and Ireland joined in 1973, Greece in 1981, Spain and Portugal in 1986.

The aims of the treaty were principally the elimination of trade barriers and the creation of a common market, but the long-term goals of the community are integration of policies across a broad range of decision-making. An important step towards achieving these goals was the Single European Act, which came into force in 1987. This act firstly permits decisions to be made in the Council of Ministers by a qualifying majority rather than the unanimous agreement previously required. It also covers a broad spectrum of community law in such areas as economic and social cohesion (including the single European market of 1992), environment, co-operation between institutions and political co-operation.

The procedures and checks for decision-making in the community are complex, designed to give each member country a proportionate voice. The chart above is a simplified representation of the bodies involved in those decisions.

free-trade area which had no overtones or future plans for political ties. The European Free Trade Association came into being in 1959 after negotiations with the EEC failed.

Nevertheless, the EEC remained a tempting prospect and Macmillan tried to negotiate entry again in 1961 but the European nations hoped to gain concessions on political unification. Only in 1963 did the government, under the inspiration of Edward Heath, decide to ask for unequivocal membership. This time France's President de Gaulle suggested that Britain's co-operation with the United States on nuclear weapons would lead to a destabilisation of the European balance of power. Harold Wilson's government made

further attempts to enter the community but de Gaulle's opposition was insurmountable, despite the eagerness of other countries.

It fell to Edward Heath's Conservative government in 1971, helped by de Gaulle's absence from the stage, to gain admission and on 1 January 1973 Britain became a member of the EEC at the same time as Eire and Denmark. The Heath government was glad of the success of the European policy. At home they proved unable to control the pressures of wage rises. The country was hit by waves of strikes in the major industries and the nation was forced to work three-day weeks in 1973. The coal miners' strike wrecked the supply of power and the people were forced to endure periodic power cuts through the winter. Even the mail stopped at one point as the post office workers went on strike. It was against this background of chaos that Heath went into the 1974 election and lost.

It was apparent there was a lot of opposition to the European Community within the country and the new Labour government promised a referendum on the issue. In 1975 the people of Britain voted in favour of remaining in the Community. The Conservative governments of Margaret Thatcher, which initially took power in 1979, fought many holding actions, firstly to reduce Britain's financial contributions to the Community, and then to slow down the moves towards full economic and political union which the Conservative Party had accepted in theory in 1963. The Labour Party remained until the mid-1980s largely opposed to the Common Market, but a realisation of the economic advantages and the growing concern for social and welfare rights in the Community changed the party attitude, and by the time of the European Parliament Election of 1989 Labour was perceived as the pro-Europe party and won the majority of the British seats in the EC, overturning a substantial Conservative majority. In late 1990 on the eve of a Party Conference, dogged by a low position in the polls, the Conservative government took Britain into the Community Exchange Rate Mechanism and progress towards political unity quickened, much against the wishes of the Prime Minister, Mrs Thatcher.

ALTERNATIVE CULTURES

IN THE 1960s the youth of Britain was attracted to a variety of alternative cultures. These cultures were often blamed for a breakdown in the social order. Rock music gave rise to several alternative youth groups. 'Mods' and 'Rockers' fought their way across various British beaches, many in the south of England, during the mid-sixties. The Mods or moderns followed bands like The Who and rode highly decorated mopeds or scooters, and fought the leather-clad motorcycle-riding Rockers as each attempted to hold rallies at the seaside. Whilst the Mods and the Rockers, and later the 'Skinheads' who graced the streets in

Most sports in international competition in the twentieth century originated in Britain, though cricket has tended to be popular only in Commonwealth countries.

Above: The Queen, Prince Andrew, Prince Philip and Prince Edward at Balmoral, Aberdeenshire.

Opposite: The wedding of Prince Charles and Lady Diana Spencer at St. Paul's Cathedral on 29 July 1981.

The Royal Family

The present royal family is a foremost example of the adaptability of the British monarchy, for great changes have been thrust upon it during the reign of Elizabeth II. Like other British institutions it has been popularised and democratised. Many of its members have married commoners – Princess Anne, Princess Margaret, Prince Andrew and Princess Alexandra. As a result, royalty is no longer so exclusive, nor is it allowed to be: and it is remarkable that it has managed to survive this drive to make its members more accessible, without loss of dignity or public esteem.

Elizabeth II, then a young mother of two, came to the throne in 1952 at the age of twenty-five. Although she was naturally somewhat inexperienced in her role, this did not save her from criticism. At the time, this provoked indignation and controversy, but by the 1960s royal protocol began to show signs of a policy of relaxation. This was greatly helped by the Duke of Edinburgh who brought a forceful commonsense and a directness of manner to his difficult role as the Queen's consort. It was he who was called (by the Conservative politician,

Norman St. John Stevas) 'the driving force behind the necessary modernisation of the monarchy'.

In the 1960s the first royal documentary was made for television, broadcast in 1969 as *The Royal Family.* For the first time, the private life of the monarch and her family was on display. The 'royals' were even shown at a barbecue, which was a watershed in public presentation.

Public image has always been considered of great importance by the Palace and, one by one, complaints have been addressed, whether institutional or personal. An example of the former was the controversy over the cost of the monarchy. Payments are made to it by means of the Civil List and must rise to keep up with inflation. Formerly, a required increase was received through extraordinary requests to Parliament, which would result in an embarrassing and often unfair debate. It was sometimes contested, for example, that the Queen was the richest woman in Britain, and not always pointed out in her defence that her assets were held in trust and not realisable. These regular financial disputes were only brought to an end by, first, the introduction of a regular review of the Civil List, and, second, the Queen's agreement that no savings on the Civil List would accrue to the privy purse.

Personal complaints were not so straightforward to address. For years the Princess Royal (Princess Anne) had a poor public image. As her horsemanship and, more worthily, her stalwart work for Save the Children Fund began to win public admiration, her status improved. But her image was also helped by the Palace's idea that Thames TV should broadcast a documentary on her life.

The marriage of Prince Charles in 1981 to Lady Diana Spencer forced these younger members of the royal family into a glare of publicity that has often been abused by the tabloid newspapers. This potentially harmful democratisation of the monarchy has proved hard to eradicate, though the Palace has combated it by the increasing use of television (it can control this medium more effectively than newspapers) and thereby helped to offset any destruction of the royal image. At the same time, the family's essential decency, the seriousness with which most members undertake their onerous duties, and Prince Charles's unusual combination of earnest sincerity and charm, have consolidated their beneficial influence. Their position as a national asset, often envied by other nations, is as secure as it has ever been.

the early 1970s with their close-cropped hair and Dr Martens airwear boots, were working-class phenomena, the 'Hippies' of the mid-sixties to whom the Beatles appealed were middle-class, often members of, or drop-outs from, higher educational institutions. The message of these Hippies was more political and social, proposing an end to conflict and the adoption of an era of peace and love. The hippie culture was often linked to drug culture and prominent members of bands like the Rolling Stones were arrested on drugs charges. The era of 'Flower Power' died out after 1968 when these same social groups became involved in the student riots against the repression of the educational and govern-mental hierarchy which had it most violent expression in France and parts of the United States. Hippies did not simply disappear; many individuals remained true to their ideals and communes, some of which lingered on (often in Wales) long past the 1960s.

THE WOMEN'S MOVEMENT

THE WOMEN'S MOVEMENT made its appearance in Britain in the later sixties with a demand for total equality for women. The winning of the vote had not greatly enhanced the position of women. Despite being over fifty per cent of the population, there was still only a tiny minority of women MPs and even after the equal opportunities legislation of the 1970s, women still received lower wages in some industries and represented a minority in the professions. For a long time, advertising still portrayed women as housewives or vamps and the permissive era allowed for more explicit sexist advertising, which was challenged in the 1980s. Women's Studies courses in the adult education sector and later in the mainstream of higher education made the issue a topic for academic study. Prolonged and increasingly successful campaigns to restore to the forefront women who were significant in British history and culture grew out of the consciousness-raising of the early seventies, led by Germaine Greer and other pioneers.

Rhodesian Independence

In the 1950s, the British government began to pursue the policy of allowing self-determination for the black colonies of Africa. As a result, the white-dominated colony of Southern Rhodesia grew disturbed by Britain's apparent acceptance that there should be majority rule in colonies before independence. Racial equality was not part of the white settlers' immediate plans.

The British government distanced itself from the ambitions of the white minorities. South Africa was forced to withdraw from the Commonwealth after its apartheid policies became increasingly abhorrent. But, as Britain recoiled from the consequences of racial division, Southern Rhodesians moved closer to South African ideals. After a series of negotiations with the Conservative government which ended without agreement on potential independence, the newly emerged Rhodesian Front, led first by Winston Field and then by Ian Smith, gained a large majority in Rhodesian elections. Following the British Labour party's election in 1964, Smith made a unilateral declaration of independence (UDI).

Britain's reaction was to impose sanctions on the wayward colony, although there were attempts at negotiation when Harold Wilson, the Labour Prime Minister, met Ian Smith for two waterborne discussions on board HMS Tiger and Fearless. Sanctions were never securely imposed and Smith's Rhodesia survived into the late 1970s despite guerilla warfare. By now the British were beginning to recognise that a settlement with the black leaders in favour of black majority rule must be achieved. In the Conservative manifesto for the 1979 election in which Margaret Thatcher first came to power, the party was committed to a lasting settlement, and in August Mrs Thatcher confirmed in Lusaka that Britain's aim was to bring Rhodesia to legal independence on a basis which the Commonwealth and international community would find acceptable. Within six months this had been achieved. In February 1980, elections were called: the outcome was a landslide victory for Robert Mugabe and the ZANU party (Zimbabwe African National Union). On 19 April 1980, after fourteen years of illegal independence, the republic of Zimbabwe (renamed from Zimbabwe Rhodesia) became the forty-third member-state of the Commonwealth.

A DISUNITED KINGDOM

WHILST BRITAIN may have become a part of a wider community in 1973, there were sections of the United Kingdom which were not wholly happy at being a part of Britain. Eire which had been given self-government in 1922 became fully independent in 1948, proclaiming itself the Irish Republic on 18 April 1949. In Northern Ireland the Irish Republican Army continued to fight with the aim of making the remaining six counties secede from Britain too. In the Northern Ireland province there was and still is a majority of Protestants, decendants of Scottish settlers of the seventeenth century. Most of these have no wish to be joined to a nation which is overwhelmingly Catholic and, to their mind, economically less advanced, Eire being dependent to a greater extent upon agriculture. As a result, the terrorist activities of the IRA have been matched within Ulster by those of the Protestant loyalist terrorist groups. In the aftermath of the trouble stirred up by the Irish Civil Rights Movement, which aimed to gain legal and social equality for the oppressed Catholic community, the British Army moved in to protect the Catholic community from the violence of Protestant extremists. In 1991 that army is still there. The IRA targeted mainly these forces, which it and many other Catholic Irish see as an occupying army. Occasionally, as in the mid-seventies and the late eighties, their campaigns have spilled onto the mainland. In 1974 bombing campaigns claimed many civilian victims in England. In 1985 Mrs Thatcher's government signed an agreement with the Eire Goverment aiming at closer co-operation in the affairs of the province and the ending of terrorism there, but by 1991 there still appears to be no solution.

Wales and Scotland have also witnessed moves towards devolution during the latter part of the twentieth century. In the 1960s the Welsh Nationalist Party, Plaid Cymru, began to win against the Labour Party in some of its traditional strongholds. The Cymdeithas yr Iaith Gymraeg, Welsh Language Society, was formed in the same decade, campaigning on the grounds that the loss of the language was the loss of the culture. There was even a threat of militant action, too; English place names

Exploitation of the oil and gas fields of the North Sea began in the 1970s, and during the 1980s Britain was a net exporter of oil.

and signs were blotted out and replaced with Welsh. Campaigns were launched to broadcast the Welsh language on television; eventually in 1982, the Welsh Channel Four was formed specifically to do this, even though the independent station HTV and BBC Wales broadcast some Welsh language programmes after the 1973 Welsh Language Act, which had reversed Henry VIII's legislation in the Act of Union.

Plaid Cymru eschewed the violence of the militant factions which burned down the Welsh holiday homes of the English, but attempted to discourage further settlement by outsiders and this contributed to its success in the 'seventies. As the recession of the later 1970s began to bite and forced the Labour government into difficulties and a programme of wide-scale borrowing from the International Monetary Fund, Labour began to search for new areas of support. To try and pull the rug from under Plaid Cymru in Wales and the Scottish National Party in Scotland, both countries were offered a devolved national assembly. Whilst the Scottish assembly would have given the country a wide range of powers, ending much of the Act of Union of

This famous Conservative poster, produced by Saatchi & Saatchi, was used during the election campaign of 1979.

1707, the Welsh assembly would have been less effective. Nevertheless, there would have been a significant change to the relationship established in the 1534 Act of Union. The bills for the devolution passed the Houses of Parliament stages in 1978 and a referendum was set in Wales for St David's Day 1979. The Scots had already voted; only 45 per cent supported the plan. Now, in Wales only 13 per cent gave their assent. It was a crushing and unexpected defeat.

MRS THATCHER'S GOVERNMENT

THE SUDDEN INCREASE in the price of oil in 1974 and again in 1979, caused havoc in world markets, and the Labour government, allied because of its small majority with David Steel's Liberal Party, found great difficulties in managing the economy. The winter of 1978 – 9 saw many strikes and the rejection of pay policies aimed at trying to curb rising inflation. In the general election of 1979 the Conservative Party, under the dynamic leadership of Margaret Thatcher, achieved a working majority after an effective campaign based on the seeming failures of Labour. 'Labour isn't working' read one of the posters from the campaign alongside a picture of a dole queue.

To those in that queue who saw the Conservative Party as a beacon of hope, there was a cruel shock. The Thatcherite group within the party, which had not yet achieved domination within the power structure, pressed for monetarist policies. A tight control of the money supply and a refusal to spend money on ailing industrial sections saw inefficient manufacturing industries plunged into a spiral of collapse. The Thatcherites opposed massive public spending; they cut direct taxes and tried to reduce excessive spending in the social services. At the beginning of the new decade businesses closed at a rate never before seen in Britain's history and unemployment grew to heights not witnessed since the Great Depression. In this atmosphere the government quickly lost support and as the mid-term approached it looked as if there might be a sudden end to Thatcherism.

The government was saved by several things. First, the Labour Party tore itself apart. The shift in the party leftwards to a more traditional socialist base, away from the acceptance of capitalism, drove elements of the hierarchy into revolt. Four of them, Shirley Williams, Roy Jenkins, David Owen and William Rogers, left to form the Social Democratic Party. Meanwhile, the Labour Party's trouble with the left-wing element – the Militant Tendency – left it weak and not a potential vote-winner. In the election of 1983 the SDP and the Liberals gained almost as many votes as Labour, but the two-party system crushed them just as the Liberals had

Margaret Thatcher

Mrs Margaret Thatcher, leader of the Conservative Party from 1975–1990, was both Britain's first woman Prime Minister and the longest-serving Prime Minister in the twentieth century.

Margaret Roberts was born in 1925 in the county town of Grantham in Lincolnshire, daughter of a shopkeeper who had enjoyed a minor political career as a local independent councillor. She won a scholarship to Kesteven and Grantham Girl's School, read chemistry at Somerville College, Oxford, and finished her pupillage as a barrister in 1955. By now she had married the divorced Denis Thatcher and was the mother of twins. They were delivered by Caesarian and their mother entered her papers for the Bar Finals from her hospital bed, a characteristic gesture of determination.

By this date she had also long since become involved with the Conservative Party: she was a conference delegate from Oxford and an unsuccessful candidate for Dartford, Kent. She made efforts to secure another nomination, but was consistently turned down until her acceptance by Finchley in London. Her first job in 1961 was Parliamentary Secretary to the Minister of Pensions and National Insurance. She subsequently served under Alec Douglas-Home and, when he stepped down, supported Edward Heath's leadership. His reward was to move her into the Shadow Treasury team, though he subsequently switched her from her primary interest of economics to Power, then Transport, then Education.

By now she had impressed her colleagues with her capacity for enormously hard work, her verbal dexterity, her grasp of detail and, not least, her political aggressiveness. After Edward Heath failed the second time to win the election for the Conservatives in 1974, Margaret Thatcher won the leadership election within the Tory Party. A full term in opposition followed during which she clarified the central issues for her Party: trade union reform was the most urgent. During Mrs Thatcher's combative period in opposition, she also organised a press lobby, reconstructed her party policy management and established her team. Hers was a marketing approach to politics which was entirely new to Britain.

On 3 May 1979, Mrs Thatcher was elected Britain's first woman Prime Minister. She would hold continuous power for the next eleven and half years, exercising increasing personal authority over her Cabinet, until forced to stand down by her own party members. Few leaders can have been so adulated by their supporters or so loathed by their detractors. Her electoral status in the eyes of the unpoliticised general public was subjected to similar extremes. Rising from a nadir of personal unpopularity in 1981, in the midst of a deep recession and high unemployment, she was to win the 1983 General Election with an increased majority, unprecedented in twentieth century British politics.

As a conviction politician, she set out with the intention of changing a Britain which she described in 1979 as a country of 'high inflation, high unemployment, high taxation, appalling industrial relations, the lowest productivity in the Western world'. In the process of change she was prepared to confront without flinching those who opposed her. Her beliefs, her authority, her ultimately long experience and her close relationship with Ronald Reagan, the President of the United States, were to earn her world status as a statesman. Indeed, it was often claimed that she was more popular abroad than at home.

No premier has been more controversial than Margaret Thatcher. This was perhaps inevitable. She was a woman, she took risks, she confronted. She had also been raised to be different. Years before, her father had declared: 'You do not follow the crowd because you're afraid of being different. You decide what to do yourself and, if necessary, you lead the crowd, but you never just follow'. It was a statement that Mrs Thatcher often quoted.

Scots Guards on Goat Ridge, the Falkland Islands, June 1982.

been crushed since 1924 and they gained only a few more seats than the Liberals had held on their own. The same happened in the 1987 election when Labour, now under Neil Kinnock, performed better, but did not materially increase its vote. In the following two years the Liberals and the majority of the SDP merged into the Social and Liberal Democrats and the remains of the SDP under David Owen disintegrated.

The second factor which saved Mrs Thatcher's first government was the war in the South Atlantic. There had been a series of diplomatic blunders in the attempts to settle the future of the Falkland Islands, the ownership of which was disputed by Argentina. The military regime in Argentina launched an invasion on the Falklands, which they called the Malvinas, in the spring of 1982. The Thatcher government went to war. The better-trained and equipped British invasion force recaptured the islands, inflicting heavy casualties on the Argentine army. Despite the swift victory there were dreadful incidents in which the Royal Navy vessels were shown to

be inadequately protected against air-launched missiles. There were about 250 British casualties out of the 10,000 British troops.

The war, a little war like the colonial wars of the nineteenth century, was popular. It seemed to show that Britain was great again. It was a partial explanation, along with Labour's disarray, for the return of Mrs Thatcher's government, now fully dominated by her faction, in the 1983 election. In confident mood the government prepared to deal with the difficult problem of closing uneconomic coal mines. The miners went on strike to save their industry. It was a violent year. The police tried to prevent mass picketing; infringements of new union laws led courts to seize mining union assets. The strike ended in failure, the mining union was split and the mass closures of pits went ahead. It looked as if massive strikes would always fail under the Conservative government, until the successful ambulance drivers' strike of 1989–90 showed that the ability to challenge the power of the government was still there.

From 1983 onwards the country witnessed

The miners' president, Arthur Scargill, addressing a rally during the miners' strike.

the privatisation of nationalised industries which were sold one by one in order to remove them from the political arena and to staunch their financial losses, which had been subsidised by the tax-payer. One result of these privatisations was the widening of share ownership among the general public. Popular capitalism has taken from national control gas, electricity, steel production, the British Petroleum Company and even the water supply, as well as many other minor industries.

In the mid-eighties an unsustainable boom began which helped, together with falling unemployment figures, to sustain Mrs Thatcher's government through another election. However, the revelation that this boom was largely ephemeral as the country headed towards economic decline again at the end of the decade limited the government's popularity. The closure of businesses in the early 'eighties was exceeded at the end of the decade. House prices rose to exorbitant heights and the government's policy of selling council houses, though highly popular, did not address the problem of the homeless in a

325

Above: Aerial view of the site near Dover from where the Channel Tunnel is constructed.

Left: The breakthrough of the French and UK service tunnels on 1 December 1990 connected Britain and the rest of Europe for the first time since the last Ice Age.

society where stable family life was on the decline. 1990 saw Poll Tax riots as the English people reacted to the introduction of a flat rate community charge instead of the rates which had themselves become discredited. Scotland had been the testing ground for this experiment and the Poll Tax introduced there in 1989 had proved very difficult to collect and organised popular groups continued to prevent the collection methods of the bailiffs.

The intransigence over political union with Europe also contributed to the government's unpopularity. In November 1990 Mrs Thatcher was seen as a political liability for a government struggling to maintain credibility. A challenge was made and after she had failed to win a convincing first-round ballot in the leadership election, Mrs Thatcher resigned. The Conservative MPs, conscious that Mrs Thatcher and her policies had less credibility, voted for John Major, Chancellor of the Exchequer in her government, to replace her as Prime Minister.

It may appear as though the loss of an empire and the introspective preoccupation with her own development have emphasised British insularity. Until recently this was arguably the case, but now as the third millenium approaches, this accusation can no longer be justified. Whilst it is true that the British are still withdrawing from their dependencies – Hong Kong will be handed over to China in 1997 – the loss of an empire has been balanced by stronger links with the rest of the world. Britain is no longer even a true island, but connected to France by the Channel Tunnel, a project revived by Mrs Thatcher though financed by private money. Britain is also a more committed member of Europe than in the past. Finally, her links with America remain stout. In the Gulf War against Iraq in 1991, a war sanctioned by the United Nations, Britain has proved to be still America's most staunch ally.

British troops were the third largest contingent among the Allies in the Gulf War.

The Gulf War

Within a few weeks of John Major's election as Prime Minister, Britain was at war. Mr Major inherited a situation which had erupted during the previous year. On 2 August 1990 the Iraqi dictator, Saddam Hussein, had invaded Kuwait with is troops, claiming that this oil-rich country was Iraq's 19th state.

At the time of the invasion, there were about 3,000 British expatriates working in Kuwait, the most recent examples of a long British trading history in the Gulf. The town of Kuwait had become a British base in 1793 and the territory had subsequently been taken into British protection (1899–1961) until its full independence was recognised. Iraq had then immediately claimed the area, whereupon British troops intervened until they were replaced by Arab League forces. Saddam Hussein's invasion of Kuwait was therefore an attempt to repeat an old claim.

In August 1990, at a crucial joint meeting, Mrs Thatcher and the American President, George Bush, took the decision that Saddam Hussein must leave Kuwait voluntarily or by force. The United Nations, with an unprecedented degree of international accord, demanded Iraq's withdrawal and the renunciation of Saddam Hussein's claim. Sanctions were imposed and an alliance of troops from different nations including Egypt, Syria and Saudi Arabia was built up in the Gulf, under the leadership of the American General Norman Schwarzkopf. Britain provided the third largest contribution of forces and the second largest navy, with 45,000 men in the arena under the command of Lieutenant General Sir Peter de la Billiére.

The deadline for Saddam Hussein's withdrawal passed shortly after the New Year of 1991. It was with the greatest reluctance that the allied parties declared war but in the night of 16 January they opened fire on Iraqi targets. Their offensive enacted the fifty-year old doctrine of strategic bombing, and proved the greatest aerial bombardment in history. The latest weapons technology was to ensure success, for the superpowers were able to use satellites to intercept intelligence and to oversee targets. On 22 February, the ground war began, a development which had been anticipated with public dread as heavy casualties seemed inevitable, despite military interventions to keep allied losses to a minimum. In the event the fears were unfounded and the conflict proved to be one-sided. In a classic campaign, the allies cut the escape route of the Iraqi troops. By 28 February a provisional cease-fire brought the war to a rapid conclusion, due in part to the controversial incident at Mutla Ridge, north-west of Kuwait City. Here the allies bombed th fleeing army of Saddam Hussein, with the military justification that it was impossible to predict whether the enemy was in genuine retreat or planning to regroup.

KINGS AND QUEENS OF ENGLAND SINCE 871

The year of accession is given after each monarch. Numbering began afresh with the conquest in 1066 by William, Duke of Normandy.

KINGS OF WESSEX AND ENGLAND
Alfred	871
Edward (I) The Elder	899
Aethelstan	924
Edmund I	940
E(a)dred	946
Eadwig (Edwy)	955
Edgar	959
Edward the Martyr	975
Aethelred II 'The Unready'	978
Edmund Ironside	1016

DANISH
Cnut	1016
Harold I Harefoot	1037
Harthacnut	1040

ENGLISH
Edward II The Confessor	1042
Harold II Godwinson	January, 1066

NORMAN
William I The Conqueror	December, 1066
William II	1087
Henry I	1100
Stephen	1135

PLANTAGANET
Henry II	1154
Richard II	1189
John	1199
Henry III	1216
Edward I	1272
Edward II	1307
Edward III	1327
Richard II	1377

LANCASTER
Henry IV	1399
Henry V	1413
Henry VI	1422

YORK
Edward IV	1461
Edward V	1483
Richard III	1483

TUDOR
Henry VII	1485
Henry VIII	1509
Edward VI	1547
Mary I	1553
Elizabeth I	1558

STUART
James I	1603
Charles I	1625

THE COMMONWEALTH 1649–60

STUART (RESTORED)
Charles II	1660
James II	1685
William III and Mary II	1689
Anne	1702

HANOVER
George I	1714
George II	1727
George III	1760
George IV	1820
William IV	1830
Victoria	1837

SAXE-COBURG
Edward VII	1901

WINDSOR
George V	1910
Edward VIII	January, 1936; abdicated December 1936
George VI	1936
Elizabeth II	1952

KINGS AND QUEENS OF SCOTLAND SINCE 1005

Malcolm II	1005
Duncan I	1034
Macbeth	1040
Lulach	1057
Malcolm III	1058
Donald Bane	1093; deposed May 1094; restored November 1094
Duncan II	1094
Edgar	1097
Alexander I	1107
David I	1124
Malcolm IV	1153
William I	1165
Alexander II	1214
Alexander III	1249
Margaret	1286
John Balliol	1292; abdicated 1296
Robert I	1306
David II	1329
Robert II	1371
Robert III	1390
James I	1406
James II	1437
James III	1460
James IV	1488
James V	1513
Mary	1542
James VI	1567;

became King of England in 1603.

PRIME MINISTERS

OF THE

UNITED KINGDOM

The names of political parties are given in brackets, though before the 1830s these were loose associations rather than the cohesive groups of today. The dates are the years in which prime ministers first assumed or resumed office.

Sir Robert Walpole (Whig)	1721
Earl of Wilmington (Whig)	1741
Henry Pelham (Whig: Broadbottomed administration)	1743
Duke of Newcastle (Whig)	1754
Duke of Devonshire (Whig)	1756
Duke of Newcastle (Whig)	1757
Earl of Bute (Whig)	1762
George Grenville (Whig)	1763
Marquess of Rockingham (Whig)	1765
Earl of Chatham (Whig)	1766
Duke of Grafton (Whig)	1768
Lord North (Tory)	1770
Marquess of Rockingham (Whig)	1782
Earl of Shelburne (Whig)	1782
Duke of Portland (Whig)	1783
William Pitt (Court Whig 1783; Tory 1784)	1783
Henry Addington (Tory)	1801
William Pitt (Tory)	1804
William Wyndham Grenville (Coalition)	1806
Duke of Portland (Whig; Pittite)	1807
Spencer Perceval (Tory)	1809
Earl of Liverpool (Tory)	1812
George Canning (Tory)	1827
Viscount Goderich (Tory)	1827
Duke of Wellington (Tory)	1828
Earl Grey (Whig)	1830
Viscount Melbourne (Whig)	1834
Duke of Wellington (Tory)	1834
Sir Robert Peel (Tory)	1834
Lord John Russell (Liberal)	1846
Earl of Derby (Conservative)	1852
Earl of Aberdeen (Coalition)	1852
Viscount Palmerston (Liberal)	1855
Earl of Derby (Conservative)	1858
Viscount Palmerston (Liberal)	1859
Earl Russell (Liberal)	1865
Earl of Derby (Conservative)	1866
Benjamin Disraeli (Conservative)	1868
William Ewart Gladstone (Liberal)	1868
Benjamin Disraeli (Conservative)	1874
William Ewart Gladstone (Liberal)	1880
Marquess of Salisbury (Conservative)	1885
William Ewart Gladstone (Liberal)	1886
Marquess of Salisbury (Conservative)	1886
William Ewart Gladstone (Liberal)	1892
Earl of Rosebery (Liberal)	1894
Marquess of Salisbury (Conservative)	1895
Arthur James Balfour (Conservative)	1902
Sir Henry Campbell-Bannerman (Liberal)	1905
Herbert Henry Asquith (Liberal)	1908
David Lloyd George (Coalition)	1916
Andrew Bonar Law (Conservative)	1922
Stanley Baldwin (Conservative)	1923
James Ramsay MacDonald (Labour)	1924
Stanley Baldwin (Conservative)	1924
James Ramsay MacDonald (Labour, then National Government)	1929
Stanley Baldwin (Conservative)	1935
Neville Chamberlain (Conservative)	1937
Winston Churchill (Conservative)	1940
Clement Attlee (Labour)	1945
Winston Churchill (Conservative)	1951
Sir Anthony Eden (Conservative)	1955
Harold Macmillan (Conservative)	1957
Sir Alec Douglas-Home (Conservative)	1963
Harold Wilson (Labour)	1964
Edward Heath (Conservative)	1970
Harold Wilson (Labour)	1974
James Callaghan (Labour)	1976
Margaret Thatcher (Conservative)	1979
John Major (Conservative)	1990

Acknowledgements

The publishers are grateful to acknowledge the following contributions from Frances Welland:
Expeditions to North America (165–6); Samuel Pepys (182); Lancelot 'Capability' Brown (203); The British Atlantic Empire in the mid-eighteenth century (209); The British Empire in Australasia (216); Medicine (217); The 1812 War with America (225); Benjamin Disraeli (253); Charles Darwin (256); William Gladstone (257); Lord Salisbury (258); Queen Victoria (261); David Lloyd George (284); James Ramsay MacDonald (286); The Battle of Britain (295); Sir Winston Churchill (296); The Commonwealth (306); The National Trust and the National Trust for Scotland (314–5); The European Community (316); The Royal Family (318); Margaret Thatcher (323); The Gulf War (327).

Illustrations are reproduced by kind permission of the following. Colour illustrations are given in italics.
The pictures on pages *142–3*, *178–9*, *186–7*, *206–7*, *243*, and *246–7* are reproduced by gracious permission of H.M. the Queen.
Abbot Hall Art Gallery, Kendal; 219, 225, 226. Aberdeen Journals: 318, 321. Ashmolean Museum: 77. Bath Museums Service: 36–7. Bede Monastery Museum: 63. Conservative Central Office: *323*. Martyn Bennett: *19*, *39*. Ernest Powell Blood: *58–9*, *75*. Bodleian Library: 108. Bodleian Library filmscript reproduced by kind permission of the President and Fellows of Corpus Christi College, Oxford: *83(i)*, *83(ii)*, 84(ii), 85. J. M. Brereton: 13. Anthea Brian: *98*, *98–9*. British Library: 56–7, 81, 96, 97, *107*, 116. British Museum: 14, 16(i), 16(ii), 17, 20(i), 20(ii), 20(iii), 21, 29, 31, 41, 45, 53, *54(i)*, *54(ii)*, 58, 60–1, 71, 72. Camera Press (photograph by Patrick Lichfield): *319*. Cardiff Castle: *263*. Colchester and Essex Museums: 46, 48. Corinium Museum, Cirencester: *34–5*, 38, 44, 47, 49. The Master and Fellows, Corpus Christi College, Cambridge: 64, 101, 109, *123*. Robert Ditchfield Ltd: 65, *67*, *78–9*, *86–7*, *87*, *90*, *95*, *102*, *110*, *111*, 112(i), 112(ii), 114, *119*, 121(i), *130*, *134–5*, 137, *139*, 145, 146(ii), *150*, 189, *194*, 200, 201, *203*, 205, 206, 208, 217, *223(i)*, 223(ii), 224(ii), *227*, *231(i)*, 236(i), 236(ii), 238(ii), 240, 245, 248, 249, *251*, 252, 253, 257, 258, *259*, *262*, 274(ii), 284, 286, *287*, 288, 290, 304, 305, *314*, *315*. Property of Lord Forteviot on loan to Brooks's: 202. Geffrye Museum: 291. Bob Gibbons: *10–11*. Grosvenor Museum, Chester: *31*. Jerry Hardman-Jones: 40–1, *67*, *103*, *115*, *174*. Harris Museum and Art Gallery, Preston: 175. Trustees of the Imperial War Museum: 272–3, 276, *279*, 280, 280–1(i), 280–1(ii), 281, *282–3*, 293, 294, 295(ii), 296, 299(i), 299(ii), 300–1, 308, 324. Jorvik Viking Centre: 76. Kent & Sussex Courier: 309. Kitchenham Ltd. 18, *26*. David McKeown: *23*, *43*, *50–1*, *127*, 128, *171*, 209, *298*, *306–7*. Mansell Collection: 24, 25, 72–3, 74, 82, 84, 88–9, 91, 92–3, 100, 104–5, 117, 118, 120, 121, 122, 124, 125, 126, 132, 132–3, 136, 138, 140, 141(i), 141(ii), 144(i), 144(ii), 146(i), 147, 149, 151, 152(i), 152(ii), 153, 155, 156, 157, *159*, 163, 164–5, 176, 179, 180, 182, 182–3, 184(i), 184(ii), 185(i), 185(ii), 188, 192–3, 193, 195(i), 195(ii), 196(i), 196(ii), 197, 198, 212, 213(i), 213(ii), 216, 221, 224(i), 228–9, 230, 231(ii), 232–3, 238(i), 241, 244, 254(i), 254(ii), 256, 260, 262(i), 264, 265, 269–70, 273, 275(i), 275(ii), 277, 283, 285, 288, 292. Museum of London: *183*, 274. Museum of Antiquities of the University and Society of Antiquaries of Newcastle upon Tyne: 27, 28, *42*, 68(i), 68(ii), 69(i), 69(ii). National Council for Civil Liberties: 313. National Gallery, London: *147(i)*. National Maritime Museum: 6. National Museum of Wales: 30, 32–3. National Portrait Gallery: *131*, *154*, 160–1, *162*, *199*, *211*. © National Trust Photographic Library: *2*. Private collection: *167*. Powys County Council, Offa's Dyke Officer: 71. QA Photos: *326(i)*, *326(ii)*. Public Record Office: 94. Reed Midland Newspapers: 317. Saatchi & Saatchi Advertising: *322*. Reproduced by permission of the Trustees of the Science Museum: 190–1, 204. Scottish National Portrait Gallery: *214*, *234–5*, *239*. By courtesy of Sothebys: 177. Tate Gallery, London: *255*, *266*. The Times Newspapers: 310, 327. United International Pictures (photograph courtesy of British Film Institute): *311*. By courtesy of the Board of Trustees of the Victoria & Albert Museum: *250*. Weintraub Films (photograph from BFI): *303*. Jeremy Whitehouse: 168, 172, 222, 295. Wiltshire Archaeological and Natural History Society: *15*. York City Art Gallery: 173. Yorkshire Post Newspapers: 325.

Index

Italics indicate that the entry is illustrated.